Science, Language, and Reform in Victorian Poetry

I0592952

Barrow's timely book is the first to examine the link between Victorian poetry, the study of language, and political reform. Focusing on a range of literary, scientific, and political texts, Barrow demonstrates that nineteenth-century debates about language played a key role in shaping emergent ideas about popular sovereignty. While Victorian scientists studied the origins of speech, the history of dialects, and the barrier between human and animal language, poets such as Elizabeth Barrett Browning, Alfred Tennyson, and Thomas Hardy drew on this research to explore social unrest, the expansion of the electorate, and the ever-widening boundaries of empire. *Science, Language, and Reform in Victorian Poetry* recovers unacknowledged links between poetry, philology, and political culture, and contributes to recent movements in literary studies that combine historicist and formalist approaches.

Barbara Barrow is Assistant Professor of English at Point Park University in Pittsburgh. Her journal articles have appeared or are forthcoming in *Journal of Victorian Culture*, *Victorian Poetry*, *Victorian Periodicals Review*, *Nineteenth Century Contexts*, and *Victoriographies*. In 2016, she was a Visiting Scholar at Baylor University's Armstrong Browning Library.

The Nineteenth Century Series

Series editors: Joanne Shattock and Julian North

The series focuses primarily upon major authors and subjects within Romantic and Victorian literature. It also includes studies of other nineteenth-century British writers and issues, where these are matters of current debate: for example, biography and autobiography; journalism; periodical literature; travel writing; book production; gender; non-canonical writing.

Recent in this series:

For more information about this series, please visit: https://www.routledge.com

Science, Language, and Reform in Victorian Poetry
Political Dialects

Barbara Barrow

Routledge
Taylor & Francis Group

NEW YORK AND LONDON

First published 2019
by Routledge
52 Vanderbilt Avenue, New York, NY 10017

and by Routledge
2 Park Square, Milton Park, Abingdon, Oxon, OX14 4RN

Routledge is an imprint of the Taylor & Francis Group, an informa business

First issued in paperback 2021

Library of Congress Cataloging-in-Publication Data
A catalog record for this title has been requested

ISBN: 978-0-367-19185-6 (hbk)
ISBN: 978-1-03-209233-1 (pbk)
ISBN: 978-0-429-20092-2 (ebk)

Typeset in Sabon
by codeMantra

Contents

Acknowledgments

This project began as a doctoral dissertation and was supported by funding from The Graduate School of Washington University in St. Louis. I am grateful to my supervisor, William McKelvy, and to my committee members, Miriam Bailin, Guinn Batten, Lynn Tatlock, and Julia Walker, for their guidance; encouragement; and rigorous, generous feedback. Ashley Maher, Lauren McCoy, Kevin Beverage, Heidi Pennington, and David Holloway offered friendship and commentary that strengthened this project. The Washington University Center for the Humanities provided a graduate fellowship and a vibrant space of intellectual companionship. My thanks go to Erin McGlothlin and to the affiliated faculty and staff at the Center for their support.

My research on the Brownings was made possible through a one-month Visiting Scholars Research Fellowship at Baylor University's Armstrong Browning Library. I am grateful to Josh King, Rita Patteson, Jennifer Borderud, Cynthia Burgess, Christi Klempnauer, and Melvin Schuetz for their hospitality and expertise.

This project has benefited from the support and advice of my colleagues at Point Park University. My thanks go to Kirstin Hanley, Jess McCort, Sarah Perrier, Karen Dwyer, Chris Girman, Kim Bell, P.K. Weston, Sera Mathew, and Colleen Hooper. The faculty, staff, and student workers at the Point Park Library helped me at all stages of the research process. Attendees, moderators, and co-panelists at annual conferences of the North American Victorian Studies Association and the Interdisciplinary Nineteenth-Century Studies Association offered feedback that helped me improve the arguments in this book. The Provost's Office at Point Park awarded faculty development funding that allowed me to present at these conferences.

Parts of the Introduction and the first chapter were published as journal articles. Material from the Introduction appeared as "Speaking the Social Body: Language-Origins and Thomas Carlyle's *The French Revolution*" in *Journal of Victorian Culture* 19.1 (May 2014): 79–92. Part of the first chapter appeared as "Gender, Language, and the Politics of Disembodiment in *Aurora Leigh*" in *Victorian Poetry* 53.3 (Autumn 2015): 243–262. I am grateful to the anonymous peer reviewers for their feedback and to the journals and their editors for permission to reproduce this material here.

At Routledge, warm thanks are due to Joanne Shattock, Julian North, Michelle Salyga, and Bryony Reece. It has been a pleasure to work with such collegial and supportive people. I'd also like to thank the two anonymous readers who offered thorough and helpful suggestions that stimulated my thinking and helped me improve the manuscript.

My mother, Lisa Smith, and my brother, Jake Smith, have always encouraged me. John Zeller's good humor and companionship makes everything possible.

Introduction

Language, Poetry, and Radical Reform in Victorian Britain

Standing in a crowded lecture hall at London's Royal Institution in 1861, the popular philologist Friedrich Max Müller linked language change to periods of revolutionary upheaval:

> It is mostly by political commotions that this surface of the more polite and cultivated speech is broken and carried away by the waters rising underneath. It is during times when the higher classes are either crushed in religious and social struggles, or mix again with the lower classes to repel foreign invasion; when literary occupations are discouraged, palaces burnt, monasteries pillaged, and seats of learning destroyed—it is then that the popular, or as they are called, the vulgar dialects, which had formed a kind of undercurrent, rise beneath the crystal surface of the literary language, and sweep away, like the waters in spring, the cumbrous formation of a bygone age.[1]

In Müller's account, renovating, revolutionary, vernacular languages periodically rise and sweep away the ossified language of the church and state. For all of their violence, such moments of political upheaval are themselves rhythmical, occurring with the regularity of the seasons ("like the waters in spring") and fitting a discernible pattern ("It is during times when..."). These moments of linguistic overflow and excess are distinct from the stasis of an elite governing language, the "cumbrous" and lasting inheritance of previous eras.

Müller's imagery of torrential language echoes many nineteenth-century theories of poetry. In the "Preface" to *Lyrical Ballads* (1802), William Wordsworth cautions readers about the "danger" of an "excitement [that] may be carried beyond its proper bounds" and offers meter, the "co-presence of something regular," as a means of "tempering and restraining the passion."[2] Coventry Patmore's "Essay on English Metrical Law" (1857) identifies a "perpetual conflict between the law of the verse and the freedom of the language."[3] Recently, Caroline Levine, Julia Saville, Anna Barton, and other scholars have read these formal properties of poetry in the context of Victorian political and social movements.[4] Levine writes that Victorian poetry, in the eyes of the New

Critics, "appeared not balanced, not tightly organized, but *excessive*," with an "earnest social message."[5] At the same time, these qualities offered poets like Elizabeth Barrett Browning the opportunity to engage with a "prosody that is notably incommensurable with the forms of the social world."[6] One especially distinctive feature of poetic language for the Victorians, then, is a rhythmical quality that allows such moments of excess to be thrown into stark relief. At the same time, the popularity of accounts like Müller's offered poets new ways of theorizing about the political effects of language in a time of dramatic social change.

Building on these claims, this book proposes that the nineteenth-century study of language played a key role in shaping the emergence of popular sovereignty. While Victorian scientists studied the origins of speech, the history of dialects, and the barrier between human and animal language, the Brownings, Tennyson, and Hardy harnessed these debates to explore social unrest, the expansion of the electorate, and the ever-widening boundaries of empire. Scholars of language and linguistics have long recognized that popular sovereignty emerged in tandem with widespread challenges to the notion of Standard English in the nineteenth century.[7] More recently, poetry scholars have shown how Victorian poets used their craft to engage with liberalism, civic discourse, cosmopolitanism, and transnational republican movements, while a revived emphasis on new formalism has inspired scholars to link these political movements to innovations in poetic meter and structure.[8] Barton, for example, understands the "formal discipline of poetry as both analogous to and also frequently identical with liberalism's ongoing mediation between law and liberty."[9] This book argues that it is Victorian poetry's lack of orderliness, its passages where poetic language spills over or exceeds its meter or formal confines, that works to challenge this balance of freedom and restraint, and to open up oppositional possibilities. Through moments of stylistic excess, expressed in formal choices that include metrical irregularities, unconventional syntax, and unusual diction, poets work to make visible the blind spots and exclusions of liberal reform. In so doing, they bring together new ideas about language with the materials of poetic craft, including epic, monodrama, and the dramatic monologue. At stake, I argue, was the democracy of language and the language of democracy as Britain rebuilt its political structure over the course of three major electoral reforms.

Despite evidence that Victorians read and thought deeply about the history and structure of language, both literary critics and historians of science tend to sideline Victorian philology, emphasizing instead the sister sciences of geology, evolutionary biology, and anthropology.[10] As Christine Ferguson notes, this critical neglect may stem from the "unsavoury political dimensions" of a science that habitually relies on socially constructed hierarchies of the primitive and the civilized.[11] However, this explanation can only partially account for the relative lack of scholarly work on Victorian philology. After all, the same charge can be made against the sciences of geology and biology, which routinely command attention in scholarly monographs, special journal issues, and centenary celebrations. Moreover, as Ferguson's own research on the "brutal tongue" in popular fiction demonstrates, many authors and scholars did find ways to disrupt such binaries, emphasizing instead expressive and liberatory dimensions of human expression that defy or challenge categorization.[12] Will Abberley likewise observes that "racial and linguistic essentialism cannot be simply equated....Philology had the potential to collapse barriers between speakers as well as enforce them."[13] Without disputing philology's role in perpetuating racial, social, linguistic, and imperial hierarchies, we can also recover textual moments that nuance our perceptions of Victorian philology as a bulwark of standardized usage and as a national hallmark of Englishness. Sarah Ogilvie's *Words of the World: A Global History of the Oxford English Dictionary* (2013), for example, shows that the dictionary's editors were more interested in World Englishes and in coverage of words coined beyond Britain than has generally been recognized.[14] Ogilvie argues that the creation of the dictionary was "a transnational effort" not confined to English volunteers. "Not only were some members of the small band of Englishmen actually Scottish, not English," she writes, "but they were supported by hundreds of men and women from around the world. The *OED* text was created by the work of hundreds of contributors worldwide. It is a distinctly global product, in a sense the original Wikipedia, coordinated by Royal Mail."[15]

It is more likely that we can trace literary criticism's relative neglect of philology to two factors. For one, the speculative, often pseudoscientific nature of the science is at odds with a scholarly tradition historically interested in empiricism and its effects on the realist novel. This tradition, begun by Gillian Beer and George Levine, and more recently extended by critics like Anne Dewitt and Adelene Buckland, often takes as its starting point a material embeddedness in scientific and literary culture, and an emphasis on realism as the gradual accumulation of ordinary events.[16] Victorian language-study, with its search for lost origins and its fanciful ideas about roots and divine meaning, may seem far afield from these concerns. Yet the science's vexed, constantly shifting balance between speculation and scientific inquiry was also central to the development of political culture in the period. For example, competing accounts of language as a divine gift on the one hand and as a product of evolutionary development on the other hand helped authors imagine political revolutions and reforms both as heaven-sent mandates and as inevitable stages in the progressive, secular unfolding of history. In attending to these politically influential accounts of language, *Political Dialects* joins works by Srdjan Smajić, Martin Willis, and Sarah Alexander that emphasize the importance of speculative, pseudoscientific, non-objective, and theoretical approaches in nineteenth-century science and culture.[17]

A second reason for philology's neglect stems from a historical turn that dismisses questions of language and reference as twin facets of a moribund deconstruction. While Hans Aarsleff and Linda Dowling read John Locke and Müller as heralds of the linguistic turn during theory's academic heyday in the 1980s, the ascendancy of new historicism rejected this emphasis on language and indeterminacy in its focus on culturally resonant artifacts.[18] As George Levine puts it in *The Realistic Imagination* (1981), the Victorians "did write with the awareness of the possibilities of indeterminate meaning...but they wrote *against* the very indeterminacy they tended to reveal," and this impatience with a suspicious deconstructive impulse shapes not only his rebuttal but also the more recent turn to "surface reading" espoused by Victorianists like Sharon Marcus and Dewitt.[19]

If the historical turn tended to sideline questions of language and reference in Victorian literary and cultural texts, recent calls for a revived, politically alert formalism invite us to reconsider language's role. For Levine, literary forms as diverse as sonnets, rhyming couplets, and narrative clash and intersect with social and political formations like patriarchy and bureaucracy. Language plays a briefly acknowledged but central role in this excitingly dynamic collision of forms: "Literature is not made of the material world it describes or invokes, but of language, which lays claims to its own forms—syntactical, narrative, rhythmic, rhetorical... Every literary form thus generates its own, separate logic."[20] If language constitutes the world it seeks to describe, then it is uniquely positioned to alter, challenge, or affirm the political forms of that world. As we will see, the poets discussed in this book draw on a range of forms—from the epic to the closet drama to the dramatic monologue—in their responses to reform. In doing so, they retain a keen awareness of language's creative potential for writing and reshaping political formations, from the poet-heroine's embrace of a radical, language-reforming, and proto-feminist Christ in Barrett Browning's *Aurora Leigh* (1856) to the re-appropriation of dialect as a tool of resistance to nationalism in Hardy's *Wessex Poems*. A heightened attention to contemporary debates about language uncovers a little-acknowledged relationship between poetry, philology, and politics, and sheds fresh light on this rich interplay of literary, cultural, and political forms.

Radical Dictionaries, Non-Standard English, and the Specter of Revolution

Victorian poets' knowledge of philology was wide-ranging. Both Barrett Browning and Browning incorporated the principles of language and liberty espoused by Locke, Tennyson's poetry about the imperial empire took its lead from Charles Darwin's theories of language evolution, and Hardy had a career-long interest in the composition of the *New English Dictionary (NED)*, later the *Oxford English Dictionary (OED)*. For their part, both lay and professional scientists and word-collectors were keenly attuned to the relationship between their research and the political upheavals of the present. Their highly politicized accounts of language-study mirrored developments in the sister science of evolutionary biology. Peter Bowler writes that evolution's model of gradual change in nature shifted away from older ideas about a relatively static, God-given social hierarchy and fostered the belief that individuals could challenge aristocratic power.[21] The steady-state changes on the earth's surface described in Charles Lyell's *Principles of Geology* (1830–1833) and Darwin's *On the Origin of Species* (1859) reflected liberal ideas about incremental progress.[22] Many Victorian philologists, inspired by evolutionary thinking, came to see language as an autonomous, self-regulating system that, much like the successive stages of evolutionary development, could eventually lead to improvements in the social order. One might say they even contributed more explicitly to the project of speaking the *polis* as their own material—language—had a direct and immediate effect on the formation of concepts in the public sphere. As the exiled German newspaper correspondent Lothair Bucher put in in 1858, "political philology" concerned itself with "terms originating in speculative politics; notions which, when first propounded, have no corresponding reality, but are to be 'realized'; words, first placed on the lips, then filling the mind, then guiding the hand to good or to evil, destined, may be, to overturn a world."[23] A political philology acts as a point of origin for social change, an exploratory site for the testing-out of new, and potentially radical, ideas.

For many nineteenth-century philologists, the radical philology of the French Revolution acted as a counterpoint to this gradualist model, recalling the role of language in a time of rapid political change. "The French Revolution may be called...the avatar of the word *equality*," declared Bucher.[24] Across the Atlantic, William Dwight Whitney argued in his *Language and the Study of Language* (1867) that the "speakers of language...constitute a republic, or rather, a democracy, in which authority is conferred only by general suffrage and for due cause."[25] Like Karl Marx, who wrote in 1852 that people on the verge of large-scale revolutions look back to the "borrowed language" of their history, Victorian poets and philologists looked to the neologisms and radical dictionaries of the earlier part of the century in their responses to reform.[26] The idea that people rather than governments might be the proper authorities on language, an idea fostered by people's grammars and treatises by William Cobbett and John Thelwall, persisted throughout the nineteenth century.[27]

In order to explore this nexus between language, philology, and politics, I turn for the remainder of this introduction to Thomas Carlyle's *The French Revolution* (1837), a text that both documents and performs, in its fragmentary, violent structure, the struggle between the old feudal and colonial order and a nascent popular sovereignty. Published just five years after the First Reform Act, *The French Revolution* is not technically a work of poetry but rather a long, experimental epic in prose. However, *The French Revolution* is an influential Victorian text deeply concerned with both scientific and metaphysical accounts of language, and as such provides valuable insights into key, foundational issues of philology and politics in the period.

A second and crucial reason for including *The French Revolution* has to do with Carlyle's reputation, among his contemporaries, as a writer of stylistic extravagance. For Lady Sydney Morgan, *The French Revolution* was a book of "transcendental excess"; William Makepeace Thackeray noted its "strange epithets, and choking double words"; Herman Merivale lamented its "bastard English."[28] Like the poets who were inspired by his work, Carlyle engages with political ideas in moments of stylistic overflow, an overflow expressed in convoluted syntax, interjections, and extended metaphors of embodiment. Perhaps this verbal excess is why *The French Revolution* was received by contemporaries as a poem rather than a work of prose. John Stuart Mill described the work as an "Epic Poem" that fulfilled Carlyle's aim to show the "poetry" of history as it shaped early Victorian ideas about reform.[29] Barrett Browning shared this assessment, calling Carlyle a "great prose poet" and describing *The French Revolution* as "a great poem," while Thackeray found among its "prose run mad" moments of "noble poetry."[30] Drawing on a rich history of revolutionary debates about language and liberty, Carlyle's sprawling, experimental history insists that an account of the Revolution cannot be written in any "living political dialects," and the idiosyncratic style of *The French Revolution* represents Carlyle's insistence that democracy requires a new distinct language of its own.[31]

Carlyle's merging of scientific and speculative accounts of language also invites us to reconsider his seeming aversion to scientific thought and, more broadly, to question the supposed division between scientific and speculative thought in the early Victorian period.[32] Critics have long regarded Carlyle as stubbornly resistant to nineteenth-century scientific rationalism. For Hans Aarsleff, he is a mystifying and incomprehensible sage figure, a "prophet of words" who turns away from the freethinking philology of Locke and Étienne Bonnot de Condillac in order to focus on the divinity of language and its unknowable "true meaning."[33] More recently, Frank Turner and John Ulrich have challenged this too-rigid division between Carlylean mysticism and contemporary science, showing how Carlyle both influenced and was influenced by scientists working in the fields of biology, physics, and paleontology.[34] Extending this debate to philology, the science of language, reveals how Carlyle's attention to both more materialist and more speculative approaches to the scientific study of language helped shape philology's interactions with radical politics.[35] Far from dismissive of the science of language, Carlyle remained deeply invested in philology, and perhaps no branch of inquiry was more influential on his political thinking than the debates about words, meaning, and sovereignty that raged during the Revolution and in its aftermath.

Carlyle's interest in language throughout *The French Revolution* showcases the crucial role the Revolution continued to play in the British political imagination on the eve of the First Reform Act. Researched and written during the Reform Crisis and during heated public debate over the bill, Carlyle's massive revolutionary history contributes to a British political discourse that raises the specter of revolutionary upheaval as a threatening alternative to electoral reform.[36] While some commentators— most famously, Edmund Burke—looked back to the Glorious Revolution of 1688 as an event that worked to promote civil liberties in England, others pointed to the events across the Channel as representations of grievances that Britons also shared.[37] Carlyle continues to draw this comparison throughout the Reform Crisis and its aftermath, declaring in *Chartism* (1839) that "These Chartisms, Radicalisms, Reform Bill, Tithe Bill, and infinite other discrepancy, and acrid argument and jargon that there is yet to be, are *our* French Revolution."[38] Moreover, as his dismissal of the Reform Bill as mere "jargon" suggests, he also elevates revolution over reform as a more dramatic and sweeping, if violent, means of social renovation.

In staking this implicit claim, Carlyle looked back to heated, cross-Channel and transatlantic debates about the relationship between language and political liberty, debates that arose in response to an eighteenth-century tradition of prescriptivist philology concerned with fixing language in a static or ideal state.[39] As Haruko Momma explains, prescriptivism "authorized certain lexical usage and labelled all others as incorrect. For the prescriptivists, therefore, the semantic web of each word consisted of one or a few 'correct' meanings situated in the middle and surrounded with the muddle of 'errors' and 'solecisms.'"[40] For many admirers and detractors, Samuel Johnson's *A Dictionary of the English Language* (1755) was the most visible symbol of this prescriptivist lexicography. In the "Preface" to the *Dictionary*, for example, Johnson had explained his decision to privilege ancient over modern principles of spelling, advising his readers to preserve "the orthography of their fathers" and to recognize that there "is in constancy and stability a general and lasting advantage" that outlasted the constant flux of linguistic change.[41] Instead of drawing on more contemporary sources to furnish examples of each word, he looked to writers before the Restoration, whose works were *"the wells of English undefiled"* and the "pure sources of genuine diction."[42] In a lexicographical anticipation of Burke's claim in the *Reflections on the Revolution in France* (1790) that tradition and not innovation must structure politics, it is tradition, not innovation, which informs Johnson's literary examples.

This model of philology underwent radical changes during the Revolution. The catastrophic theories of eighteenth-century geology had long begun to unravel the static, harmonious vision of nature and society ordered on the aristocracy, finding in the imagery of geological disaster a way of describing the sudden overthrow of the *ancien régime*.[43] These revolutionary ideas found their way into the sister science of philology, where some Revolutionary sympathizers, such as the American lexicographer Noah Webster, the French dramatist Louis-Sébastien Mercier, and the English philologist and political agitator John Horne Tooke, urged their readers to overthrow the shackles of the aristocracy with new words, spellings, and phrases. In his two-part *The Diversions of Purley* (1786, 1805), a philological treatise that takes the form of a dialogue among learned men at an English manor house, Horne Tooke shows how the Johnsonian tradition acts as a prop for aristocratic power and a barrier to the revolutionary principles of liberty and equality. In the midst of a heated debate over the term "rights," the men consult Johnson's *Dictionary* and conclude that Johnson's careful etymologies reinforce hereditary power by omitting important meanings of the term:

F.—...Let us see how Johnson handles it. He did not indeed acknowledge any RIGHTS of the people; but he was very clear concerning Ghosts and Witches, all the mysteries of divinity, and the sacred, indefeasible, inherent, hereditary RIGHTS of Monarchy. Let us see how he explains the term.
RIGHT——
RIGHT——
RIGHT——
NO. He gives no explanation: —Except of RIGHT hand.[44]

The dialogue works to demystify the veneration and divine authority granted to the aristocracy in a time of revolution. "But seek no further for intelligence in that quarter," concludes one of the men, "where nothing but fraud, and cant, and folly is to be found—misleading, mischievous folly; because it has a sham appearance of labour, learning, and piety."[45] According to the *Diversions*, a proper understanding of language-study's role to political freedom lies not in Johnson's dictionary but rather in etymologies that sought to rescue original, liberatory meanings of words and in a simplification of grammar aimed at making the study of language more widely accessible to all users, for whom a proper understanding of language is necessary in order to understand "religion and civil society."[46]

Horne Tooke's use of etymologies and grammar to challenge the outmoded English aristocracy also resonates in the work of Noah Webster, which Carlyle was reading in 1833.[47] In his *Dissertations on the English Language* (1789), Webster writes that the American Revolution had dramatically changed the rules and standards of English across the Atlantic. "As an independent nation," Webster declares, "our honor requires us to have a system of our own, in language as well as government. Great Britain, whose children we are, and whose language we speak, should no longer be *our* standard; for the taste of her writers is already corrupted, and her language on the decline."[48] Webster pushes for a new form of American English that would disregard the fading, obsolete words of the old regime. Webster's dictionaries put this goal into practice by standardizing and codifying distinct forms of American spelling and pronunciation.[49] His "Preface" to *An American Dictionary of the English Language* (1828) further explains his rejection of English political terms:

> Thus the practice of hawking and hunting, the institution of heraldry, and the feudal system of England originated terms which formed, and some of which now form, a necessary part of the language of that country; but, in the United States, many of these terms are no part of our present language,—and they cannot be, for the things which they express do not exist in this country. They can be known to us only as obsolete or as foreign words. On the other hand, the institutions of this country which are new and peculiar, give rise to new terms or to new applications of old terms, unknown to the people of England; which cannot be explained by them and which will not be inserted in their dictionaries, unless copied from ours.[50]

In Webster's estimation, the feudal traditions of the English elite, expressed in heraldry and hunting, are inexpressible in the context of American democracy. Such terms can only be "obsolete," while the distinct institutions and symbols of American politics require their own unique definitions.[51] Political difference is the origin of linguistic difference, the main force that drives the creation of new words, terms, and meanings in the wake of a fading aristocracy.

In France, the revolutionary dictionary emerged in response to the institution of the French Academy and its longstanding relationship to the royal court. Founded in 1635 by Cardinal Richelieu, chief minister to King Louis XIII, and temporarily suppressed during the Revolution, the French Academy was responsible not only for overseeing French grammar and spelling but also for producing the authoritative dictionary of the French language, the *Dictionnaire de l'Académie française*, which entered into its sixth and seventh editions in the Victorian period.[52]

During the Revolution, Mercier called for language reform in *Panorama of Paris* (1781–1788) and *The New Paris* (1789), works that Carlyle frequently cites in *The French Revolution*.[53] "The people have too long been prevented from understanding each other by the change in the signification of words," he writes in *The New Paris*. "The Parisian is afraid of the abuse of words, and suffers things to proceed."[54] For Mercier, the revolution is a linguistic as well as a political rebellion. He distances himself from the top-down, hieratic language of the French Academy, whose first rule was that language should be defined by the standards of the royal court.[55] In *Panorama of Paris*, Mercier provides a lively account of Parisian street life that vies with the history of the city in the official dictionary:

> Anyone who expects to find in this work a *topographic* description of public squares and streets, or a history of the city's past, will be disappointed. I have concentrated on customs and their rapidly changing nuances. Moutard, the Queen's book-publisher, sells a dictionary in four enormous volumes, approved by the censors and with a privilege from the king, in which one will find the story of every castle, college, and alleyway. If the monarch ever thinks of selling his capital, this fat dictionary would serve, I think, as a catalogue or inventory.[56]

In Mercier's hands, the dictionary is a tool of monarchical wealth and oppression. His own account, on the contrary, is composed of episodic, eyewitness vignettes of Parisian life, among them street lighting, markets, street singers, and barbers' shops, all of which influence Carlyle's own panoramic descriptions of revolutionary Paris. In keeping with this inventory of urban street life, Mercier promotes an understanding of language as a creative force that emerges not from the court but from the speech of the people. "I call the people the sovereign judge of language," he writes in his own *La Neologie*, a non-prescriptive dictionary compiled from new coinages.[57]

By way of his reading in Johnson, Webster, and Mercier, Carlyle encountered both the prescriptivist tradition of the eighteenth century and the philology of revolution that followed it. By the 1820s and 1830s, when Carlyle was just at the beginning of his writing career, philology in the British Isles had yet to achieve the kind of methodological precision it was gaining on the Continent.[58] While Franz Bopp in Germany and Rasmus Rask in Denmark were both pioneering a more systematic approach to the study of the Indo-European languages, one "severed" from "the Romanticism that midwifed it," the study of language in Britain was less streamlined and more speculative, a heady and sometimes incongruous mixture of grammatical treatises, Anglo-Saxon scholarship, and theological accounts of the dispersion at Babel.[59] At the same time, early Victorian writers were keenly attuned to the revolutionary implications of the philology that had inaugurated their century. The "want of fixity [in English pronunciation]," warns W.H. Savage in *The Vulgarisms and Improprieties of the English Language* (1833), "creates an everlasting contention, and leaves to the arbitrary caprice of individuals a power, in which the ignorant assume a want of claim equally forcible with the learned."[60]

Carlyle's 1832 *Fraser's* review of John Wilson Croker's edition of *Boswell's Life of Johnson* acknowledges these opposing tensions between prescriptive and radical philology, and between the linguistic past and the linguistic present. Carlyle portrays Johnson as a genuine speaker of the truth and a preserver of tradition in an age already "boiling" toward the epoch-defining forces of revolution and reform.[61] "If England has escaped the blood-bath of a French Revolution," he writes, "...let Samuel Johnson, beyond all contemporary or succeeding men have the praise" for making England "*Toryish*, Loyal to the Old."[62] At the same time, Carlyle presents Johnson as a conservative foil to the inexorable forces of revolution. In *Sartor Resartus* (1833–1840), for example, Johnson is no match for the "Sansculottist" energies of the radical anti-hero, Diogenes Teufelsdröckh.[63] *Sartor Resartus* contrasts Johnson's genteel formality with Teufelsdröckh's strict principles of equality. "I would fain carry it farther than most do;" writes Teufelsdröckh, "and whereas the English Johnson only bowed to every Clergyman, or man with a shovel-hat, I would bow to every Man with any sort of hat, or with no hat whatever" (181). The narrative structure of *Sartor Resartus* mimics the tension between tradition and revolution in the language of its fictional English Editor. In the end, it is not the dignified language of Johnson but rather the infectious radicalism of Teufelsdröckh that begins to affect *Sartor's* narrator: "What a result, should this piebald, entangled, hyper-metaphorical style of writing, not to say of thinking, become general among our Literary men! As it might so easily do. Thus has not the Editor himself, working over Teufelsdröckh's German, lost much of his own English purity?" (221). In this satirical account of the danger that Teufelsdröckh's German poses to English "purity" and, earlier, to the social values of Johnson, *Sartor Resartus* holds Johnson up as a figure of rapidly diminishing influence under the force of the revolutionary energies streaming across to Britain from the Continent.[64]

Like Mercier, Carlyle celebrates demotic speech and rejects the dictionary of the French Academy as a tool of elite court culture. In a letter to Mill in 1833, Carlyle criticizes the exclusionary lexicography of the French Academy:

> Another thing I need, perhaps attainable enough: a good French Dictionary! I have got old *Richelet* in two folios, very useful for

my *Bayle* and whatever is earlier; and then three or four wretched French-English ones, which daily in attempting to use them I feel inclined to burn. The Academy Dictionary is not of my sort; a little vocabulary of any sort that contained *all* kinds of words, vulgar and royal, and gave even the feeblest interpretation were far better for me than your *Cruscan* ("sifting") sort, for often the "siftings" are the very thing I am in quest of.[65]

Carlyle's rejection of the limited entries of the Academy Dictionary and his frustration with the "sifting" process of the *Accademia della Crusca*, the linguistic academy founded at Florence in 1583, show his desire for a more capacious register of the French language that contains both elite and vernacular forms of expression.[66] Like Horne Tooke and Mercier, Carlyle takes aim at standard dictionaries as censors of the broader social panorama.

We can also trace Carlyle's defense of his own style back to Mercier's passionate investment in neology. Defending his writing in an 1835 letter to John Sterling, who had called Carlyle's language "barbaric," Carlyle writes, "If one has thoughts not hitherto uttered in English Books, I see nothing for it but that you must use words not found there, must make words,—with moderation and discretion, of course." He goes on:

> But finally do you reckon this really a time for Purism of Style; or that Style (mere dictionary style) has much to do with the worth or unworth of a Book? I do not: with whole ragged battalions of Scott's-Novel Scotch, with Irish, German, French and even Newspaper Cockney (when "Literature" is little other than a Newspaper) storming in on us, and the whole structure of our Johnsonian English breaking up from its foundations,—revolution there as visible as anywhere else![67]

With equal measures of delight and anxiety, Carlyle anticipates an impending linguistic revolution, a dialogic stampede of languages that will overturn the literary standard of Johnsonian English. Carlyle insists that the structures of established usage are changing and that these changes are intimately connected to changes in the social order. He dismisses what he calls "dictionary style," a correct linguistic standard, as an adequate vehicle for expressing political upheaval. In *The French Revolution*, language generates meaning in opposition to the received wisdom of the dictionary. "Men and Knitting-women repeat Fédéraliste with or without much Dictionary-meaning; but go on repeating it," Carlyle writes, "till the meaning of it becomes almost magical" (II: 249). Carlyle substitutes for the authoritative dictionary a neology that speakers gradually internalize and comprehend through affective processes of repetition. His revolutionary invasion of languages blends a characteristically distasteful assessment of linguistic corruption—the "newspaper Cockney"—with a genuine belief in the providential, regenerative force of the vernacular.

Carlyle's satirical references to "English Purity" and his inclusion of "Scott's Novel-Scotch" among the invasive languages mentioned earlier also underline how the prescriptivist approach created metropolitan standards that marginalized and dismissed Scottish languages. As Robert Crawford notes, Carlyle's indebtedness to Sir Walter Scott is pervasive throughout his work, with Scott standing in for "the first of a number of linguistic precursors of his own inventive, eclectic, non-Standard English diction."[68] This idea that there was one "Standard English," a phrase which, Tony Crowley has shown, first appeared in an 1836 *Quarterly Review* article, would present lasting barriers to the recognition of Scots as an independent language within the British Isles.[69] In Scotland, this notion of a "standard" national language, in turn, would fail to account for the regional complexity of linguistic differences between the Scots Gaelic spoken in the Highlands and the Lowlands Scots language.[70] The marginalization of Scottish accents would prompt a self-improvement literature that remained in print throughout the Victorian period and that aimed to teach Scots how to cultivate a metropolitan English accent.[71]

In his writing on the Scottish literary tradition, Carlyle resists this association of metropolitan English accents with upper-class status. In his 1828 essay on Robert Burns's poetry, for example, Carlyle writes that Burns's work offers a vision of egalitarian sincerity that affects readers regardless of "casual varieties in outward rank or inward."[72] Like the writing of the fictional Teufelsdröckh, Burns's poetry offers, for Carlyle, a radically leveling vision of social life. Burns's "appearance among the sages and nobles of Edinburgh must be regarded as one of the most singular phenomena in modern Literature; almost like the appearance of some Napoleon among the crowned sovereigns of modern Politics."[73] By politicizing Burns's literary debut in this way, Carlyle suggests that his use of Scots dialect works to challenge and dismantle an established Standard English much in the same way that Napoleon's early career worked to challenge and dismantle the structures of hereditary power.

Carlyle's encounters with the rhetorical tradition at Edinburgh further shaped his awareness of the class prejudices associated with regional dialects. His disdain for the rhetorician and Chair of Rhetoric and Belles Lettres at the University of Edinburgh, Hugh Blair, is widely discussed, but Carlyle also developed his vision of language in response to lesser-known figures like the Aberdeen-born philologist and schoolmaster Alexander Crombie.[74] While Crombie's philological study *The Etymology and Syntax of the English Language* (1802) openly renounces prescriptivism, observing that the job of the grammarian is "not to dictate forms of speech, or to prescribe law to our modes of expression," his insistence on looking to learned rather than lay speakers does seek to establish standards of correct and incorrect usage that are inherently bound up with class divisions.[75] Crombie advocates for a literary standard based on the use of "reputable authors" as a stay against the diverse sociolects of the poor, whose speech, he complains, differs too widely from province to province:

> The vulgar in this, as in every other country, are, from their want of education, necessarily illiterate. Their native language is known to them no farther, than is requisite for the most common purposes of life. Their ideas are few, and consequently their stock of words, poor and scanty. Nay, their poverty, in this respect, is not their only evil. Their narrow competence they abuse, and pervert. Some words they misapply, others they corrupt; while many are employed by them, which have no sanction, but provincial, or local, authority. Hence the language of the vulgar, in one province, is sometimes hardly intelligible in another.[76]

Crombie equates material poverty with a poverty of vocabulary, showing how regional and provincial variations work against a reputable, national standard for the English language. As Crombie's complaint of trans-regional unintelligibility suggests, the biblical story of the dispersion at Babel was a frequent reference in nineteenth-century accounts of linguistic difference. Ethnological research into the study of languages reinvigorated the story of the dispersion at Babel in accounts like James Cowles Prichard's *The Eastern Origin of Celtic Nations* (1831), a volume that attempted to link the Indo-European languages to the Eastern languages to suggest an aboriginal connection that was lost after a period of separation.[77] In Crombie's account, however, Babel stands not for a global dispersion of peoples but for a provincial distribution of the rural poor, one that stands in the way of a comprehensive, unified national tongue.

For Carlyle, however, no hieratic linguistic authority could unite the scattered dialects of a modern, revolutionary polity. Rather, these dialects played a necessarily chaotic in overturning received conventions of language and calling attention to class divisions. Carlyle disliked Crombie, declaring to Robert Mitchell in 1821, "Do you take...your Crombie...and let me be doing with Lake poets, Mystics."[78] He was familiar with recently published ethnological references to Babel, having apparently borrowed Prichard from the etymologist Hensleigh Wedgwood (Darwin's cousin) in 1837.[79] In *The French Revolution*, linguistic variations take on a providential revolutionary significance that highlights Carlyle's dislike of standardized language: "To the ends of France; and in as many dialects as when the first great Babel was to be built!" he declares of the divine "voice of the People" (1:329). In stark contrast to Crombie's trans-regional unintelligibility, Carlyle presents this historical clash of voices as a chaotic and necessary force of political mobilization.

However, while Horne Tooke dismissed divine-origins theories of language as mere forms of mystification, in which the notion of "divine rights" worked to legitimize a corrupt aristocracy, Carlyle was determined to show that such divine rights continued to exist, not in an exploitative, rotten monarchy but in the providential voices of the long-silenced underclass, who acted as agents of God's righteousness. In a more extreme and sustained way than Mercier, Webster, and Horne Tooke, Carlyle wanted to create what we might call a political theology of language, in which the populist neologisms of the Revolution become messianic expressions of a divine will. In *The French Revolution*, for example, he describes the bill-stickers of Paris, with their paste pots and placards, as a "Sacred College" who reveal, beneath the ever-changing messages of their placards, the spiritual basis of human communication (1:331):

> They made the walls of Paris didactic, suasive, with an ever-fresh Periodical Literature, wherein he that ran might read: Placard Journals, Placard Lampoons, Municipal Ordinances, Royal Proclamations...What unutterable things the stone-walls spoke, during those five years! But it is all gone; To-Day swallowing Yesterday, and then being in its turn swallowed of To-morrow, even as Speech every is. Nay what, O thou immortal Man of Letters, is Writing itself but Speech conserved for a time? The Placard Journal conserved it for one day; some Books conserve it for the matter of ten years; nay some for three thousand: but what then? Why, *then,* the years being all run, it also dies, and the world is rid of it. Oh, were there not a spirit in the word of man, as in man himself, that survived the audible bodied word, and tended either Godward, or else Devilward, for evermore, why should he trouble himself much with the truth of it, or the falsehood of it, except for commercial purposes?
>
> (1:331)

In the tattered placards of Paris, Carlyle locates a divine spirit that, elsewhere in *The French Revolution*, also fills the voices of the revolutionaries themselves, prompting them to act as agents of a heavenly mandate. This spirit precedes the words that express it, taking temporary form in "audible bodied" placards and chants, and eventually outlasting these momentary casings.

Carlyle's combination of radical philology and theological accounts of language was central in producing the emergent form of the "social body" in the Victorian political imagination. Mary Poovey writes that the phrase "the social body" emerged in the nineteenth century as part of a linguistic shift from the metaphor of the "body politic," understood as the king and Parliament, to the metaphor of the "social body," widened to include the laboring classes.[80] *The French Revolution* is a powerful meditation on the modern polity as a sovereign body and on the new forms of linguistic representation this body demands. Carlyle's theological reading of language turns to a long tradition of associating political power with the doctrine of the Incarnation, or the "word-become-flesh" in the language and body of Christ, in order to describe the emergence of political power vested in the people as part of a divinely ordained plan. This description of language as a type of holy incarnation draws on the prologue to the Book of John, in which Christ's body takes human form: "And the Word was made flesh, and dwelt among us, (and we beheld his glory, the glory as of the only begotten of the Father,) full of grace and truth."[81] In this account of language-origins, the spirit precedes the flesh, and the word comes before its material embodiment in the figure of Christ, much as in Carlyle's Sacred College, where the spirit in the word outlasts the "audible bodied word" of the Revolutionary placards. Throughout *The French Revolution*, this idea of the word-made-flesh animates individual bodies, the collective bodies of the revolutionaries, and even comes to express the divine energies of the Revolution itself.

Carlyle's language of incarnation takes aim at empiricist accounts of language that minimized the question of its divine origins. Influential works of Enlightenment language-philosophy, including "Of Words" from Locke's *An Essay Concerning Human Understanding* (1689), had downplayed biblical accounts of language-origins by referring external knowledge to sensory perception or to "common sensible ideas," as Locke wrote, which emerged from "organs...*fit to frame articulate sounds*, which we call words."[82] Linda Dowling has shown how Locke's empiricism would give rise to later materialist accounts of language and to the alarming supposition that language was "little more than another physical reality in a universe now wholly governed by physical laws."[83] *The French Revolution* emphatically rejects the Lockean claim that language derives from the evidence of sensory perception alone: "But if the very Rocks and Rivers...are, in strict language, made by those outward Senses of ours, how much more, by the Inward Sense, are all Phenomena of the spiritual kind" (1:8). Much as the word precedes the flesh in the Johannine account of the Incarnation, the spiritual senses precede the outward senses.[84]

If the Book of John was an important antecedent for Carlyle's reworking of the Incarnation, Edward Irving's sermons popularized and expanded upon this doctrine for an eager and devoted audience. Born in Dumfriesshire in 1792, educated in the ministry at Edinburgh, and eventually made master of a Kirkcaldy academy, Irving came to know Carlyle as the rival schoolmaster of a neighboring school in Annandale before he went on to a sensational career as a premillenialist preacher in London.[85] There, Irving performed the apocalyptic sermons that inspired his congregation to speak in "tongues," attracting both inquisitive audiences and heavy criticism from the press, and eventually undergoing a trial and deposition from the Church of Scotland. Carlyle watched the apocalyptic ecstasy of Irving's congregation with horror, writing in 1832 that Irving remained "enveloped in the vain sound of the 'Tongues'.... I pity poor Irving, and cannot prophecy of him: his 'Morning Watch' he gave me yesternight is simply the howling of a Bedlam."[86] In a commemorative piece on Irving written thirty-two years after the latter's decease in 1834, Carlyle lamented that his friend's controversial sermons led him to be "scornfully forgotten at the time of his death" and had caused him, long before, to fall "out of the notice of the more intelligent classes."[87]

However, as Stewart J. Brown reminds us, Irving had first roused controversy and even accusations of heresy, not for his later cultivation of the "tongues" but rather for his belief in Christ's human nature.[88] Irving's collected *Sermons, Lectures, and Occasional Discourses* (1828), for example, expands upon the Johannine doctrine of the word-made-flesh, arguing that "grace and truth came, not by the *word* but by the *Word Incarnate*...For it was in the act of becoming flesh that all grace and all truth was embodied."[89] On this point, Carlyle and Irving were apparently in agreement. As Irving wrote to his wife in 1829, lamenting his Edinburgh companions' resistance to his views, there was in Annan "a strength" where different acquaintances were "firm as to the human nature of Christ, which none here is, except Thomas Carlyle."[90] Early in Irving's controversial career, Carlyle shared with his friend a belief in the dual nature of Christ, finding in the doctrine of the Incarnation a way of bridging the boundary between the material and the divine realms.

If Irving's views on incarnation offered an account of language that bridged the material and the divine realms, Coleridge's writings drew out the underlying political theology of this connection by linking the story of the Incarnation to the structure of the aristocratic body politic. Carlyle's letters show that he visited Coleridge at Highgate in the years leading up to Coleridge's death in 1834; he admired the *Aids to Reflection* (1825), despite characterizing Coleridge himself as a "round fat oily yet impatient little man" who spoke in "half intelligible Kantianism."[91] Most importantly, Coleridge shared Carlyle's insistence on the divine nature of language. In his "Preface" to the *Aids to Reflection*, Coleridge distances himself from Horne Tooke's materialist etymologies in the *Diversions*, explaining that he likewise wants to bring readers' attention to the "science of words [and] their use and abuse"; however, where Horne Tooke titled his work "winged words," Coleridge would substitute "living words," meaning those such as Ezekiel saw in the visions of God.[92]

Coleridge's metaphysical account of language was inseparable from his interest in the divinely inspired political community.[93] In *On the Constitution of Church and State* (1829), a tract that later became the subject of a lengthy analysis by Mill in the *London and Westminster*

Review (1840), Coleridge uses the concept of the incarnate Word as shorthand for the hereditary aristocracy. Coleridge is concerned throughout with describing the power of the King as the head of the church, the nationality, and the clerisy, and in explaining the symbolic composition of the body politic. He observes that it is difficult to find "in the whole compass of language... a metaphor so commensurate...as that of *Body Politic*, as the exponent of a State or Realm"; in a brief and suggestive note, he offers "the WORD (*Gosp. of John*, 1.1)" as the most fitting metaphor for "the Divine Alterity."[94] Much as word bridges the divine and material worlds, the monarch bridges the sacred realm and the realm of the state.

Coleridge's model of the incarnate Word as a symbol of the monarch's divine power anticipates Ernst Kantorowicz's classic study of political theology, *The King's Two Bodies* (1957). Kantorowicz demonstrates how the twofold nature of Christ as both human and divine influenced perceptions of the monarch's body in medieval times so that the feudal king was endowed with both a physical body and an immortal super-body.[95] The notion of Christ's two bodies emerged as a response to the reading of the Eucharist, which came to symbolize dialectically both the natural body or the host on the altar and the mystical body of the Church; this mystical body would evolve into the early modern body politic with the king at its head.[96] Similarly, in Coleridge's account, the monarch's ability to access both the human and divine realms finds its model in the metaphor of Christ's dual nature as both essence and body. Language bridges this boundary between the heavenly and the political realms as the monarch acts as a divinely appointed communicant of the sacred word. In the aftermath of the Revolution and the reforms that followed it, this model of the incarnate body politic came under pressure as Western European monarchies grappled with the emergence of democratic and republican movements. The language of the aristocratic body politic gradually gave way to the language of the social body, with its greater inclusion of non-noble and non-aristocratic subjects.[97]

Throughout *The French Revolution*, Carlyle develops his model of a messianic language based in the emergent social body, finally advocating for a revolutionary new political dialect in place of the static jargoning of Victorian reforms. *The French Revolution* takes up this historical transition from the body politic to the body social and recasts it in linguistic terms, radically assigning a messianic and world-historical power to the language of the underclasses. Carlyle shares Coleridge's language of the polity as a form of incarnation, but he emphatically rejects the aristocracy's potential to act as a spiritually viable force. Carlyle instead radicalizes Coleridge's model of the body politic by relocating the divine word of the monarch to the French subjects who body forth into political collectives, extending the idea of the word-become-flesh to a broader portion of revolutionaries whose activities, in turn, create a new political idiom. In *The French Revolution* the word-become-flesh not only becomes a metaphor for communicating the divine potential of language but also describes the historical emergence of the social body whose new forms of speech overturn the structures of the monarchical order, creating a "living political dialect" of the modern polity. He begins by identifying the weakened elements of the feudal body politic: the Church has "for centuries seen itself decaying"; now, when yoked to a rotting monarchy the two institutions will "stand and fall together" (1:13). Carlyle contrasts the decadent monarchy with the plight of the silent poor, whose voices are heard only "in Heaven," where "the answer too will come,--in a horror of great darkness, and shakings of the world, and a cup of trembling which all nations shall drink" (1:16). Carlyle links the decline of the body politic to the providential, gathering, and as-yet silent powers of the underclasses.

Carlyle makes the hereditary order the target of this linguistic regeneration by equating language decay with the royal flesh. For example, he connects the demise of King Louis XV to a weakness in the somatic authority of the monarchy: it is through a "lazy habit of body" that hereditary institutions deteriorate (1:31–32). This somatic decrepitude even extends to the weary and macabre self-awareness of King Louis XV himself, who, with a "spasmodic antagonism," goes riding out in his carriage to gaze wearily at graveyards (1:21). The narrator conflates physical and verbal embodiment by extending these descriptions of sickness and decay to language. Drawing on the terminology of prescriptivist grammars, he calls Louis a "Solecism Incarnate," literally a language-blunder, a violation of grammatical rules (1:23). Genteel language works to index the ruined feudalism that the king represents. Expressions such as "Sir" are "Tatters and fibres of old Feudality; which, were it only in the Grammatical province, ought to be rooted out!" (2:59). This fading language also influences the period's written literature. Carlyle cites two fashionable novels published in 1789 as "the last-speech of old Feudal France," gesturing toward the decline of the written standard (1:62). Echoing his description of the revolutionary dispersion in his letter to Sterling, Carlyle envisions a new linguistic revolution that will overturn a sick monarchy whose corruptions saturate the period's literary productions.

Far from being a wholly democratic transfer of sovereign authority to the people, however, Carlyle's language-metaphors also caution readers that the newly formed structures of the French government may threaten to replicate despotisms experienced under the old regime. In this regard, he takes after Mercier, who was cautious about positing too great a breach between the old and the new order.[98] For both commentators, the Revolution threatened to overshadow or obscure continuities of injustice and the ways new structures of the polity could replicate them. "Are Representative Governments merely at bottom Tyrannies too?" Carlyle asks (1:226). *The French Revolution* is also suspicious of political incompetence, describing the National Assembly as a body whose members gather to *"cancel" one* other with "jargon and hubbub" (1:226) and that wastes time trying to "get its theory of defective verbs perfected" (2:320).

The French Revolution suggests that the voice of the people has the power to overturn the National Assembly, much as it overturns the Bastille. Carlyle symbolizes the force of this anarchic vocabulary by describing the French Revolution as a confusion of tongues: revolutionary Paris is filled with "jargon as of Babel, in the hour when they were first smitten (as here) with mutual unintelligibility, and the people had not yet dispersed!" (2:105). Yet this is not a lasting chaos. In all human movements, Carlyle writes, there is "order, or the beginning of order" (2:126). The order that emerges from this Babel is the emergent form of the social body, and its power of linguistic regeneration lies in the symbolic corporeal power the underclasses now manifest as newly embodied subjects. Carlyle reminds us again of the new signification of the social body when he wonders about the signification of the phrase "Revolution" itself. He writes, "What then is this Thing, called La Révolution, which, like an Angel of Death, hangs over France" (2:377). At first a mere chain of empty signs, Carlyle gives the Revolution a definition and a body. "La Révolution," he writes, "is but so many Alphabetic Letters, a thing nowhere to be laid hands on...where is it? what is it? It is the Madness that dwells in the hearts of men" (2:377). The narrator converts language into flesh, collapsing signification into the collective body of the revolutionaries and into a grotesquely rendered language of political violence.

In order to describe this "Madness," Carlyle draws on Mercier's perplexed linguistic characterizations of the Revolution, using them to justify his proposition for the historian's new role as a neologist, as someone who must "make make words," as he described in his letter to Sterling. Like Mercier, Carlyle acknowledges that the available language of history is inadequate to describe the Revolution: the fanaticism Carlyle sees as inspired by the Reign of Terror is a "wonderful, tragical predicament;—such as human language, unused to deal with these things... struggles to shadow out in figures" (2:246–247). History, attempting to describe the Terror, "babbles and flounders" (2:332). Carlyle's narrator finally concedes that the historian's task is that of Adamic naming: "It is thus...that History, and indeed all human Speech and Reason does yet, what Father Adam began life by doing: striving to name the new Things it sees of Nature's producing" (2:333). And yet the Terror baffles even the creative powers of neology:

> But what if History were to admit, for once, that all the Names and Theorems yet known to her fall short? That this grand Product

of Nature was even grand, and new, in that it came not to range itself under old recorded Laws of Nature at all, but to disclose new ones? In that case, History renouncing the pretension to name it at present, will look honestly at it, and name what she can of it! Any approximation to the right Name has value: were the right Name itself once here, the Thing is known henceforth; the Thing is then ours, and can be dealt with.

(2:333)

In this landscape of fallen language, which Vanden Bossche characterizes as a "Babelian fragmentation," to name new things after the principle of Adam is to participate in the Revolution's own anarchic idioms without bringing about order.[99] The historian's task is "helpless" not only because all attempts to name the acts of the Revolution are mere approximations but also because the existing languages of history contain no ordering principles with which to represent the Revolution. Because neology is inherently destabilizing, the very attempts to name the events with a new historical idiom perpetuate the chaos this language seeks to describe.

Carlyle's answer to this problem of representation is in the act not only of speaking but also of embodied, physical witnessing: to "look honestly," echoing Mercier's declaration that "everything is optical."[100] "How will the historian get out of this labyrinth?" writes Mercier. "How will he avoid the sway of his own opinion, when those who have the most penetrating eyes have had such difficulty in seizing the point of view, and of fixing an object in such extreme and continual change of position?"[101] Carlyle, dismissing the "Dryasdust" histories of Blair, answers this vertiginous procession of history by making his narrator-historian an embodied figure in the text. If "everything is optical," then the act of historical narration must be a dynamic act of eye-witnessing, an act that necessarily involves the historian's own physical presence. Describing gala-day at Versailles, Carlyle tells his readers, "Yes, friends, ye may sit and look: bodily or in thought, all France, and all Europe, may sit and look; for it is a day like few others...It is the baptism day of Democracy...the extreme-unction day of Feudalism!" (1:139–140). Carlyle's figurative placement of his own body and those of his readers within the text, his emphasis on the act of looking, reveal how this seminal transition from the body politic to the social body relies on a complex political dialect of embedded physicality. For Carlyle, modern history is the history of the social body. To "speak" the social body is to speak a new incarnational and historical language whose embodied properties symbolically express the relocation of hereditary authority to the underclasses.

The French Revolution, in turn, documents this transfer of power through its own linguistic excesses that challenge the static and bureaucratic language of reform. In so doing, Carlyle's text is an instance of a literary form that is, in Levine's phrase, "incommensurable with the forms of the social world."[102] It thus has the potential to oppose that world and specifically to dispute the gradualist agenda that would come to shape Victorian political reform. To be sure, Carlyle's account also has serious and alarming limitations. Throughout his writings, he represents political subjects in Ireland and the West Indies as needing immediate suppression, while political subjects in England and France band together to effect sweeping changes before they retreat from their world-historical positions as revolutionary agitators. One might split Carlyle's writing career into distinct radical and less radical phases, as Raymond Williams has done: on this model, the monumental works of the 1830s gradually deteriorate into the racist, bigoted diatribes of the *Latter-Day Pamphlets* (1850) as a more disillusioned Carlyle shifts away from "genuinely social thinking" and toward a "contemptuous absolutism."[103] However, as Simon Gikandi and Lowell T. Frye remind us, the seeds of his reactionary thinking are already present in his earlier career.[104] It is important to consider how the opposing forces of revolution and containment are also already present in the language Carlyle uses to express his vision of a new political dialect. For in looking to a divine Providence to effect dramatic changes through the voices and actions of the revolutionaries, Carlyle saw the underclasses as temporary renovators of the social and political order rather than the lasting agents of their own hardly won sovereignty. *The French Revolution* does take seriously the providential role of the social body, and Carlyle's radical relocation of a divinely authorized, incarnated speech in the populace sought to amplify their real sufferings and demands. The ending of *The French Revolution* offers a potentially radical, if quieter, appeal to the reader as an agent of dramatic political change. In the new revolutionary landscape of Carlyle's epic, the Parisian *sans-culottes* incarnate a divine power like that once granted to the monarch in feudal times. Carlyle suggests that this power is also available to his Victorian readers by addressing them directly:

> To me thou wert as a beloved shade, the disembodied or not yet embodied voice of a Brother. To thee I was but as a Voice. Yet was our relation a kind of sacred one; doubt not that! For whatsoever once sacred things become hollow jargon, yet while the Voice of Man speaks with Man, hast thou not there the living fountain out of which all sacrednesses sprang, and will yet spring? Man, by the nature of him, is definable as 'an incarnated Word'.

> (2:453)

Carlyle suggests the reader's own potential in effecting revolutionary change, anticipating the reader's gradual embodiment as a linguistic—and hence, political—agent. His theory of language anticipates Müller's description of necessary, renovating "political commotions" expressed through language, which, like Müller's flooding waters, act as a "living fountain." In the post-Revolutionary order, man, generically understood, is an "incarnated Word": a bearer of untapped revolutionary potential and a newly embodied subject of the modern polity. In extending this political agency to the reader, Carlyle suggestively parallels his closing warning of the *sans-culottes* energies that will continue on in "one bodily shape into another" after the Revolution, those forces of the "unhealthy" peace that worked to destroy the old regime. Carlyle implies that this same revolutionary force is available to contemporaries whom he saw as languishing in Reform-era Britain. Against an inefficient and bureaucratic stasis, or what he termed "National Palaver" in his epic history (1:329), Carlyle anticipates the reader as a potential agent in cycles of regeneration and change. The polity follows Mercier's logic of neology and, in so doing, perpetuates what Philip Rosenberg calls Carlyle's "doctrine of permanent revolution."[105] Carlyle's contemporary reader, the "disembodied or not yet embodied voice of a Brother," bears the incarnate Word of the *sans-culottes*, both embodying and threatening to unleash the providential language of revolutionary upheaval into the stagnant political theater of British reform.

This same providential authorization, however, also contains the agents of the social body in reiterated acts of formation and destruction. Like the dialectical play of the sovereign body, at once a sacred essence and a material force, the revolutionary polity swells with divinely sanctioned vengeance and acts out its destructive forces in the political sphere without establishing a coherent new order. In other words, by shuttling back and forth between silent formation and revolutionary action, this movement of the social body generates its own form of political stasis. The embodied, modern polity is destructive but never creative, a product of historical forces but unable to direct or organize its own energies in any lasting way. The trope of incarnated, sovereign authority, the "incarnate Word" that completes *The French Revolution*, suggests that the polity is always directed by a divine power that is just beyond it and inaccessible. Carlyle's positioning of the revolutionaries as sources of untapped, embodied potential paradoxically sets the terms for a Victorian conception of the modern polity that is always mediated by an elite authority, for a living political dialect that harnesses the vital, necessary, but "not yet embodied" agency of the speaking body social.

While the other authors I discuss deploy a range of different poetic forms, they all embrace philology in their own calls for a new political dialect. Chapter 1 shows how debates about the origin and development of language could offer imaginative solutions to the question of women's participation in the political and the domestic spheres. Specifically, I argue that Elizabeth Barrett Browning's juvenile poem *An Essay on Mind* (1826), her verse play *A Drama of Exile* (1844), and her epic

Bildungsroman *Aurora Leigh* (1856) build on Carlyle's language of incarnation and on the language-philosophy of Locke and Condillac in order to claim a voice for the politically engaged woman poet. While Barrett Browning is often read as a poet of overflowing physicality, I show how her imagery of disembodiment and linguistic effacement stresses the political silencing of women. Enlightenment philology, as refracted through the forms of the closet drama and the verse epic, helped Barrett Browning further register her opposition to women's exclusion from the electorate officially codified in the 1832 Reform Act.

Chapter 2 takes up Robert Browning's representations of antisocial speech in *The Ring and the Book* (1868–1869). The mid-Victorian period saw a great outpouring of research on the relationship between language and sociability. Looking back to Locke's characterization of language as a tool of "fellowship" for "sociable creature(s)," prominent Victorians, such as Müller and Darwin, emphasized the role of the community in shaping word forms, dialects, language-origins, and human-animal communication.[106] At the same time, the newly founded Philological Society pitched its plans for the massive collective project of the *NED* as a fundamentally social and democratic enterprise. I consider these developments in light of the Second Reform Act of 1867, and I argue that Browning's startling diction, jagged prosody, and excessively wicked characters work to make visible the lingering, authoritarian presence of aristocratic rule and the millions of subjects still left unenfranchised by liberal reform. This chapter challenges post-structuralist accounts of Browning's poetry as inherently multi-vocal, instead demonstrating how philology informs his opposition to triumphant contemporary accounts of democracy imagined through the shared national project of the *NED*.

Chapter 3 considers how debates over language and political sovereignty informed the Victorian poetic engagement with the empire. I demonstrate how Alfred Tennyson's monodrama *Maud* (1855) and his epic *Idylls of the King* (1859–1885) take up debates about human and animal language in light of contemporary works by Robert Chambers, Müller, Darwin, and other scientists and anthropologists who speculated on the language of ancient *homo sapiens*. I show how the figure of the epic "wild man" troubles the human-animal boundary and raises the specter of a lawless primordial past, one that tugs apart the poems' attempts at formal coherence and vies with the *Idylls'* representations of Arthur's absolutist body politic. In this way, the disruptive animal presence, registered through metrical irregularities, sound patterns, metonymic substitutions, and canine imagery, consistently undermines the "excessive ease" that Alice Meynell finds in Tennyson's prosody.[107] By keeping the wild yells and animal-like language of the knight Balin, "the Savage," always at the margins of the court, Tennyson's poem reveals anxieties that the polity is always on the verge of reeling, as Arthur says, "back into the beast" and collapsing its own class- and race-bound hierarchies. At the same time, by constructing both the neighborhoods of the British underclass and the colonies as lawless primal spaces, Tennyson's poetry imagines such sites as outlets for the failures of social reform. This chapter shows how scientific and philological debates inform the *Idylls*' critique of a democratically reforming society that continues to perpetuate atrocities in the empire.

While Tennyson's *Idylls* engages with evolutionary accounts of speech, Thomas Hardy's *Wessex Poems* (1898) and *Poems of the Past and Present* (1902) take up the long-delayed and long-awaited release of the first fascicle of the *NED* in 1884—the same year the third and final Reform Act would extend the franchise to agricultural laborers. Both of these events worked to incorporate the rural districts into the national community: while the *NED* and later the *OED* included many provincial and dialectal words, the Third Reform Act extended the vote to rural working men. In Chapter 4, I argue that Hardy's poetry uses repeated motifs of lovers' speech and sympathetic interlocutors to resist the philological and political appropriation of the rural districts into a national whole and, in so doing, contributes to recent critical efforts to "provincialize" Europe. While philologists like Frederick Elworthy looked to regional dialects as traces of a romantic past recoverable through language, Hardy's use of diction, imagery, and meter all insist on the irreducibility of rural life and its multiple, complicated histories, creating an excess of signification that cannot be simplistically applied to models of nationhood. While the Philological Society had long encouraged and promoted the incorporation of dialectal words into the dictionary project, Hardy's formal experimentation in his Wessex poetry challenges the Society's representations of the provincial districts as simplified homes of linguistic tradition and as safe havens from the ravages of industrial capitalism and the dislocations of global war.

The Conclusion examines the changing landscape of philology around the turn of the twentieth century, when a shift toward Saussurean linguistics and the bifurcation of philology into linguistics and literary studies changed the nature of the interactions between poets and philologists.[108] At the same time, the influence of Victorian philology persisted in early twentieth-century poetry and beyond. I show how the Victorians helped transmit this nexus of philology, politics, and versification to a new generation of Modernist poets, and I consider recent calls for a new or revived philology in the humanities.

Notes

1 Müller, *Lectures on the Science of Language*, 61–62.
2 Wordsworth, Preface to *Lyrical Ballads*, 110.

3 Patmore, "Essay on English Metrical Law," 9.
4 See Caroline Levine's *Forms*, Julia F. Saville's *Victorian Soul-Talk*, and Anna Barton's *Nineteenth-Century Poetry and Liberal Thought*.
5 Levine, "Formal Pasts and Formal Possibilities in Victorian Studies," 1242.
6 Levine, *Forms*, 79.
7 See, for example, Hans Aarsleff, *From Locke to Saussure* and Susan Romaine's "Introduction," to *The Cambridge History of the English Language*, 1–56. Examples of literary criticism that discuss the relationship between philology and revolution include John Beer's *Romanticism, Revolution, and Language* and Alexander Regier's *Fracture and Fragmentation in British Romanticism*.
8 See, for example, Isobel Armstrong's *Victorian Poetry: Poetry, Poetics, and Politics*, Herbert Tucker's *Epic*, Meredith Martin's *The Rise and Fall of Meter*, Edward Adams's *Liberal Epic*, Christopher M. Keirstead's *Victorian Poetry, Europe, and the Challenge of Cosmopolitanism*, Saville's *Victorian Soul-Talk*, and Barton's *Nineteenth-Century Poetry and Liberal Thought*. On the turn to new formalism, see Susan J. Wolfson's *Formal Charges*, Tucker, "The Fix of Form," Armstrong's *The Radical Aesthetic*, Marjorie Levinson, "What is New Formalism?" Levine's "Strategic Formalism" and her book *Forms*. See also Carolyn Dever's "Strategic Aestheticism," Tucker's "Tactile Formalism," and Levine's "Scaled Up, Writ Small," all contributions to a review forum on Levine's work in *Victorian Studies*, 49, no. 1 (2006). For the need to investigate liberalism before attempting to revive notions of aesthetic appreciation, see David Wayne Thomas, *Cultivating Victorians*.
9 Levine, "Formal Pasts and Formal Possibilities in Victorian Studies," 1242 and Barton, *Nineteenth-Century Poetry*, 2.
10 Recent exceptions to this general tendency include Christine Ferguson's *Language, Science, and Popular Fiction in the Victorian Fin-de-Siècle: The Brutal Tongue* and Will Abberley's *English Fiction and the Evolution of Language*. For individual studies of philology and individual poets, see Cary H. Plotkin, *The Tenth Muse*, Donald S. Hair, *Tennyson's Language* and *Robert Browning's Language*, and Dennis Taylor, *Hardy's Literary Language*. While these excellent single-author studies shed light on each poet's investment in the science, their focus necessarily narrows the discussion to exclude the broader nexus of poetry, philology, and reform across the century. Martin's *The Rise and Fall of Meter* has deeply informed my understanding of poetry and philology in the period. Martin, however, is mainly interested in philology's "profound impact on the study of the English language and the perception that the English language…should and could reflect the greatness of the nation" (43). I also focus on moments when poetry complicates or resists this equation of language with nation.
11 Ferguson, *Language, Science, and Popular Fiction*, 4. See, for example, Edward Said's assertion that Orientalism was "secularized, redisposed, and re-formed by such disciplines as philology" (122). The role and status of language is a major subject of research and analysis in postcolonial literary studies. See, for example, the essays on language collected and edited by Ashcroft, Griffiths, and Tiffin in *The Post-Colonial Studies Reader*, 261–396, Ramanathan, *The English-Vernacular Divide: Postcolonial Language, Politics, and Practice*, and Schneider, *Postcolonial English: Varieties Around the World*. I discuss philology's relationship to racism and imperialism in greater detail in Chapter 3.
12 Ibid., 1–12.

13 Abberley, "Race and Species Essentialism in Nineteenth-Century Philology," 45.

14 Ogilvie, *Words of the World*, xv. For an example of a critical view that equates the *OED* with linguistic standardization, see Dennis Taylor, *Hardy's Literary Language*, 1–28. John Willinsky's study of the citation selections of the *OED* is an example of a reading that stresses the dictionary's imperial ideology. He shows how the first edition works to "integrate...nation and empire" through its chosen print sources, which promote Protestantism, middle-class values, and the growth of capitalism; consequently, the dictionary represents "that particularly English claim on science and civilization, merit and accomplishment" that stood in opposition to the primitivism of the rest of the world. See *Empire of Words*, 5–6. More broadly, the field of linguistics has been enriched by a greater attention to cross-cultural influences and the way they shape the language known as English. Today, linguists speak not of one monolithic "English" but rather of "world Englishes" that are the product of acculturation and nativization in African, Asian, and Latin American contexts. See Kachru, "World Englishes in World Contexts," 567–568.

15 Ibid., xiii.

16 See Beer, *Darwin's Plots*, Levine, *Darwin and the Novelists*, Dewitt, *Moral Authority, Men of Science, and the Victorian Novel*, and Buckland, *Novel Science*.

17 Examples of monographs that challenge the empiricist paradigm include Srdjan Smajić's *Ghost-Seers, Detectives, and Spiritualists: Theories of Vision in Victorian Literature and Science*, Martin Willis's *Vision, Science, and Literature 1870–1920: Ocular Horizons*, and Sarah C. Alexander's *Victorian Literature and the Physics of the Imponderable*.

18 See Aarsleff's *From Locke to Saussure* and Linda Dowling's *Language and Decadence*. For a condensed overview of this shift from theory to new historicism, see Tucker's "The Fix of Form."

19 Levine, *The Realistic Imagination*, 4. On "surface-reading," see Best and Marcus's "Surface Reading: An Introduction" and Dewitt's introduction to *Moral Authority*, 5–6.

20 Ibid., 10.

21 Peter Bowler, *Evolution*, 54–57.

22 For a discussion of how pre-Darwinian science aligned with notions of reform and respectability, see James A. Secord's introduction to Lyell's *Principles of Geology*, ix–xliii, as well as his introduction to Robert Chambers's *Vestiges of the Natural History of Creation*, ix–xlv. For a discussion of Darwin's *Origin of Species* and political reform, see Bernard Lightman, "The Popularization of Evolution and Victorian Culture," 292–300. In Chris Vanden Bossche's apt summary, the "principle that meaning can only be determined by examining words in context, the principle of historical philology, implied that language gains its meaning by reference to itself, not to some authority outside of itself.... In the domain of language, the individual became free to create meaning." See Vanden Bossche, *Carlyle and the Search for Authority*, 7. In general, I see this shift to historical philology as more uneven and contested than Vanden Bossche suggests here.

23 Bucher, "On Political Terms," 44.

24 Ibid.

25 Whitney, *Language and The Study of Language*, 38.

26 Marx writes of "borrowed language" that "the beginner who has learnt a new language always translates it back into his mother tongue, but he has

assimilated the spirit of the new language and can produce freely in it only when he moves in it without remembering the old." See "The Eighteenth Brumaire of Louis Bonaparte," 595.

27 See Cobbett's *Grammar of the English Language*. On both Cobbett and Carlyle as commentators on the condition of England, see Ulrich, *Signs of Their Times*. On Thelwall's democratic politics as it relates to his oratory, elocutionary writings, and elocutionary practices, see Scrivener, *Seditious Allegories* 167–204 and Solomonescu, *John Thelwall*, 95–119. See also Julius Charles Hare and Augustus William Hare's *Guesses at Truth, by Two Brothers* (1827). Armstrong notes that Julius Hare's interest in philology, among other fields, was important to the Cambridge circle that influenced Tennyson. See Armstrong, *Victorian Poetry*, 60.

28 Morgan, review of *The French Revolution*, 47; Thackeray, review of *The French Revolution*, 69; Merivale, review of *The French Revolution*, 77.

29 Mill, "*The French Revolution*: A History," 17.

30 EBB to Mary Russell Mitford, 1 April 1842, in Kelley and Hudson, *The Brownings' Correspondence*, 5: 301 and "A New Spirit of the Age" in *The Brownings' Correspondence*, 8: 356. Thackeray, review of *The French Revolution*, 71.

31 Carlyle, *The French Revolution*, 1: 168. Hereafter, all volume and page references appear in parentheses within the text.

32 For recent work in literature and science studies that move away from empiricism to embrace speculation and pseudo-science, see Smajić, *Ghost-Seers, Detectives, and Spiritualists*, Willis, *Vision, Science, and Literature*, and Alexander, *Victorian Literature and the Physics of the Imponderable*.

33 Aarsleff, "Introduction" to *From Locke to Saussure*, 37–38.

34 For Carlyle's influence on prominent men of science, see Turner, "Victorian scientific naturalism," 325–343. On paleontology and its influence on Carlyle's historiographical writings, see Ulrich, "Thomas Carlyle, Richard Owen, and the Paleontological Articulation of the Past," 30–58.

35 While literary critics have long argued that Carlyle's idiosyncratic style is linked to politics, they have tended to overlook the central influence of the developing science of philology both on his work and, more broadly, on early Victorian debates about revolution and reform. For Catherine Gallagher, contemporary politics reveals the "ironic degradation of the symbol," causing Carlyle to relocate the symbol's divine potential in the heroic realm. See *The Industrial Reformation of English Fiction*, 195. Chris R. Vanden Bossche reads the circular structure of *The French Revolution* as evidence of Carlyle's skepticism that the French would ever author a new social order. See *Carlyle and the Search for Authority*, 81.

36 For British responses to the Revolution, see Thompson, *The Making of the English Working Class*, Emsley, *Britain and the French Revolution*, and Philp, *The French Revolution and British Popular Politics*. For an argument that focuses on how Britain avoided a massive revolutionary outbreak like France, see Christie, *Stress and Stability*.

37 Claeys, *The French Revolution Debate*, 1–10.

38 All references to *Chartism* are to the second edition (London: James Fraser, 1840), and will appear in parentheses within the text.

39 Detailed accounts of Romanticism's relationship to philology include Smith's *The Politics of Language*, Tomalin's *Romanticism and Linguistic Theory*, and Beer's *Romanticism, Revolution, and Language*.

40 Momma, *From Philology to English Studies*, 1–2.

41 Johnson, "Preface" to the *Dictionary*, 1: n.p.

42 Ibid.

43 For the analogy between apocalyptic geological catastrophes and the Revolution, see Aarsleff's introduction to *From Locke to Saussure*, 32. Rudwick examines the relationship between geology, historiography, and the shifting definitions of "revolution" in *Bursting the Limits of Time*.

44 Horne Tooke, *The Diversions of Purley*, 2: 303.

45 Ibid., 2: 303–304.

46 Ibid., 2: 3. For more on Horne Tooke's politicized accounts of etymology and grammar, see Smith, *Politics*, 111–113. See also Lamarre, "John Horne Tooke," 188–207.

47 For Carlyle's familiarity with Webster see Thomas Carlyle to John A. Carlyle, 1 October 1833, *CLO*, DOI: 10.1215/lt-18331001-TC-JAC-01; CL 7: 3–10.

48 Webster, *Dissertations*, 20. For more on Webster's work and its relationship to American independence, see Micklethwaite, *Noah Webster*.

49 Brewer, "Johnson, Webster, and the *New English Dictionary*," 303–312.

50 Webster, Preface to *An American Dictionary*, 1: n.p.

51 Ibid.

52 For an overview of the history of the French Academy, see Murray, "The Académie Française," 267–273.

53 Harrold records that *Nouveau Paris* is cited 26 times and *Tableau de Paris* 3 times in Carlyle's history. See "Carlyle's Sources for *The French Revolution*," 582–584.

54 Mercier, *New Picture of Paris*, 1: xiii.

55 Daniel Rosenberg discusses Mercier's views of the French court in "Louis-Sébastien Mercier's New Words," 372.

56 Mercier, *Panorama of Paris*, 23.

57 Qtd. in Rosenberg, "Louis-Sébastien Mercier's New Words," 378.

58 See Turner's overview of the period in *Philology*, 133–143.

59 Ibid., 131–132.

60 Savage, *The Vulgarisms and Improprieties*, i. Bailey discusses this text and its political conservatism in "British English since 1830," 240.

61 Carlyle, "Boswell's *Life of Johnson*," 103.

62 Ibid., 122.

63 Carlyle, *Sartor Resartus*. 180. All citations are to the Oxford World's Classics edition (Oxford University Press, 1987) and will appear in parentheses within the text.

64 Carlyle treats Johnson at greater length in *On Heroes*, praising his dictionary as "the best of all Dictionaries" (152).

65 Thomas Carlyle to John Stuart Mill, 24 September 1833, *CLO*, DOI: 10.1215/lt-18330924-TC-JSM-01; CL 6: 444–450.

66 For an overview of the history of the *Accademia della Crusca*, see Beltrami and Fornara, "Italian Historical Dictionaries," 357–384. Also see the note to the letter cited in n. 65 above.

67 Thomas Carlyle to John Sterling, 4 June 1835, *CLO*, DOI: 10.1215/lt-18350604-TC-JOST-01; CL 8: 134–138.

68 Crawford, *Devolving English Literature*, 139.

69 Crowley, "Class, Ethnicity, and the Formation of 'Standard English,'" 307. Crowley treats the topic of Standard English at greater length in *The Politics of Discourse*. McClure gives a historical overview of the struggle in the United Kingdom to see Scots recognized as an independent language and to take accounts of both national and regional speech forms within Scotland. See "English in Scotland," 358–365.

70 Sorensen discusses how the notion of a national tongue based on national borders overlooks the differences between Scots Gaelic, Scots, and English in *The Grammar of Empire*, 2.

71 Mugglestone, "The Rise of Received Pronunciation," 243–244. See also her *Talking Proper.*
72 Carlyle, *Essay on Burns*, 19.
73 Ibid., 72. For more on Burns's poetics, see also Leask, *Robert Burns and Pastoral.*
74 Crawford notes Carlyle's antipathy to Blair in *Devolving English Literature*, 140. For Carlyle's meditations on the uninspired dullness of "Dryasdust" history, see his prologue in Vol. 1 of *Oliver Cromwell's Letters and Speeches*, 3–74. Carlyle, anticipating adverse responses to his writing, wrote to Mill in 1836 that if only some small portion of readers had "a feeling that the form after all perhaps came from within, and was what it best could be, and only contradicted Blair's Lectures...I shall reckon it much." See Thomas Carlyle to John Stuart Mill, 2 March 1836, *CLO* 8: 316–318. DOI: 10.1215/lt-18360302-TC-JSM-01). See also Blair's *Lectures on Rhetoric and Belles Lettres* (1783).
75 Crombie, *The Etymology and Syntax of the English Language*, 316.
76 Ibid., 318.
77 Prichard, *The English Origin of Celtic Nations*, 11–13.
78 Thomas Carlyle to Robert Mitchell, 16 March 1821, *CLO*, DOI: 10.1215/lt-18210316-TC-RM-01; *CL* 1: 343–346.
79 Carlyle apologizes for his late return of an unnamed "Pritchard" text in an 1837 letter to Hensleigh Wedgwood. See also n. 2 to this letter in Thomas Carlyle to Hensleigh Wedgwood, 1 February 1837, *CLO*, DOI: 10.1215/lt-18370201-TC-HWE-01; *CL* 9: 136–137.
80 Poovey, *Making a Social Body*, 7–8. Pamela Gilbert, John Ulrich, and Catherine Hall have persuasively shown how this model of the social body shaped Victorian convictions about social class, race and ethnicity, medical discourse, and liberalism, but their accounts do not investigate the origins of this model. See Gilbert, *Mapping the Victorian Social Body*, 4–5, Ulrich, *Signs of Their Times*, 4, and Elaine Hadley's discussion of "abstract embodiment" in *Living Liberalism*, 14. Hall uses Poovey's model of the social body in "The nation within and without," 179–233. For an account of Carlyle's use of the discourse of disease and the social body in *Chartism*, see Martin, "Blood Transfusions," 83–102.
81 John 1.14.
82 Locke, *An Essay Concerning Human Understanding*, 361–362.
83 Dowling, *Language and Decadence*, xiv.
84 Carlyle anticipates the significance that the doctrine of the Incarnation would come to play in later Victorian responses to the sister sciences of geology and biology. Both Boyd Hilton and Michael Wheeler write that the Incarnation became more important to many spiritually inclined Victorians as they grappled with the materialist implications of geology and evolution: because the Incarnation was an originating force that came before the material world, it animated the empirical fossil record with a divine significance. See Hilton, *The Age of Atonement*, 299 and Wheeler, *St. John and the Victorians*, 237. Much as later writers would turn to the book of St. John as a response to the controversies over evolution, Carlyle used the trope of the word-become-flesh to counter materialist accounts of language. This vision of language as a spiritual essence could govern and sacralize the empirical study of etymological histories, vocal organs, and sensory data.
85 Brown's biographical entry on Irving provides an overview of his training and career; see "Irving, Edward (1792–1834)." For an analysis of Carlyle's and Irving's friendship, see McCracken-Flesher, "Carlyle, Irving, and the Problematics of Prophecy," 25–52.

86 Thomas Carlyle to John A. Carlyle, 16 February 1832, *CLO*, DOI: 10.1215/lt-18320216-TC-JAC-01; CL 6: 119–128.
87 Carlyle, *Reminiscences*, 37.
88 See Brown, "Irving, Edward (1792–1834)."
89 Irving, "Beginning or Origin," 15.
90 Edward Irving to Isabella Martin, 19 May 1829, in Oliphant, *The Life*, 2: 79.
91 See Thomas Carlyle to Thomas Murray, 24 August 1824, *CLO*, DOI: 10.1215/lt-18240824-TC-TM-01; CL 3: 137–140 and Thomas Carlyle to John A. Carlyle, 7 March 1825, *CLO*, DOI: 10.1215/lt-18250307-TC-JAC-01; CL 3: 296–300. For Carlyle's familiarity with the *Aids to Reflection*, see, for example, Thomas Carlyle to Henry Crabb Robinson, 25 April 1826, *CLO*, DOI: 10.1215/lt-18260425-TC-HCR-01; CL 4: 79–83.
92 Coleridge, *Aids to Reflection*, 6–7. McKusick discusses Horne Tooke's influence on Coleridge in *Coleridge's Philosophy of Language*, 33–52.
93 King discusses Coleridge's *On the Constitution of Church and State* and *Aids to Reflection* as key texts in the development of a divine republic of letters in *Imagined Spiritual Communities*, 21–56.
94 Coleridge, *On the Constitution of Church and State*, 84.
95 Kantorowicz, *The King's Two Bodies*, 3–23.
96 Ibid., 193–206.
97 Recently, Santner has taken up Ernst Kantorowicz's study to argue that the aftermath of the French Revolution in Europe saw a period of struggle to reconstitute the body politic in the transition to popular sovereignty. See *The Royal Remains*, xi. See also Poovey, *Making a Social Body*, 7–8.
98 Daniel Rosenberg, "Louis-Sébastien Mercier's New Words," 371.
99 Vanden Bossche, *Carlyle and the Search for Authority*, 83.
100 Mercier, *New Picture of Paris*, 2: 411.
101 Mercier, *New Picture of Paris*, 2: 412.
102 Levine, *Forms*, 79.
103 Williams, *Culture and Society*, 83.
104 Gikandi, *Maps of Englishness*, 57–59, Frye, "Vocables, Still Vocables," 196–216. It is worth mentioning in this context that Carlyle's next major political statement, *Chartism* (1839), seems to retreat from his position in *The French Revolution*, arguing instead for education reform and a dubious scheme of emigration as solutions to poverty throughout the British Isles, the Irish Famine, and Chartist agitation. Carlyle's understands Chartism as an extension of revolutionary sentiments that had been gathering since 1789 (42). Language, again, is a symptom of the social upheaval in industrial Britain, much as it had been the symptom of corruption in revolutionary France. Chartism speaks a "most loud though inarticulate language" (40), and the members of a reformed Parliament fail to speak effectively for their constituencies: "friends of the people; chosen with effort, by the people, to interpret and articulate the deep dumb want of the people! To a remote observer they seem oblivious of their duty.... They are either speakers for that great dumb toiling class which cannot speak, or they are nothing that one can well specify" (5). Much as Carlyle feared that democracy had led to despotism in revolutionary France, he feared that ballot-boxes, and parliamentary reform would only pave the way for extremist, undemocratic leaders. What the people really wanted, under the "democratic turbulence," was a "true leader" (55); barring this, better education and the opportunity to leave Europe and emigrate abroad to regions "vacant or tenanted by nomades" would supposedly relieve the class tensions and the poverty that democratic reform could not (112). *Chartism*, then, differs

from *The French Revolution* in conceding that some gradual reform is necessary—although in the realm of education rather than Parliament—as well as in advancing a genocidal vision of the Empire as an open stretch of territory waiting to be emptied of its inhabitants and re-settled by Britain's poor. Again, the role of the social body as a political and linguistic force structures Carlyle's analysis, but here, we see the seeds of idealized leadership he would describe more fully in *On Heroes, Hero-Worship, and the Heroic in History* (1841), in which great men, rather than a providentially authorized underclass, effect large-scale social and political change. For the history of the Chartist movement, see, for example, Jones, *Languages of Class*, Chase, *Chartism*, and Vanden Bossche, *Reform Acts*.

105 Philip Rosenberg, *The Seventh Hero*, 201. For a discussion of Carlyle's hero-theory in the context of his rejection of democracy, see 176–203.

106 Locke, *An Essay Concerning Human Understanding*, 361.

107 Meynell, "Some Thoughts of a Reader of Tennyson," 7.

108 On the shift to Saussurean linguistics, see Ferguson, *Language, Science, and Popular Fiction*, 3; on the split into separate disciplines, see Momma, *From Philology to English Studies*, 185. I discuss both of these changes in greater length in the Conclusion.

1 "No perfect code"

Elizabeth Barrett Browning's Political Poetics and Women's Language

Readers often praise Barrett Browning's poetry for its sensory excesses. While feminist critics of the 1970s and 1980s celebrated her vividly embodied imagery, a more recent interest in the so-called Spasmodic school of poetry, with its focus on sensations, rhythms, and pulses, has further emphasized the central role of women's physical experience in Barrett Browning's work.[1] Herbert Tucker, for instance, explores how *Aurora Leigh* (1856), full of "Shudder, pulsation, outburst, and spasm," makes the predominantly male Spasmodic milieu "appear to have been, in its deepest fiber, feminine all along."[2] Julia Saville likewise demonstrates how her "poetics of the body" emerges from her republican sympathies.[3] Such analyses magnify Aurora's desire to craft a poetry that will express her own "full-veined, heaving, double-breasted Age" (5:216).

An analysis of Barrett Browning's political poetics, then, might be expected to focus on her embodiment. In this chapter, however, I take a different approach, focusing on Barrett Browning's creation of a bodiless poetry as a symbolic expression of women's exclusion from the reformed electorate. Barrett Browning draws on Enlightenment-era and contemporary debates about the science of language in order to protest this exclusion and to claim a voice for the socially engaged female poet. In her juvenile poem, *An Essay on Mind* (1826), she incorporates the language-theories of Locke and Condillac, two philosophers who emphasize the relationship between words and sensory experience, to show how language shapes and expresses the idea of the individual's liberty, autonomy, and freedom from oppression. In her poem-masque hybrid *A Drama of Exile* (1844), she connects these accounts of language to Carlyle's speculative writings on the social body as a form of incarnation, in which the divine word becomes flesh and unites the polity. While Carlyle's model of the social body emphasized the greater inclusion of the lower classes, Barrett Browning's reveals how this model of the polity marginalizes women for their supposed physical and emotional sensibilities. Finally, in *Aurora Leigh,* she develops a reading of socially engaged, poetic language that underscores women's exclusion from the social body by contrasting passages about their vivid embodiment alongside passages of women's denial and disappearance.

This opposition between a flourishing embodiment and the negation of the body highlights the contradictions of a universalizing discourse of language and liberty that ignores women, and mounts a powerful critique of women's political invisibility in the reformed electorate.

An analysis of Barrett Browning's attention to language debates throughout her poetry has two significant implications. For one, it reveals how Enlightenment and early Victorian philology animate a body of work often seen as detached from contemporary scientific debates. As Marjorie Stone and Beverly Taylor have observed, scholars generally do not read Barrett Browning as a poet with much interest in scientific developments.[4] Her frequent use of Biblical allusions and her vision of poetry as a form of spiritual communication make her an unlikely spokeswoman for Enlightenment language-philosophy. And yet her poetry was crucial in negotiating both epistemological and sacred accounts of speech characteristic of many nineteenth-century speculations about language.

Second, a closer reading of Barrett Browning's ambivalent stance toward the speaking, sensory body invites us to reconsider much recent criticism on the Spasmodic school of poetry, with its emphasis on pulses, sensations, and physical experience. *Aurora Leigh* is often taken as a pioneering example of feminist liberation expressed through the sensorium. Yet *Aurora Leigh* is also the poem that most vividly stages the female body's effacement and disappearance. By privileging corporeal experience as the foundation for *Aurora Leigh's* political interventions, such readings tend to overlook the poem's reservations about the body and its role in communicating poetic language. In so doing, they run the risk of recovering the very gendered notions of sensibility that *Aurora Leigh* contests and subverts in its explorations of disembodiment.[5] Spasmodic readings, in other words, must also reckon with a darker and less celebratory understanding of the relationship between poetry, language, and the gendered body, one articulated by Edmund Gosse's denunciation of Barrett Browning as a "spasmodic" poet expressing a "Pythian shriek" through her feminine poetics.[6] A reconsideration of Barrett Browning's intervention into debates about the social body, then, also helps us avoid recuperating a gender essentialism that her poetry itself fiercely contests. In bringing together language-philosophy, politics, and gender in this way, Barrett Browning's work reveals how the science of language shaped Victorian ideas about liberty and the political exclusion of women in the age of reform.

Enlightenment Language-Philosophy and *An Essay on Mind*

Barrett Browning's experience as a young woman growing up in an ardently Whiggish family shaped her lifelong interest in exploring women's relationships to politics.[7] The First Reform Act of 1832, which Barrett Browning's brother publicly supported in local debates near Hope End, did not invent the widespread and deeply held conviction that citizenship was synonymous with (propertied) manhood, but it did affirm and formalize that conviction by explicitly naming masculinity as a criteria for enfranchisement.[8] As James Vernon, Catherine Hall, and other historians have noted, the 1832 Reform Act explicitly defined the new body of voters as "male persons," thus inaugurating what Hall has called the "rule of difference" in which differences "encoded through gender, property, religion, and race" create inequalities both at the state and the national level.[9] This rule was in large part based in a gendered system of virtual representation: as the legal and social subordinates of men, middle- and upper-class women were thought to be represented through their fathers or husbands, the property-holding heads of the household.[10] The fact that some women had technically been able to vote before the 1832 Reform Act and that many women continued to have a great deal of influence in parish events and municipal and local politics did not significantly alter this glaring exclusion in the Victorian period, despite the best efforts of John Stuart Mill, Helen Taylor, and Millicent Garrett Fawcett in the 1860s.[11] Nor did the fact that the passage of the 1832 Act nearly coincided with the ascension of Victoria, a female monarch, in 1837.[12] Women's language and women's bodies came to index their supposed lack of political responsibility, shot through with the tremors and disturbances of feminine sensibility.

Throughout her juvenilia, Barrett Browning repeatedly triangulates this relationship between language, liberty, and the body. In "A Thought on Thoughts," a comic piece she began at age seventeen and published in the *Athenaeum* in 1836, Barrett Browning describes a feud that involves a noble family of "Thoughts" and an "ignoble house of...Words."[13] Made up of Philosophical Thought, Poetic Thought, and Scientific Thought, among others, this family of Thoughts lost its ability to communicate with the house of the Words in ancient times, when "several of the Thoughts were falling fast into poverty" and

> the Words came benevolently to their help...in return for which compassion they did however exact so servile an attention...that the Thoughts, who are of kingly blood, could bear it no longer: and thus, a coldness having arisen between the Thoughts and Words, no well-bred person ventures to invite them to the same hearthstone.
>
> (277–278)

In this passage, Barrett Browning locates the origins of linguistic disharmony in the tensions among different social classes, explicitly linking the philosophy of language to the conditions of politics. She concludes the piece with a series of questions that raise issues of individual freedom and expression:

> In conclusion, let me entreat you to consider the wrongs of our family. Are we to be for ever oppressed by that branch of words called Epithets? Are we to be left in obscurity by words who are obsolete? Are we to be misrepresented by words of double meaning? Are we to be thrown into exile by words of no meaning at all? Are we to be absolutely knocked down by words of six syllables?
>
> (280)

With comic desperation, the young poet reads language's turmoil as a threat to personal and political autonomy. The domestic image of the family suggests an intimate relation among members later divided by conflict, but it also stresses the embodied nature of language, showing how these family members are "thrown into exile," or "knocked down" by the violent drama of miscommunication. The family drama stands in for the larger community of readers as well: this is "our" family, the poet suggests, and "we" all share its plight. "A Thought on Thoughts" locates the origin of conflict in the relationships among sensory, perceiving individuals, and shows how disputes arise from the language choices they make. Nevertheless, words with all their distortions and limitations are still the foundation of society.

Barrett Browning's ambitious juvenile poem *An Essay on Mind* elaborates on this problem, exploring how attention to the spiritual dimensions of language can work to heal the rifts in communication among embodied individuals. A 1,262-line poem in rhyming couplets, *An Essay on Mind* contemplates the powers of the mind, and celebrates the contributions of historians, scientists, and philosophers to the human quest for knowledge. Both the Biblical story of language fallen from Paradise and the influence of Enlightenment language-philosophy are central to this account. Book 2 opens by lamenting the difficulties of communication among speakers, observing that thoughts without language are obscure, while thoughts translated into words fail to accurately express the thoughts behind them. Words give ideas a "body" (644) even as they drastically alter the "spiritual essence" of unspoken thoughts (639). In this early poem, Barrett Browning uses Enlightenment language-philosophy to align language with political freedom while also insisting on the divine potential of human communication. This combination, in turn, acts as an early illustration of Barrett Browning's developing political aesthetic, and anticipates her creation of a bodiless poetry.

Barrett Browning's interest in communication in her juvenile poetry dramatizes many of Locke's politicized statements about language. Barrett Browning was well-read in Locke's works, and his language-treatise, "Of Words," remained a key source text for philologists throughout the Victorian period.[14] For the Victorians as well as for his own contemporary readers, "Of Words" offered a model of language that was intimately connected to the political and social liberty of the sensing, perceiving individual. One of the central tenets of the *Essay* is that sensation and reflection are the sources of all ideas: "Our observation employed either about *external sensible objects; or about the internal operations of our minds, perceived and reflected upon by ourselves, is that, which supplies our understandings with all the materials of thinking*" (109).[15] This emphasis on sense experience also informs Locke's account of words and their meanings. Locke notes "how great a dependence our *words* have on common sensible ideas; and how those, which are made use of to stand for actions and notions quite removed from sense, *have their rise from thence, and from obvious sensible ideas are transferred to more abstruse significations*" (362). The first origin of a word is to be found in sense experience: Locke gives the example of the word "spirit," which means "breath" (362). As Donald Hair explains, in this empiricist account of language "etymology means tracing words back to their source in sensations. Sensations, the data produced by our senses, crowd in upon our minds, where, in ways that Locke explains, they become ideas, those generalizations from experience that make up our knowledge. To these ideas, we attach sounds," and it is this "arbitrary connection of spoken word and idea" that forms the basis of Locke's theory.[16] For a young poet interested in language, knowledge, and the senses, then, Locke's *Of Words* was a key source of inspiration. As Anna Barton observes, Barrett Browning's rendering of Locke's ideas in pentameter couplets "encourages the reader to reflect on the relationship between Locke's philosophy and the work of poetic composition."[17]

Furthermore, Locke's theory offered Barrett Browning a means of thinking through the connections between the speaking individual and the broader community. Locke begins his account by asserting that language's primary purpose is to act as the "great instrument, and common tie of society" (361). Because God "designed man for a sociable creature" (in Locke's gendered formulation), he has organs with which to produce articulate sounds, and the capacity to "*use these sounds, as signs of internal conceptions; and to make them stand as marks for the ideas within his own mind, whereby they might be made known to others, and the thoughts of men's minds be conveyed from one to another*" (361). Within this general framework, there is room for variation based on individual knowledge and experience. Locke explores at some length how the meanings of words signify only insofar as they mean something in the mind of the individual user. Whereas a child might use the word "gold" to refer to the substance or the color, a more learned speaker might add "weighty substance," "malleability," and so on, so that each speaker uses this work in reference to his own distinct idea (364–365). Communication is built on the shared illusion that one speaker's ideas are the same as the ideas in the minds of his listeners, and that the words any speaker uses are assumed to refer to reality, even though actual words themselves result from an *"arbitrary imposition"* of meaning (366).

At the same time, these heterogenous communities of speakers do abide by conventions that are stronger than any political authority. Locke writes,

> every man has so inviolable a liberty, to make words stand for what ideas he pleases, that no one hath the power to make others have the same ideas in their minds, that he has, when they use the same words, that he does. And therefore the great Augustus himself, in possession of that power which ruled the world, acknowledged, he could not make a new Latin word: which was as much as to say, that he could not arbitrarily appoint, what idea any sound should be a sign of, in the mouths and common language of his subjects. 'Tis true, common use, by a tacit consent, appropriates certain sounds to certain ideas in all languages, which so far limits the signification of that sound, that unless a man applies it to the same idea, he does not speak properly: and let me add, that unless a man's words excite the same ideas in the hearer, which he makes them stand for in speaking, he does not speak intelligibly.
>
> (366)

"Common use" and "tacit consent" furnish the necessary conditions of communication among members of a society. Locke's account of conventions brings language firmly into the domain of political life, relating individual words and meanings to communal consensus. "Of Words" thus takes language's state of imperfection, its rootedness in the separate experiences of different speakers, and its adherence to shared conventions, and translates it into a statement about individual liberty and freedom from absolute political domination.[18]

Working across the Channel, Condillac offered a sensationist account of idea formation that further deepened Barrett Browning's insights into the connection between knowledge, liberty, and the sensing, perceiving individual. Where Lockean empiricism maintains that there are no innate ideas, Condillac asserts that there are no innate abilities, either: our capacities to remember, reason about, and judge our surroundings all stem directly from our experiences of sensory perception.[19] Condillac's *Traité des sensations*, or *Treatise on the Sensations* (1754) traces the origins of knowledge back to the gradual awakening of the senses, showing how alternating experiences of pleasure and pain eventually teach the individual about bodily awareness, memory, ideas, and passions. Condillac describes a hypothetical statue that gains its senses of smell, hearing, taste, sight, and touch in gradual succession, learning to combine and distinguish among the different sensory experiences until the statue understands that he is separate from the external objects he perceives (88–89). Like Locke's perceiving individual, Condillac's statue gains knowledge from immediate, concrete objects. "The statue has no general idea which was not a particular idea," Condillac writes (217).[20] If the statue holds an orange, for example, his understanding of that object stems entirely from the smell, color, weight, and other sensory data he takes in as he handles it. Condillac asks readers to see themselves as statues, and to understand how they, too, are gradually awakened to knowledge and ideas through such experiences of perception.

Like Locke, Condillac links his account of sensory perception to the liberty and autonomy of the individual. In his "Dissertation on Freedom" appended to the end of the *Treatise,* Condillac explains how the statue learns through pleasure and pain, and through attendant sensations of fear and danger, the power of deliberation and the power to make sound decisions based on the risks that might arise when he seeks to fulfill his desires for food, warmth, and other bodily needs. Through experience, the statue learns to forgo some desires and to weigh whether he should act or not act; consequently, he comes to understand individual liberty. Like an experienced pilot, the statue learns "to control his desires, direct his movements, hold the balance, and when needful cast the anchor. So he obtains an empire which only violent passions can overthrow" (250). Condillac's presentation of the sensory individual as a kind of private empire resembles Locke's presentation of the isolated, perceiving speaker resistant to outside domination and control.

Both Locke's and Condillac's writings shaped Barrett Browning's early written reflections on the nature of language and the perceiving self. In "A Thought on Thoughts," as we have seen, Barrett Browning echoes Locke's point that confusion and misunderstanding emerge from the physical and mental boundaries that divide sensory, perceiving individuals from one another. In that piece, Condillac's private empires of individuals collapse under the Lockean deceitfulness of words. In an early autobiographical fragment, "My Own Character" (1818), Barrett Browning grapples with, and ultimately concedes, Locke's claim that there are "no innate principles," while in a second fragment, "Glimpses into my Own Life and Literary Character" (1820), she credits Locke for offering her insights into the workings of metaphysical knowledge: "I accompanying Locke thro his complex reasoning & glorious subjects my mind seems more enlarged more cultivated & more enlightened!"[21] *An Essay on Mind* proceeds from this premise that the relationship between thoughts and words is like the relationship between the mind and the body, and encourages readers to revere language even in its fallen, imperfect state. The orderliness of the poem's end-stopped rhyming couplets works to give body and shape to chaotic thought, much as the bodies of "A Thought on Thoughts" impose physical form upon the abstract concepts they represent:

> Ah! spurn not words with reckless insolence;
> But still admit their influence with the sense,
> And fear to slight their laws! Perchance we find
> No perfect code transmitted to mankind;
> And yet mankind, till life's dark sands are run,
> Prefers imperfect government to none.
>
> (653–659)

Much as Locke presents words and their meanings as collective, shared illusions that approximate reality, Barrett Browning presents language as a distorting medium in which words have no innate or natural relationships to the thoughts they express. Yet the lack of a "perfect code" for language does not mean giving up on language altogether. Much as Barrett Browning sees "imperfect government" as preferable to anarchy, the distortions and flaws of language are troublesome but necessary impediments to the expression of one's thoughts. The opening exclamation and its initial caesura declare the poet's determination to forge her art out of imperfect materials, a mission these lines also suggest through the series of active, transitive verbs and verbal phrases ("spurn not," "admit," "fear to slight," "find"). The shift to a passive construction ("no perfect code transmitted") resists the possibility that language's origins are knowable to the perceiving and embodied self. The fifth quoted line stands out all the more for its hint of spondaic disruption to the otherwise regular iambic pentameter; it also reiterates the imagery of a fallen dynasty from "A Thought on Thoughts," thereby suggesting the flawed and fallen condition of language. Elsewhere in the poem Barrett Browning addresses at length Locke's notion of the individual speaker governed by his senses: "Mind is imprison'd in a lonesome tower: / Sensation is its window" (739–740), as well as to Condillac's "mimic statue" with its soul "Composed of sense" (731–731).[22] Imprecise or imperfect communication is the price one pays for engaging with the sensory world and moving through that world as an alert, perceiving individual.

Barrett Browning is also wary of this sensory and embodied experience of language, insisting that her readers recognize the divine properties of human communication. Her prefatory remarks to her discussion of Locke and Condillac warn readers that "Language from its material analogy deteriorates from spiritual meaning" ("Analysis of the Second Book," 97), and her own note to her lines on Condillac observe that Condillac's statue "is very cleverly put together, but is a *statue* after all" (note B, 116). The narrator of *An Essay on Mind* elevates a silent, wordless communion in the heavenly sphere over the material world of confused, fallen speech. She imagines a future state where bodiless souls communicate to each other in a perfect and universal language, and where the divisions between the soul and the body, and between thoughts and words, no longer apply:

> Thus Thought must bend to words! - Some sphere of bliss,
> Ere long, shall free her from the alloy of this:
> Some kindred home for Mind – Some holy place,
> Where spirits look on spirits, 'face to face,' –
> Where souls may see, as they themselves are seen,
> And voiceless intercourse may pass between,
> All pure – all free! as light, which doth appear
> In its own essence, incorrupt and clear!
> One service, praise! one age, eternal youth!
> One tongue, intelligence! one subject, truth!
>
> Till then, no freedom, Learning's search affords,
> Of soul from body, or of thought from words.

> (659–670)

These lines echo the crisis of "A Thought on Thoughts," with their gendered personification of Thought and their imagery of the "kindred home." Yet they also extend the possibility of bodily transcendence, diverging sharply from Locke and Condillac in order to praise the "One tongue" or perfect language that can only be gained by sundering the ties between language and the body. Anaphora and parallel structure ("One tongue," "One service") emphasize the unitary nature of this sacred exchange between spirits. The narrator anticipates a "holy place" where "voiceless intercourse may pass between" souls; the lack of a punctuated caesura in this line suggests the seamlessness of this divine communication. In place of a flawed linguistic communication is an imagined state of being that transcends the disappointments and imperfections of language and meaning through an unspoken, ungendered communion of souls.[23] In this new dispensation, everything is as free as the light that appears "in its own essence" and is not mismatched to an arbitrary sign. The "One tongue" of intelligence hints at the many tongues of the dispersion at Babel and suggests that this future state of providential communion will bring about a universal reconciliation of speakers, while her claim that all "souls may see" seeks to elevate language above the body's sensorium and to endow the soul itself with capacities for vision.

Like Locke and Condillac, Barrett Browning longed to unite the sensory body with language and political freedom, but she wished to do so in ways that deeply affirmed language's sacred power. While

Enlightenment language-philosophy provided a means through which Barrett Browning and other Victorians conceived of the freedom of the sensory, speaking individual, Barrett Browning's later poetry would turn to Biblical accounts of language, God's divine breath, and Christ's incarnation in order to express the spiritual and otherworldly nature of human communication. At the same time, as we will see, these accounts had little to recommend them to a female poet seeking to craft her own political and poetic language within a male literary and philological tradition. This issue leads Barrett Browning, in *A Drama of Exile*, to uncover and perform the tension between embodiment and disembodiment, between Locke's and Condillac's universal, sensory, male individual and the supposedly disordered and excessive female sensorium.

Language-Origins, Women, and Incarnation in *A Drama of Exile*

Barrett Browning's mature poetry often seeks a connection to the divine through the haptic ecstasy of Christ's touch. Her essay "Some Account of the Greek Christian Poets," published in installments in the *Athenaeum* in 1842, calls for a new poetry suffused with the grace of Christ's incarnate body:

> Religious 'parcel-poets' we have, indeed, more than enough; writers of hymns, translators of scripture into prose, or of prose generally into rhymes, of whose heart-devotion a higher faculty were worthy. Also there have been poets, not a few, singing as if earth were still Eden; and poets, many, singing as if in the first hour of exile, when the echo of the curse was louder than the whisper of the promise. But the right 'genius of Christianism' has done little up to this moment, even for Chateaubriand. We want the touch of Christ's hand upon our literature, as it touched other dead things - we want the sense of the saturation of Christ's blood upon the souls of our poets, that it may cry *through* them in answer to the ceaseless wail of the Sphinx of our humanity, expounding agony into renovation.
>
> (371–372)

Speaking not only for herself but also for her larger community of readers, Barrett Browning describes how composing, translating, and singing—the activities of the poet—lack the animating grace of divine form, making language, in effect, into an art form sundered from spiritual meaning. Her hybrid dramatic-masque poem, *A Drama of Exile*, which appears as the lead work in *Poems* (1844), explores this problem at length. In this retelling of the Miltonic story of exile from Paradise, Barrett Browning equates God's breath with divine speech, explores the Adamic account of language both before and after the

Fall, and foregrounds the role of Eve's body and language in this new, post-lapsarian world. The closet drama form, with its hint of communal performance redirected into individual acts of reading, allows Barrett Browning to address the collective or the "we" of "Some Account of the Greek Christian Poets." At the same time, the story of Eve coming to terms with her own role in the expulsion and with this troubled, post-lapsarian language enables Barrett Browning to test out and gender the model of the awakening statue proposed by Condillac. Ultimately Barrett Browning revises the story of the Fall by anticipating the redemptive incarnation of Christ. This revision allows her to assert the divine essence of language as a worldly manifestation of Christ's Word while also preserving her emphasis on the marginalized role of women's bodies and women's language.

Barrett Browning looks to Romantic philology in order to assert the spiritual meaning of language in response to accounts like Locke's and Condillac's. As Dowling notes, the publication of Locke's *Essay* threatened the idea of human communication as part of a providential will or intelligence, and works such as J.G. Herder's *On the Origin of Language* (1772) reaffirmed the spiritual underpinnings of language by showing written letters to be animated by an otherworldly, divine breath.[24] For example, Herder writes that the vowels of Hebrew, the "so-called divine, the first language," remained unwritten because they were too sacred to be constrained by an alphabet:

> With us, vowels are the first, the most vital things, the hinges of language, as it were. With the Hebrews, they are not written. Why? Because they could not be written. Their pronunciation was so alive and so finely articulated, their breath so spiritual and etherlike that it evaporated and eluded containment in letters. It was only with the Greeks that these living aspirations were pinned down in formal vowels, though these still required a seconding by the spiritus signs and the like, whereas with the Orientals speech as it were was a continuous breath, nothing but spiritus, the spirit of the mouth, as they so often call it in their depictive poems. What the ear caught was the breath of God, was wafting air; and the dead characters they drew out were only the inanimate body which the act of reading had to animate with the spirit of life.[25]

Herder equates divinity with speech and breath, and with the embodied acts of inhalation and exhalation. Aspiration becomes a means of channeling God; the divine communal breath evades the material sphere of written characters and physical bodies. The act of reading restores to language its sacred character, and completes the divine connection between spiritual breath, the embodied speaker, and the community of listeners.

The notion of "God's breath" animating the material world continued to shape philology in the Victorian period and especially in the 1840s, in the wake of the publication of Robert Chambers's notorious work of popular science, *Vestiges of the Natural History of Creation* (1844). Chambers presents an evolutionary account of human speech in which language is not a divine gift but a function of physical development. While "there is a great inclination to surmise a miraculous origin for it," Chambers writes, "...there is no proper ground...for such an idea in Scripture."[26] Chambers's rejection of language's divinity prompted a rebuttal from William Whewell, whose *Indications of the Creator* (1845) borrows from natural theology the idea of God as a First Cause whose work was manifest in the intricate designs of nature: "We must needs believe...that the First Cause which produced air and organs of articulation produced also language and the faculties by which language is rendered possible....Nor can we think otherwise than that the Being who gave these faculties, bestowed them for some purpose."[27] Barrett Browning seems to have shared this sentiment: in 1845 she declared that *Vestiges* was "one of the most melancholy books in the world."[28] For Barrett Browning, philosophical and scientific elaborations of language's relationship to the evolutionary, physiological body threatened to displace language's sacred character.

This sacred relationship between the divine realm and the sensing individual is also central to her understanding of the social importance of poetry and the relationship between writers and readers. In an 1844 essay on Thomas Carlyle co-authored with Richard Hengist Horne, she invokes the image of Locke's individual mind, a "prisoner in a dark room, or in a room which would be dark but for the windows of the same, meaning the senses."[29] Carlyle's language acts on the "general mind" as the senses act on the individual mind, "strik[ing] a window out here, and another there" and awakening readers.[30] This pairing is central to Carlyle's ability to affect his audience, and it also informs Aurora Leigh's youthful encounters with a poetry that "burns you through" and "shakes the heart / Of all the men and women in the world" (1:905, 906–907). Here Locke's writings on language and sensation help Barrett Browning develop a view of poetry as a means of physically startling readers and inviting them to contemplate new political and social ideas. By invoking the story of the divine breath first breathed into Adam in the Book of Genesis, Barrett Browning also revises Locke's emphasis on the senses to endow the body with a spiritual impulse. Carlyle's prophetic, otherworldly language reveals "God's breath" working through his words: "there was a divinity at the shaping of these rough-hewn periods" (258). Following in a tradition of Romantic philology that would be re-animated by the controversial statements of *Vestiges*, Barrett Browning invokes the Biblical imagery of God's breath working through writers and creating a bond of providential communication between writers and readers.

However, while Barrett Browning borrows the trope of divine breath from Romantic philology, she also radically revises this trope by underscoring its patriarchal history. In 1845, she lamented that England had had many learned women, "and yet where were the poetesses? The divine breath which seemed to come and go...why did it never pass, even in the lyrical form, over the lips of a woman?"[31] Where God's breath enables the muscular or "rough-hewn" prose of Carlyle, it is absent or displaced from the scant history of the English poetess, an absence Barrett Browning indicates by further eliding the body of the female poet through the metonymic image of her lips. This incorporeal poetics, with its marginalization of the female body, exists in direct antithesis to the image of Christ's firm hand renovating the poet's soul, and to the startling sensory aggression of Carlyle's prophetic language.

A Drama of Exile intensifies these themes by granting a central place to Eve's language and to her sensory awakening. The drama takes place immediately after the Fall from Paradise and from the lost, divine language spoken in the Garden of Eden.[32] As Aarsleff notes, the Genesis story of Adam's name-giving stresses a harmonious, pre-lapsarian relationship between sign and signifier. The Adamic language-theory "held that languages even now, in spite of their multiplicity and seeming chaos, contain elements of the original perfect language created by Adam when he named the animals in his prelapsarian state. In the Adamic doctrine the relation between signifier and signified is not arbitrary; the linguistic sign is not double but unitary."[33] For Aarsleff, Locke's argument about language's imperfection was aimed primarily at this doctrine. As Locke insists, words stand in for ideas "not by any natural connexion...for then there would be but one language amongst all men; but by a voluntary imposition, whereby such a word is made arbitrarily the mark of such an idea" (363). Barrett Browning addresses these ideas in a passage where Adam recalls his name-giving:

> Lo, my voice,
> Which, naming erst the creatures, did express
> (God breathing through my breath) the attributes
> And instincts of each creature in its name,
> Floats to the same afflatus....
>
> (1825–1829)

Adam's channeling of God's divine breath rehearses the story of an originary, Biblical "divine breath" as the origin of language, one first bequeathed unto the first male speaker. Adam discerns a harmony of expression in which "the attributes / And instincts" of each named animal are manifest in his designations. His linguistic authority comes across in his confident parenthetical statement as well as in his use of "afflatus" to express his creative impulse. Adam's body, too, works in harmony with this language. God's breath works through Adam and recalls Herder's remarks on the divine spiritus.

In keeping with the Adamic doctrine, Barrett Browning shows how language after the Fall loses its sense of harmony, and how the sensorium, too, becomes disordered and instable. *A Drama of Exile* genders this experience, suggesting that Eve is especially sensitive to this linguistic and physical chaos. The Fall brings to the characters, and most especially to the guilt-stricken Eve, a "new apocalypse of sense" that contrasts with the placid breath and language of Adam's name-giving (161). She observes that the earth "is crazed with curse" and "wanders from the sense / Of those first laws affixed to form and space" before the age of sin (910–913). Eve's observation of changes in the physical landscape also brings a heightened attention to her own sensory experience. She begs God not to shut her and Adam away

> From verity and from stability,
> Or what we name such through the precedence
> Of earth's adjusted uses, - leave us not
> To doubt between our senses and our souls,
> Which are the more distraught and full of pain
> And weak of apprehension.
>
> (958–963)

Eve's plea questions the results of designation and naming, the province of Adam before the Fall, acknowledging that verity and stability may not be concrete states in themselves but only "what we name such." The opposition between "our senses and our souls" underscores a physical relationship to experience that foregrounds the role of bodily perception.

Eve continues to question the origins of speech and perception. Confronted with a circle of zodiac figures, she addresses Adam, "Thou who didst name all lives, hast names for these?" (974) and, upon receiving his explanation, asks, "By dream or sense, / Do we see this?" (990–991). The lost, unitary language of Paradise gives way to a fallen, imperfect tongue and a disordered sensorium. With this preoccupation Eve anticipates *Aurora Leigh's* Marian Erle, who wonders of Lady Waldemar: "*Did* she speak," or did she "only sign? / Or did she put a word into her face / And look, and so impress you with the word?" (6.963–966). Barrett Browning suggests that the *Drama's* apocalypse of sense is deeply related to women's physical sensibility, revealing a gendered responsiveness to physical experience that is a distinct condition of the fallen tongue or "imperfect government" of language in exile. Eve bears this burden physically more so than Adam, both in her own repeated allusions to the chaotic body and in the pains of childbirth, the "Peculiar suffering" or "pang paid down for each new human life" that she will experience in exile (1858–1859).[34]

Because this fallen state further removes words from the "spiritual essence" Barrett Browning sought to attain through her poetry, *A Drama of Exile* shifts its emphasis from a post-Adamic, imperfect language to a model of language redeemed by the words and body of Christ. At the play's climax, just as Adam and Eve are confronted by a chorus of angry Earth Spirits who seek to usurp their dominion, Christ appears in the zodiac, orders the spirits to respect "This regent and sublime Humanity" (1780), and commands Adam to bless Eve and release her from her guilt. He promises his listeners:

> That not in vain
> Nor yet ignobly ye shall serve, I place
> My word here for an oath, mine oath for an act
> To be hereafter. In the name of which
> Perfect redemption and perpetual grace,
> I bless you through the hope and through the peace
> Which are mine, - to the Love, which is myself.
>
> (1815–1820)

Christ's appearance promises not only to endow fallen humanity with a new and perpetual word, but also to reconcile the division between sense and soul so persistently lamented by Eve. He declares to his listeners that God's grace will "glorify you into soul from sense!" (1813) and thus promises, through his word, to redeem the play's "apocalypse" of the body in the new conditions of exile. He forecasts the eventual rupture between humanity and the divine word of God, a rupture that symbolically repeats the separation between God's language and man after the Fall from Paradise:

> Eternity stands always fronting God;
> A stern colossal image, with blind eyes
> And grand dim lips that murmur evermore
> God, God, God! while the rush of life and death,
> The roar of act and thought, of evil and good,
> The avalanches of the ruining worlds
> Tolling down space, - the new world's genesis
> Budding in fire, - the gradual humming growth
> Of the ancient atoms and first forms of earth,
> The slow procession of the swathing seas
> And firmamental waters, - and the noise

Of the broad, fluent strata of pure airs, -
All these flow onward in the intervals
Of that reiterated sound of – GOD!
Which WORD, innumerous angels straightway lift
Wide on celestial altitudes of song
And choral adulation, and then drop
The burden softly, shutting the last notes
In silver wings. Howbeit in the noon of time
Eternity shall wax as dumb as Death,
While a new voice beneath the spheres shall cry,
'God! why hast thou forsaken me, my God?'
   And not a voice in Heaven shall answer it.

                                   (1932–1955)

These lines open with the image of "Eternity" as the personification of endless time, while Eternity's "grand dim lips" suggest the language of the cosmos. A chain of aural elements ("murmur," "rush," "roar," "humming," "noise") heightens this emphasis on language, but these acts of expression only come at intervals in between the punctuated, regular repetitions of God's name. The image of angels who "lift" and "drop" God's word with their song implies the materiality of this word and its transformation into flesh. Christ repeats the new, fallen state of language after exile and presents the future as the antithesis of the worldless communion Barrett Browning anticipates in *An Essay on Mind*: instead of the silence of perfect, harmonious communication, Christ warns of an eternal separation between speakers, in which humans cry out to the heavens and no one answers.

   The only redemption available to Adam and Eve in this perpetual state of fallenness is the intervention of Christ's own body and being into the space between the divine and the human realms:

                   Then, at last,
I, wrapping round me your humanity,
Which being sustained, shall neither break nor burn
Beneath the fire of Godhead, will tread earth,
And ransom you and it, and set strong peace
Betwixt you and its creatures.

                                   (1968–1973)

As Adam and Eve stand in rapt attention, this speaking Christ in the zodiac gradually takes on fleshly form, prompting Adam to declare that "Thy speech is of the Heavenlies, yet, O Christ, / Awfully human are thy voice and face" (1956–1957). Unlike the divine breath that first created language in Adam's throat and that vanishes after the Fall, Christ's incarnation promises a model of speaking and being that foregrounds the role of the sensory, human body as a means through which to access and commune with the divine. By shifting her emphasis from the Biblical expulsion into fallen, discordant speech to the redeeming incarnation of Christ, Barrett Browning imagines a way to achieve the "spiritual essence" she had celebrated in her early poetry on language.

In *A Drama of Exile,* then, Barrett Browning gradually transforms the story of language after the Fall into an imagined future model of language-as-incarnation that releases Eve from her tormenting sensorium and reaffirms the status of language as a divine gift. "Some Account of the Greek Christian Poets" eagerly anticipates an age of incarnate poetry that will translate collective suffering into renewal through the figure of the poet, and *A Drama of Exile* looks ahead to the redeeming embodiment of Christ's language on earth. If Herder's account of "God's breath" would animate the dead letters of writing, Barrett Browning's haptic Christ inspires a new era of poetic language, one touched and spoken alive as his blood and body become material in the word. Her readers are all free individuals in a society of speakers working with the imperfect "code" of language, Barrett Browning suggests, and yet they are all united through the word and body of Christ, whose material incarnation or word-made-flesh animates and sacralizes the polity. Therefore, though all citizens may speak a fallen and imperfect tongue on earth, their use of language at all still connects them to the divine, universal incarnation that redeems the political community and makes it cohere.

The function of the author or poet, as she explains in her writings on Carlyle, is to use language as a medium through which to access the divine, and to use one's sensory body and prophetic language to bridge the gap between the material world and the heavenly realm. However, this more generalized or universal role of the poet or author quickly becomes problematic when the speaker is a woman. Because Eve's womanly body further aggravates the physical and emotional effects of sensory, embodied experiences, she is an untrustworthy speaker, acutely aware of her body's distortions and in need of exculpatory blessings and forgiveness from Adam and Christ.

If *A Drama of Exile* foregrounds the emotional language and physical sensibilities of the first female speaker in the Bible, *Aurora Leigh* develops these themes at even greater length by having its poet-protagonist navigate the contemporary Victorian social body, both acting as its poetic representative and noting her own exclusion from its political activities. Barrett Browning explores this vision of incarnation at length as the poet-narrator Aurora crafts her political critique of Britain's aristocracy, the Woman Question, and its treatment of the underclasses through a vatic, poetic language. However, the association between women's embodiment and women's sensibility expressed by Eve persists as a barrier to the poet's success in *Aurora Leigh* and leads Barrett Browning to an even more dramatic revision of the incarnate word, one the poem expresses through a bodiless poetics.

Language, Incarnation, and the Social Body in *Aurora Leigh*

Walking through the streets of a newly republican Paris, the young heroine of *Aurora Leigh* makes a radical claim about language as an instrument of social transformation. "Virtue's in the *word!* / The maker burnt up the darkness with His, / To inaugurate the use of vocal life," Aurora declares, adding that the poet's word, planted "deep enough / In any man's breast," can help a man more than changes in material conditions (6:218–220, 221–222). Aurora's faith in language's ability to empower its users, and her allusion to the "*word!*" of the Book of John, reflects an alliance between divine-origins theories of language and the emergent notion of the social body in the Victorian political imagination. As we saw in the Introduction, Thomas Carlyle's use of the Johannine "word-become-flesh" helped frame the transformation of the pre-Reform body politic into the more inclusive, post-Reform model of the social body, in which the lower classes or the people at large have a greater political role. Like Carlyle, Barrett Browning sees the polity as a form of social incarnation, one that brings together Aurora and Marian, and, notoriously, the ragged poor of St. Giles with the well-heeled denizens of St. James. And, like the prophetic, embodied narrator of Carlyle's *The French Revolution*, Aurora navigates this social world as its passionate witness and representative, using her poetic powers to address gender and class inequalities and to act, through her language, as a medium who communicates with the divine.

And yet this same emphasis on the body also fuels the poem's internal dismissal of women's poetry. In Book 2, the central male antagonist, Romney Leigh, points to Aurora's body as an obstacle to political expression. Catching the young Aurora in the act of crowning herself as a poet, Romney insists that women cannot write about contemporary debates over labor or slavery because they understand everything in terms of their own experience: "All's yours and you, / All, coloured with your blood, or otherwise / Just nothing to you" (2:196–198). In a powerfully essentializing gesture, Romney invalidates Aurora's poetry by means of her body. His insult articulates a larger double bind that is at the heart of *Aurora Leigh*: namely, the tension between the work's lively interest in political questions and its commitment to representing these questions in an expressive, physical language.

Aurora Leigh's political intervention, then, turns on the conflict between two kinds of bodies: the larger social body the poet seeks to represent, and the distorting presence of her own embodied, feminine language. For the remainder of this chapter, I argue that *Aurora Leigh* responds to this conflict by staking out a poetics of bodilessness as a poetic and political strategy. While acknowledging the poem's insistently physical idiom, I seek to uncover an alternative subtext of effaced language and vanishing bodies, and to show how this subtext is equally central to *Aurora Leigh*. Through the associated figures of Aurora and Marian, Barrett Browning's epic imagines an alternative potential in linguistic negations of the body, negations that offer a revitalized political poetics even as these negations disassociate women's language from women's physical experience.

In focusing on *Aurora Leigh's* interest in a transfigured poetics I join critics such as Kirstie Blair, Jason Rudy, and Charles LaPorte who underline Barrett Browning's alertness to language as an art of spiritual transformation. While Blair and Rudy analyze the spiritual underpinnings of Barrett Browning's relation between poetics and the body, LaPorte has shown how *Aurora Leigh* "genders prophecy and poetry" in ways reminiscent of related scholarship that foregrounds Aurora's relation to Victorian sage discourse.[35] *Aurora Leigh* bases its poetics on a creative attachment to language's divine potential, one that upholds an incarnational poetics to unite the material and spiritual realms.[36] Embodiment and disembodiment in *Aurora Leigh* dialectically transform each other, at times informing Aurora's desire for detached contemplation, at other times realizing her eager bodily longing for a Christ to descend and "straighten out / The leathery tongue turned back into the throat" (5:108–109).

However, while these works have convincingly demonstrated the link between the material and the spiritual realms in Barrett Browning's work, I wish to focus on *Aurora Leigh's* extensive engagement with the subject of earthly political sovereignty. If the poem understands a principle of incarnation to animate language, so too does it recognize these principles to be associated with a long tradition of political power. *Aurora Leigh* understands the Victorian social body as a formation that bears traces of its roots in an autocratic feudal hierarchy, one symbolized in the poem's representations of the French emperor Napoleon III and of Romney's phalanstery—a structure whose failure some critics have read as indicative of the work's conservatism.[37] I contend, however, that *Aurora Leigh's* imagery of disembodiment seeks to create an alternative political poetics that transcends this embodied hierarchy. Aurora's acute sensibility prevents her from entering into mainstream political discourse, and the abstracted bodies of Aurora and Marian come to assert an alternative reading of women's language that disentangles the body from notions of political and poetic authority.

Aurora Leigh extends *A Drama of Exile's* tropes of incarnation to consider language and its relationship to political life. Through this incarnational poetics, Aurora gives expression to both a vibrant fleshly aesthetic and a political trope of sovereignty. As we saw in the Introduction, concepts of sovereign authority in Britain were historically grounded in readings of Christ's body. In Ernst Kantorowicz's classic account of the king's two bodies, the feudal king was endowed with both a natural, physical body and a royal, immortal super-body. This division had its origin in the consecrated host or the Eucharist, at once the "corpus natural" or natural body and also the "corpus mysticum," or the social body of the Church. This social body would later evolve into the early modern "body politic," with the king at its head.[38] This long tradition of political theology is at the heart of Aurora's observation, as she looks back to England from post-Revolutionary Paris, that freedom's "self" comes "Fixed in a feudal form incarnately / To suit our ways of thought and reverence, / That special form, with us, being still the thing" (6:43, 45–47). Despite the ascendancy of liberal politics in Britain during this time period, Aurora understands her adopted country's political system to rest on the power structures and traditions associated with its monarchical history, traditions that distinguish British subjects from the "light" political abstractions and revolutionary impulses of the French (6:2).[39] References to incarnation in *Aurora Leigh* are the means by which Aurora both acknowledges the spiritual underpinnings of language and signifies her own entry into contemporary political discourse.

However, if Aurora draws on an incarnational discourse of sovereign authority, so too does she inherit the uneasy deployment of this political rhetoric in the wake of the French Revolution and on through nineteenth-century revolutions and reforms. As Mary Poovey has noted, the transition to political modernity brought with it a new emphasis on the "social body" as a more inclusive representation of the polity that could include the lower classes.[40] This representation, in turn, extended the incarnational logic of royal sovereignty into the unstable space of social representation in the wake of the democratic revolutions of the nineteenth century, a phenomenon Claude Lefort analyzes by showing how members of modern society remain "so captivated by the image of a body that they project it onto their own union."[41] This projection undermines the plans for reform and reconstruction that inform Romney's social work in *Aurora Leigh*. Romney's phalanstery, converted from an ancestral estate and overseen by its designated patriarch, still bears the traces and injustices of its feudal heritage. As Aurora's aunt reminds her, Romney is the "son who represents our house / And holds the fiefs and manors" (2:636–637). In its tacit replication of ancient power structures, Romney's phalanstery approximates the "feudal form" Aurora associates with British political life more broadly.

Tropes of embodiment in the writings that inform Romney's work further underline the lingering presence of incarnational rhetoric in cross-Channel political debates. The notion of society as an incarnated body is prominent in the writing of the theologian Frederick Denison Maurice, who played a leading role in the Christian Socialist movement the guests at Lord Howe's party associate with Romney in *Aurora Leigh* (5.737). In *The Kingdom of Christ* (1837) Maurice used the body of Christ to propose a vision of harmony among sects:"The Church is a body united in the acknowledgement of a living *Person*.... In that Person whom the church confesses as the Lord of Man, he recognizes the Being in whom all men are united, out of whom men are necessarily separated."[42] So too did French thinkers like Pierre-Joseph Proudhon and Charles Fourier, whom Lady Waldemar reads to ingratiate herself to Romney, draw on a secularized logic of incarnational brotherhood (3:584–585). In *Theory of the Four Movements* (1808), Charles Fourier spoke of the collective impact of economic mishaps upon the "social body."[43] Pierre-Joseph Proudhon characterized modern individualism as the source of the collective's loss of power, creating a society "like a body in which the particles had ceased to cohere and which would crumble into dust at the slightest shock."[44] The presence of these thinkers in *Aurora Leigh* reveals how the work's political discourse understands the somatic language of the body politic as an ongoing influence on alternative reorganizations of society in the nineteenth century.[45]

Aurora Leigh registers this discursive shift in ambivalent terms, using the corporeal idiom of the body politic to describe the transition to a political model of the social body that understood sovereign authority to reside within the people. As Alison Chapman has recently argued, Barrett Browning's residence in Florence during the Italian *Risorgimento* or unification movement situated her in a dynamic network of expatriate women poets seeking to craft political poetry, while Saville has demonstrated how Barrett Browning's "soul poetics" situates her within a trans-Channel political network of writers in France, Britain, and Italy.[46] This lively context of transcultural exchange also provided Barrett Browning with material for Aurora's meditations on politics as she travels through Paris under the reign of Louis-Napoléon Bonaparte, who would ascend to the throne as Napoleon III shortly following an 1851 coup later ratified by a controversial national referendum during the Browning's stay in Paris.[47] Aurora's description of Napoleon III describes his body as partly an image of absolute sovereign power and partly the symbol of popular will:

> And if last [France] sighs
> Her great soul up into a great man's face,
> To flush his temples out so gloriously
> That few dare carp at Caesar for being bald,
> What then? – this Caesar represents, not reigns,
> And is no despot, though twice absolute:
> This Head has all the people for a heart;

This purple's lined with the democracy, -
Now let him see to it! for a rent within
Would leave irreparable rags without.

(6:66–75)

The poet personifies the French as a single woman's body while collapsing the "Head" and the "people" into one body politic. The metaleptic substitution of the purple robe for the ruling body recalls associations of purple with both royalty and sacrifice, and suggests that Napoleon III yields some of his authority to the people's will.[48] Aurora also softens Napoleon III's potentially absolute body by describing it as underwritten by the intangible collective "soul" of France, a popular approval that allows her to distinguish between the opposed imperatives of reigning and representing. Aurora's presentation of a democracy grafted onto the investitures of Napoleon III's frame, with the people within his body, underlines the ways the somatic political rhetoric of incarnate authority lingers and continues to shape and define perceptions of sovereign power. Yet this same power, once granted by the people, is exercised by Napoleon III alone, suggesting Aurora's sympathy with potentially more authoritarian ideologies of leadership: "Now let him see to it!" In Aurora's representation, Napoleon's divided body reflects the competing claims of hereditary leadership and popular sovereignty.

Aurora's self-crowning, reminiscent of both Virgil's crowning of Dante in *The Divine Comedy* and the crowning of Germaine de Staël's heroine in *Corinne*, elevates the poet as a political figure who speaks for the collective social body.[49] Barrett Browning's unsent 1857 letter to Napoleon III in defense of Victor Hugo, then in exile in Jersey and openly publishing statements against the emperor, illustrates her belief in the poet's divine role within the polity. The poet should be exempt from punitive measures because the poet contains a "divine love" that justifies any perceived offenses against the state: "Make an exception of him, as God made an exception of him when He gave him genius."[50] Barrett Browning's poet is both of and beyond the polity, a central figure in the nation but also one with access to a divinity beyond it.

Barrett Browning was also familiar with this political function of the poet's language from her reading of Thomas Carlyle's *On Heroes, Hero-Worship, and the Heroic in History* (1841), a text she much admired and which situated the poet in a lineage that included that of the king. Carlyle writes that "the Hero can be Poet, Prophet, King, Priest" and that Dante and Shakespeare stand out in their "royal solitude.... They *are* canonized."[51] Aurora aspires to take part in this political tradition of canonized poets. The name of the poet, she declares, "Is royal, and to sign it like a queen, / Is what I dare not, - though some royal blood / Would seem to tingle in me now and then" (1:935–937). In these accounts and in the scene of her self-crowning the poet aspires to speak for the social body, using her own body and language to craft a political poetics.

Romney's objections to Aurora's self-crowning, however, bring Aurora's female body into conflict with the social body she seeks to represent. "None of all these things, / Can women understand" declares Romney of women's abilities to write about modern politics and social ills (2:182–183):

> 'Therefore, this same world
> Uncomprehended by you, must remain
> Uninfluenced by you. – Women as you are,
> Mere women, personal and passionate,
> You give us doating mothers, and perfect wives,
> Sublime Madonnas, and enduring saints!
> We get no Christ from you, - and verily
> We shall not get a poet, in my mind'
>
> (2:218–225)

In one sweeping gesture Romney both forecloses the possibility of a woman's political poetics and declares women's writing to be incapable of representing the deeper conceptual underpinnings of political authority—we "get no Christ" from Aurora. In Romney's view the female poet's body distorts her political views, causing her to express instead her own embodied sensibility. A rich strand of feminist criticism has analyzed the ways that *Aurora Leigh* subverts Romney's essentialist pronouncements on women's language through strategies that include intertextuality, bricolage, metalepsis, and satire.[52] Building on this criticism, I will now turn to *Aurora Leigh's* unacknowledged investment in bodilessness as a political and poetic strategy. Through the transformations and encounters of Aurora and Marian, the poem's second heroine, Barrett Browning's epic advances a desire to escape the female body and its marginalized language. This distance, in turn, acts both as a means to transcend gender categories and as a way of underlining the exclusion of women from the polity.

If Aurora's travels among Britain, France, and Italy offer her a vantage point from which to explore broader questions of political sovereignty, the triangulated marriage plot between Aurora, Romney, and Marian extends this corporeal imagery of the social body to the domestic realm. Aurora's representations of Napoleon III reveal the contradictions inherent in the emergent notions of the social body, while Romney's work revisits these contradictions in his converted feudal estate. Romney's role in this uneasy entanglement of somatic discourses is most apparent through his participation in the poem's complex symbolic networks of blood. He tells Aurora of his social program that the "common blood / That swings along my veins, is strong enough / To draw me to this duty" (2:322–324), invoking an arterial imagery that suggests that he positions himself within a communal social body.[53] Importantly, however, "duty" is also the term Aurora's aunt uses to characterize her undemonstrative caregiving: Aurora remembers that her aunt did "Her duty to me, (I appreciate it / In her own word as spoken to herself) / Her duty, in large measure, well-pressed out" (1:361–363). The poem early on establishes a connection between "duty" and acts of condescending domestic patronage, and Romney's use of the term implicates his own remaking of the feudal estate in similar terms, revealing a haphazard, freighted circulation of sovereign authority in the domestic household. Romney's reference to his own bloodline early establishes the nobility of his lineage: he is a "Leigh, / With blood trained up along nine centuries" (2:1011–1012). His association with ancient property and blood underlines the lingering presence of a body politic with its authority grounded in notions of an innate corporeal nobility.

The persistence of this feudal standard haunts Romney Leigh's social program and undermines his attempt to redistribute his own inheritance among the lower classes. As a consequence, his phalanstery offers not a remaking of the body politic but rather a reinscription of the systems of industrial labor that the new living community was intended to counter. The failure of this redistribution, in turn, suggests the failure of social reconstruction when it draws from a reified feudal economy. The poem suggests that, much as Aurora looks back from Paris on the "feudal form" that continues to shape politics in Britain, Romney's efforts to detach himself from his position in a traditional hereditary order still bear the "special form" of the body politic that lingers to undermine his social project.

Aurora's observation, then, that "We cannot be the equal of the male / Who rules his blood a little" presents the language of political modernity as a confluence of multiple, unstable meanings (2:705–706). On the one hand, to govern one's blood refers back to the feudal tradition that implicates Romney, with all of his masculinist discourse; on the other hand, it underscores women's bodies as excessive and ungovernable and, because of this, unsuited to the demands of poetic and political representation. Aurora inherits from this somatic rhetoric not only the instability of corporeal representation that haunts Romney's social project—the fraught and incomplete transfer of authority from the body politic to the body social—but also the question of how a woman poet, with her gendered body, might best speak for this collective.

Aurora Leigh tacitly merges the possibility of an expressive female poetic body with the communal body of its readers.[54] The many physical descriptions of bodies in *Aurora Leigh* approach a style of ekphrasis, reading the body at once as an intensely visual object and as the means of collective expression and self-definition. The young Aurora tells the reader to

> See the earth,
> The body of our body, the green earth,
> Indubitably human like this flesh
> And these articulated veins through which
> Our heart drives blood.
>
> (5:116–120)

Aurora invokes a communal body and anatomizes it, calling attention to the different elements of "this flesh," "these...veins," "our heart." The word "articulated" has two meanings, here designating both physical segments linked by joints and the idea of a distinct utterance, so that the "articulated veins" are simultaneously the subjects of description and the transmitters of poetic language.[55] Aurora's communal body recalls her declaration to Romney that it takes a poet's individualism to create collective feeling: "It takes a soul, / To move a body: it takes a high-souled man, / To move the masses" (2:479–481).[56] Aurora suggests that the poet's language can act as a catalyst for action in the collective social body. In a revised reading of Barrett Browning's earlier remarks on Carlyle's visceral language, the body of the narrating female poet is both the means of her individual expression and a part of her shared sensibility with her readers.

Yet if *Aurora Leigh* invokes a communal, physical sensibility it also subverts this equation of politics, language, and the body through its repeated longings for transcendence, for a poetics that does not have its origins in the body. "Let me think / Of forms less, and the external" cautions Aurora in Book 5, in the more subdued lines that follow her celebration of the "double-breasted Age" (5:223–224, 216). Her early, feverish work at improving her poetry likewise expresses not a full habitation of the body but rather a denial of it:

> Observe – 'I,' means in youth
> Just *I*, the conscious and eternal soul
> With all its ends, and not the outside life,
> The parcel-man, the doublet of the flesh,
> The so much liver, lung, integument,
> Which make the sum of 'I' hereafter when
> World-talkers talk of doing well or ill.
>
> (3:283–289)

Aurora opposes the soul to the body and further reduces the body's co-
herence through a set of metonymic divisions in the fifth line earlier. Au-
rora divides the "outside life" from the inner life and makes the inner life
the mark of her identity: the poet composes one identity or "*I*" from the
inside while the other "I" is created by the "World-talkers" who view
her externally. This external body is detached into separate elements
of "liver" and "lung" that together do not make a coherent, embodied
whole. Significantly, Aurora's "doublet of the flesh" recalls the ill-fitting
and "large / Man's doublet" of education her father wraps around her
in Book 3, subtly underlining the connection between exterior forms
and constructions of gender (1:727–728). Like the weight of classical
learning, and like the masculine sonneteer tradition in which the poet
must learn to "stand still," Aurora's doublet of the flesh is a form over-
lain with the traditions and language of others (5:89).[57] In other words,
if Aurora must learn to inhabit the ungainly masculine forms of Greek
education and of the sonnet, so too must she learn to renounce them
physically, to throw off "This dark of the body" in her creation of a
distinctive poetic voice (5:23).

    Aurora Leigh further imagines as subtext a disembodied relationship
that escapes this double inscription of language and the female body
through its heroines, constructing two fluctuating readings of women's
bodies and their relationship to language through Aurora's and Marian's
thematically intertwined but divergent poetic autobiographies. Affinities
among the physical experiences of Aurora and Marian establish their
similarities. Both women experience, albeit in different degrees, mo-
ments of physical scrutiny and shame: Aurora's discomfort with her
aunt's gaze, with the "unscrupulous eyes" that look "body and heart"
through Aurora and probe her feelings for Romney (2:686, 687), is bru-
tally intensified in Marian's memory of her cruel French mistress who
"clipped me with her eyes / As if a viper with a pair of tongs" as she
discerns her pregnancy (7:39–40). As with their exposure to physical
shame both women stumble through early encounters with written lan-
guage: as a girl Aurora "nibbled here and there" at the shut-away books
in her aunt's attic (1:838), while the young Marian "weeded out / Her
book leaves" and "made a nosegay" of the stray volumes she received
from a traveling pedlar (3:987–988, 990). Most significantly, their rela-
tionship with Romney brings the two women into homosocial relation
with Marian's vision of her role as Romney's companion. She is "Much
fitter for his handmaid than his wife" in an abject literalization of the re-
inscribed social inequality Aurora imagines as part of Romney's domes-
tic arrangements (4:227). Through such affinities, the poem introduces
Marian as a central figure in its establishment of a political poetics.

    However, if both characters are linked by gender, they are divided
by class, and this division is equally central to *Aurora Leigh's* repre-
sentation of disembodiment as a political strategy. As many scholars

have noted, the extremity of Marian's rape and exploitation fore-
ground not the liberation but rather the degradation and the abuse of
the female body, aligning Marian with a Christological narrative of
fleshly suffering.[58] Moreover, this very narrative of redemption, along
with the codes of sexual fallenness and self-effacement that accom-
pany Marian's story, essentially amounts to a negation of Marian's
body, one underscored by her abrupt departure from Aurora, Romney,
and the poem itself in the concluding Book 9.[59] Without disputing
this narrative of abjection, however, I contend that Marian's vanishing
body, the "ghost of Marian," is equally central to *Aurora Leigh's* po-
liticized fantasy of disembodiment (9:389). Marian's alignment with
Christ, and particularly with imagery of Christ's ascension, enables
a symbolic reversal of the exclusionary incarnation associated with
Romney's lingering body politic. In her reading of Marian's exploited
body Joyce Zonana argues that Marian's body teaches Aurora the
grave consequences of dividing flesh and spirit: "For Marian, utter
physical abasement results in spiritual elevation, just as Aurora's spir-
itual elevation, as disembodied muse/artist, requires her descent to
the level of her own blood."[60] While building on Zonana's character-
ization of the complementary relationship between the two women, I
would qualify this oppositional reading of Marian's abstraction and
Aurora's embodiment by underlining Marian's negated form and final
elevation as a central strand of the poem's transfigured poetics. Mar-
ian bears Aurora's desire for an abstracted and transcended body, and,
in so doing, creates a vantage point from which to critique the injus-
tices of Britain's "feudal form(s)."

In its periodic resistance to language, Marian's body challenges the
poem's broadly essentializing somatic networks. In stark contrast to the
work's physicalized language of the body politic, Marian is textually
marked by obliquity, negations, and absences. When we first encounter
Marian we are told that "She was not white nor brown, / But could look
either, like a mist that changed" (3:810–811). Aurora, for all of her po-
et's skill, cannot quite find terms to describe her: her hair is somewhere
"twixt dark and bright, not left you clear / To name the colour" (3:814–
815). In a poem that repeatedly equates poetic genres with the body,
Marian's resistance to Aurora's characterization highlights her disen-
gagement from the epic's formal systems of representation. She eludes
Aurora in Paris, where Aurora catches a fleeting glimpse of Marian as
"a face / And not a fancy, though it vanished so" (6:311–312); on their
first re-encounter Marian "fluttered from me like a cyclamen" (6:445).
Marian resists the powers of Aurora's affirmed poetic language, pow-
ers that elsewhere arouse Lady Waldemar's envy and elicit Romney
Leigh's declarations of love, even as the form of the autobiographical
poem creates a dynamic where Aurora speaks for Marian, narrating her
speech and actions. Much as Aurora learns to throw off the "doublet"

of language, Marian periodically evades it, thereby calling into question the equation of gender, language, and bodies elsewhere in the poem.

In so doing, Marian's disembodiment engages with broader cultural discourses of fallenness. Like the disappearing footsteps of Little Em'ly in Charles Dickens's *David Copperfield* (1850), the language of efface- ment that characterize Marian works to minimize and diminish her shamed body.[61] Yet Marian, unlike Dickens's character, is given a voice in the narrative to represent her own body, and her self-reflexive, de- monstrative characterizations of her physical life suggest a degree of for- mal control over its representation. This self-reflexive distancing is most apparent in Marian's descriptions of motherhood, descriptions that dif- fer from *Aurora Leigh's* opening representations of motherhood in their pointed implications of constructedness. Aurora's mother's physicality is intertwined with her language: Aurora recalls early memories of her mother "kissing full sense into empty words" (1:6). Aurora's formative encounters with language are likewise bound in acts of feminine phys- ical expression that vividly offset the repressed language of her wid- owed father's household, where "we...did not speak too loud" (1:123) and where the absence of maternal physical and linguistic expression is suggested by the "tongue-tied Springs" of Aurora's adolescent home (1:207).

In contrast, Marian's physical duties of motherhood are willed corpo- real performances. "I'm dead, I say..." she insists (6:819),

> I'm nothing more
> But just a mother. Only for the child
> I'm warm, and cold, and hungry, and afraid,
> And smell the flowers a little and see the sun,
> And speak still, and am silent, - just for him!
>
> (6:823–827)

In a passage that echoes Aurora's own anatomization of her narrating body in Book 5, Marian parses out her physical sensations and assigns them an expressive function. Yet where Aurora's body in that passage is united by language and expression—the "articulated" veins of the poet's body naturalized and underwritten by its association with a feminized earth—Marian's is a body integrated by conscious and willed acts of caretaking. Marian's reflexive distance from this maternal function, in other words, highlights mothering as a kind of demonstrative perfor- mance, one Marian assumes while insisting on her own status as a de- tached or disembodied and "dead" figure separate from the naturalized female, expressive body.[62]

Marian's tacitly acknowledged exclusion from this expressive body and its implicit relationship to language give her a vantage from which to survey the twinned relation of speech and the body in other women.

In Book 6, Marian describes Lady Waldemar's treacherous visits to her, and remembers how Lady Waldemar had worked to convince her of her unfitness to be Romney's wife. In this passage, Marian quietly highlights the relation between feminine speech and bodily expression:

> '*Did* she speak,'
> Mused Marian softly, 'or did she only sign?
> Or did she put a word into her face
> And look, and so impress you with the word?
> Or leave it in the folding of her gown,
> Like rosemary smells a movement will shake out
> When no one's conscious?
>
> (6:963–969)

Marian's description of Lady Waldemar questions whether language can be divided from her body. In its muted, sinister impact on the listener, in its act of *impressing* Marian with language, Lady Waldemar's speech is a grotesque revision of Aurora's emphatic poetry of Lockean sensation. Marian's speech implicates the female body and its accoutrements—the folded gown and the rosemary—as an unstable network of signs that highlights language's constructed, gendered relationship to feminine gestures and accessories.

The new life that Marian and Aurora build in Florence represents the establishment of a more democratic household that works in counterpart to the symbolic inequalities of Romney's phalanstery. In the concluding books of the poem, the two women have relocated from a feudalism that is "still the thing" in Britain to a republican Italy imaginatively transformed into a vantage point for the New Jerusalem. Drawing on the Revelations imagery associated with Owenite and other contemporary socialist movements, Romney offers a vision of "bodies" that are "lightened to redemption" (9:940, 941) and from which will emerge a new, more equitable, woman-centered poetics.[63] Central to this millennial scene is the image of the "woman clothed with the sun" from Revelation 12, an image critics have associated with both Aurora and Marian.[64] Building on Romney's vision of lightened bodies, I would extend this imagery to encompass Marian's evocative untouchability and its role in the poem's closing vision of a renewed and reconstructed polity.

From the vantage of the prophet John the woman clothed with the sun appears as a distant vision, a "great wonder in heaven" with "the moon under her feet, and upon her head a crown of twelve stars."[65] Marian's final apotheosis, in stark counterpoint to her earlier abjection, emphasizes this vision of physical distance. Like the woman with the "moon under her feet," Marian stands "As if the floating moonshine interposed / Betwixt her foot and the earth, and raised her up / To float upon it"

(9:189–191). Marian herself underlines this release and detachment from physical form by characterizing herself in the third person, as "this ghost of Marian" (9:389); she further performs her intangibility when Romney tries to embrace her, jumping back "with a staglike majesty / Of soft, serene defiance, - as she knew / He could not touch her" (9:290–292). In escaping the poem's political narrative of intertwined speech and bodies, such images of disembodiment reveal a transformative subtext, a reading of language that is not physically grounded in feminine somatic response. Through the intertwined experiences of Aurora and Marian, Barrett Browning presents a counterpoint of physical instability, negation, and disembodiment, a poetics that transcends the female form.

One final description of Marian, striking for its unusual imagery in the context of Aurora's more tentative characterizations, underscores the poem's investment in disembodiment as a political strategy. Aurora, on her first visit to Marian, observes of Marian's response to Romney's love that "The cataracts of her soul had poured themselves, / And risen self-crowned in rainbow: would she ask / Who crowned her? – it sufficed that she was crowned" (4:184–186). Like the star-crowned woman of Revelations, and like Aurora's birthday scene, Marian's act of self-crowning recalls the uneasy relation between bodies, poetry, and gender. Marian's ascension is the poem's answer to Romney's insistence that the world will "never get a Christ" from a female poet. The "Christ" that *Aurora Leigh* ultimately offers is one that escapes the politicized language of physical form.

Retrieving this subtext of disembodiment, in turn, challenges us to revise our own critical approaches toward a feminist poetics. *Aurora Leigh* presents us with a politics of physicality, as has long been recognized—most recently in Tucker's analysis of the work as a "somatic epic" and a "feminist charter" (378–379). Yet its even bolder feminist contribution lies in its willingness to suspend and question the relation between language, gender, and the body. Barrett Browning's epic both underlines the injustices of the lingering body politic associated with Romney's phalanstery and destabilizes the correlation between poetics and the female form. In so doing, *Aurora Leigh* raises the possibility of a radically politicized disembodiment, a woman-centered poetics that both critiques and transcends the uneasy incarnational imagery of Victorian Britain's changing social body.

Aurora Leigh, then, reworks the emphasis on sensation Barrett Browning had identified in Locke and Condillac and translates those accounts of language into the spiritual language and wordless communion she had longed for in *An Essay on Mind*. A woman-centered poetics of incarnation allows *Aurora Leigh* to acknowledge the role of the sensory body in language, perception, and communication while insisting on the spiritual origins of language and underlining the complex challenges that gendered and marginalized bodies offer to Locke's and Condillac's universal models of human communication. By further incorporating the incarnational tropes of Carlyle and subjecting them to a proto-feminist critique of women's sensibility, Barrett Browning offers a revisionary poetics that allows her politically engaged speaker to take part in debates about the social body, to insist on the spiritual origins of language, and to claim her own body as a vessel that can both facilitate communication and elevate language above the essentializing stereotypes associated with women and sensibility. *Aurora Leigh*'s uncurling of Christ's "leathery tongue" is the full and final realization of the "One tongue" of *An Essay on Mind*, a radicalized language of incarnation that both enables and empowers a women's political poetics.

If Barrett Browning's bodiless poetry responds to the exclusion of women from the First Reform Act, Robert Browning's poetry takes up the study of language in the context of the Second Reform Act of 1867. The years leading up to and following the 1867 Act saw a great outpouring of research on the relationship between language and sociability, ranging from Müller's popular lectures on speech communities to the Philological Society's call for a broad network of volunteers to begin collaborating on the *NED*. Robert Browning's poetry challenges this vision of the sociable, democratic language-community by revealing the authoritarian impulses that lay behind many of these appeals.

Notes

1 See, for example, Kaplan's "Introduction" to Barrett Browning's *Aurora Leigh*, 15–16 and Zonana, "The Embodied Muse," 257–258. Stone gives a thorough account of the poem's reception history and its feminist recovery in "Criticism on *Aurora Leigh*: An Overview." For recent accounts that link *Aurora Leigh* to the Spasmodic poets see Tucker, *Epic*, 339–384. See also the special issue on the Spasmodics edited by LaPorte and Rudy, Blair's *Victorian Poetry and the Culture of the Heart*, and Rudy, *Electric Meters*.
2 Tucker, *Epic*, 378 and 380.
3 Saville, *Victorian Soul-Talk*, 30. See also Barton, *Nineteenth-Century Poetry*, on Barrett Browning's "embodied, avowedly feminine poetic" (11).
4 Stone and Taylor, "Introduction to *Poems* (1856)," lxiv. See also Stone's corrective to critical assumptions about Barrett Browning's conservative stance toward Victorian geology in "Elizabeth Barrett Browning," 339.
5 For a discussion of Barrett Browning's ambivalent stance toward sensibility that predates the recent critical interest in Spasmody see Leighton, *Victorian Women Poets*, 91.
6 Qtd. in Tricia Lootens, *Lost Saints*, 128.
7 For Barrett Browning's Whiggish upbringing see Avery and Stott, *Elizabeth Barrett Browning*, 33–38.
8 For Bro's involvement in the 1832 Reform debates see Avery and Stott, *Elizabeth Barrett Browning*, 34. For the equation of the franchise with masculinity see Clark, "Gender, Class, and the Nation," 230–253.
9 See Vernon, *Politics and the People*, 15, and Hall, "The Rule of Difference," 109–110.

10 See Clark, "Gender, class, and the constitution," 234.
11 For women's involvement in local and parish politics see Heater, *Citizenship in Britain*, 135–136. For the organized women's suffrage movements that began in the 1860s see, for example, Blackburn, *Women's Suffrage*, Rover, *Women's Suffrage and Party Politics*, Smith, *The British Women's Suffrage Campaign*, and Nym Mayhall, *The Militant Suffrage Movement*. For women's suffrage efforts before the 1867 Act see Gleadle, *The Early Feminists*.
12 Heater, *Citizenship in Britain*, 118.
13 "A Thought on Thoughts," vol. 4 of *The Works of Elizabeth Barrett Browning*, edited by Sandra Donaldson, 277. Unless otherwise noted, all citations to Barrett Browning's poetry and prose will be to the *Works* and will be given in parentheses within the text.
14 See, for example, Müller's *Lectures*, 14. Avi Lifschitz analyzes major Enlightenment-era debates about language's relationship to the mind in *Language and Enlightenment*. Hans Aarsleff notes that Locke influenced Horne Tooke, who in turn influenced Victorian thinkers like Mill; see *The Study of Language in England*, 13–72 and also Hair, *Tennyson's Language*, 9–12. For a differently inflected reading of Locke's influence on Barrett Browning that shows how the poet's juvenilia imagines poetry as philosophy's successor and asserts the relationship between politics and aesthetic form see Barton, *Nineteenth-Century Poetry*, 8–15. On Barrett Browning's interest in Locke's ideas of sensation and reflection and the role of the senses in comprehending language see Hair, *Fresh Strange Music*, 26–40. All citations to Locke's *Essay* in this chapter are from Roger Woolhouse's edited edition (New York: Penguin, 2004) and will be given in parentheses within the text.
15 For a comprehensive analysis of Locke's epistemology see Michael Ayers, *Locke: Epistemology and Ontology*.
16 Hair, *Tennyson's Language*, 9. For a book-length study of Locke's theory of language see Ott, *Locke's Philosophy of Language*, esp. 1–33.
17 Barton, *Nineteenth-Century Poetry and Liberal Thought*, 12.
18 Abberley's discussion of "language vitalism" explores the idea of an organic, originary language at length. See *English Fiction and the Evolution of Language*, 6 and 91–127.
19 See Falkenstein, "Étienne Bonnot de Condillac." O'Neal treats the French sensationist movement and Condillac's philosophy at length in *The Authority of Experience*.
20 Carr discusses Condillac's revision of Locke's empiricism in her "Translator's Introduction," xix–xxvii. All references to Condillac will be to Carr's translation and will appear in parentheses within the text.
21 Barrett Browning, "Two Autobiographical Essays by Elizabeth Barrett," 120 and 128.
22 In identifying Barrett Browning's references to Locke I am indebted to Donaldson's editorial notes to the poem in Vol. 4 of the *Works*, 119–131.
23 This emphasis on a silent, ungendered communion of souls is also a persistent theme in Barrett Browning's *Sonnets from the Portuguese* (1850). See, for example, Sonnet XXII: "When our two souls stand up erect and strong, / Face to face, silent, drawing nigh and nigher" (1–2) in the *Sonnets* (28).
24 Dowling, *Language and Decadence*, xiii and 10–15.
25 Herder, *Essay on the Origin of Language*, 95.
26 Chambers, *Vestiges*, 310–311.
27 Whewell, *Indications of the Creator*, 160.
28 Barrett Browning to Mrs. Martin, January 1845, in Kenyon, *The Letters of Elizabeth Barrett Browning*, 1: 238.

29 Barrett Browning, "Thomas Carlyle," in Horne, *A New Spirit of the Age*, 2: 255. Barrett Browning contributed portions of this essay, which include the aforementioned passages; the rest of her contributions are identified in Vol. 8 of Kelley and Hudson, *The Brownings' Correspondence*, 353–359.

30 Ibid., 256.

31 Barrett Browning to Mr. Chorley, 7 January 1845, in Kenyon, *Letters*, 1: 232.

32 For a discussion of this poem's varied generic affiliations see Stone and Taylor's headnote in the *Works*, 1: 4–5.

33 Aarsleff, "Introduction" to *From Locke to Saussure*, 25.

34 See also Marjorie Stone's and Beverly Taylor's gloss to these lines in n.46, p.72.

35 Blair, *Form and Faith*, 153; Rudy, *Electric Meters*, 176–183; LaPorte, *Victorian Poets*, 50. Stone reads Aurora as a sage-figure in *Elizabeth Barrett Browning*, 134–188; Stott explores Aurora's role as a non-conformist sage in Stott and Avery, *Elizabeth Barrett Browning*, 205–209. Lewis approaches Aurora as a "Wisdom" figure in *Elizabeth Barrett Browning's Spiritual Progress*, 171–211, while Dieleman proposes a reading of Aurora as a "poet-preacher" rather than a prophet in *Religious Imaginaries*, 61–99.

36 For Aurora's references to incarnation see Rudy, *Electric Meters*, 170–188 and Davies, "Aurora, The Morning Star," 54–61.

37 See, for example, Kaplan, "Introduction," 11, and Reynolds, "Critical Introduction," to her Ohio University Press edition of *Aurora Leigh*, 16.

38 Kantorowicz, *The King's Two Bodies*, 3–23.

39 Parry locates the emergence of Liberal dominance in British politics in the period of 1846–1866. See *The Rise and Fall of Liberal Government*, 153. Barrett Browning's early poem "Kings" (1831) likewise registers her skepticism toward monarchical power and her equation of political rule with visions of Christ. See "Kings" and also Avery, "Telling it Slant," 407.

40 Poovey, *Making a Social Body*, 7–8. Poovey's earlier formulation of an "uneven development" also informs my reading of embodied language in Victorian political rhetoric. Poovey's concept of "unevenness" in mid-Victorian constructions of gender addresses both the contested and unstable workings of gender ideology and the ways in which this instability allowed for the formation of oppositional stances in the 1850s. See *Uneven Developments*, 1–4. Building on Poovey's term, I would suggest that political notions of the social body and its relation to gender in Victorian Britain were similarly uneven and instable, thus opening the way for *Aurora Leigh's* oppositional critique.

41 Lefort, *Democracy and Political Theory*, 242.

42 Maurice, *The Kingdom of Christ*, 2: 338.

43 Fourier, *The Theory of the Four Movements*, 243.

44 Proudhon, "The Collective Force," 113.

45 Barrett Browning's well-known remarks on contemporary socialism emphasize her distrust of political systems that, in her view, threatened individual autonomy: "I love liberty so intensely that I hate Socialism.... I would rather (for *me*) live under the absolutism of Nicholas of Russia than in a Fourier machine, with my individuality sucked out of me by a social air-pump." See Elizabeth Barrett Browning to Miss Mitford, 15 June 1850, in Kelley and Hudson, *The Brownings' Correspondence*, 16: 138. Barrett Browning's distrust of Christian Socialism on the one hand and Fourierism on the other hand is based in part on her belief that both approaches were overly abstract: "What is [Christian Socialism], after all, but an out-of-door extension of the monastic system? The religious principle, more or less apprehended, may

bind men together so, absorbing their individualities, and presenting an aim *beyond the world;* but upon merely human and earthly principles no such system can stand...." Of Fourierism she wrote that "If Fourierism could be realised...out of a dream, the destinies of our race would shrivel...I do not believe in purification without suffering, in progress without struggle, in virtue without temptation..." See Elizabeth Barrett Browning to Isa Blagden, 1850, in Kelley and Hudson, *The Brownings' Correspondence,* 16: 228.

46 See Chapman, "Poetry, Network, Nation," 275–285 and Saville, *Victorian Soul-Talk,* 29–82.

47 For more on Barrett Browning's response to Napoleon III see Woodworth, "Elizabeth Barrett Browning, Coventry Patmore, and Alfred Tennyson," 543–560.

48 On these associations with purple in Victorian color theory see, for example, George Field's 1835 work *Chromatography,* 132–138. Linda Shires discusses the influence of this work on nineteenth-century painting in "On Color Theory, 1835: George Field's Chromatography."

49 For a more extensive discussion of the influence of *Corinne* on *Aurora Leigh* see Moers, *Literary Women,* 179–183; Peel and Sweet, "*Corinne* and the Woman as Poet in England," 204–220; Lewis, *Germaine de Staël, George Sand, and the Victorian Woman Artist,* 107–116.

50 Elizabeth Barrett Browning to the Emperor Napoleon, April 1857, in Kenyon, *Letters,* 2: 262.

51 Carlyle, *On Heroes, Hero-Worship, and the Heroic in History,* 77 and 82. For more on the influence of Carlyle's *On Heroes* on *Aurora Leigh* see Woodworth, "Elizabeth Barrett Browning," 543–560 and also Taylor, "Carlyle, Elizabeth Barrett Browning, and the Hero as Victorian Poet," 235–246.

52 See Kaplan's "Introduction" for an account of how *Aurora Leigh's* language, repressed by patriarchy, "re-enters discourse with a shattering revolutionary force" (11). See also Kaplan's account of *Aurora Leigh's* intertextual relationship to works by William Wordsworth, John Milton, Madame de Staël, Charles Kingsley, and others, 15–36. Reynolds's "Critical Introduction" analyzes the poem's intricate, shifting narrative construction and its strategies of "diffusion and fragmentation" that upend the "'liberal humanist' context within which Barrett Browning wrote" (12). Stone discusses Barrett Browning's strategies of gender and genre inversion in "Genre Subversion and Gender Inversion," 101–127. See also Stone's analysis of the work's woman-centered deployment of metalepsis, allusiveness, and narrative irony in *Elizabeth Barrett Browning,* 153–188.

53 One prominent example of corporeal imagery in the poem, the wedding scene and the entry of the poor of St. Giles, has often been noted (4: 538–595). For a reading of the poem that emphasizes Aurora's class prejudices see Kaplan's "Introduction," 11–12 and 31–33. Brent Shannon analyzes Barrett Browning's depictions of the poor as a "sick and sickening mass" in the context of the social body rhetoric used by middle-class reformers in "A Finished Generation, Dead of Plague," (42). For a reading that underlines Aurora's fascinated disgust with the poor as one stage in her artistic development, a stage later subject to self-critique and irony, see Stone, *Elizabeth Barrett Browning,* 162–171. See also Reynolds's analysis of the poem's narrative structure that presents events that are always subject to revision in her "Critical Introduction," 28–54, and Stott's discussion of the scene's alertness to processes of dehumanization in Avery and Stott, *Elizabeth Barrett Browning,* 188–197. I would add to these that the overdetermined, claustrophobic representation of the social body in this scene is significant for its location in the church or the *corpus mysticum* of Kantorowicz's

account: it returns to the site of the social body's conceptual beginnings while also representing the poor as noxious invaders.

54 Barrett Browning's emphasis on embodied poetics in *Aurora Leigh* antici-
pates the analysis of women's writing and the body in work by Luce Irigaray,
Chantal Chawaf, Hélène Cixous, and others. See Irigaray, "Ce sexe qui n'en
est pas un" [The sex which is not one], 99–106, Chawaf, "La chair lin-
guistique" [Linguistic flesh], 177–178, and Cixous, "Le rire de la méduse"
[The Laugh of the Medusa], 245–264, all in *New French Feminisms: An
Anthology*, ed. Elaine Marks and Isabelle de Courtivron.

55 "Articulated," in the *Oxford English Dictionary*, 1st ed.

56 Barrett Browning's working notes for *Aurora Leigh* stress this poetic move-
ment from abstract and ideal to the external and practical: "the practical &
real...is but the external evolution of the ideal & spiritual—that...is *from
inner to outer*." Qtd. in Reynolds, "Editorial Introduction," 85.

57 In 1845 Barrett Browning wrote of the Elizabethan era, "where were the
poetesses? The divine breath which seemed to come & go...why did it never
pass, <even in the lyrical form> over the lips of a woman?" See Elizabeth
Barrett Browning to Henry Fothergill Chorley, 7 January 1845, in Kelley
and Hudson, *The Brownings' Correspondence*, 10: 14.

58 See, for example, Armstrong, *Victorian Poetry*, 360.

59 For a discussion of the figure of the fallen woman in Victorian society see
Anderson, *Tainted Souls*, 167–197. See also Leighton's "Because men made
the laws," 109–127.

60 Zonana, "The Embodied Muse," 257–258.

61 See Michie, *The Flesh Made Word*.

62 For an alternate reading of this passage see Faulk, "Destructive Maternity,"
45. Faulk reads Marian's speech as emblematic of the poem's equation of
motherhood and death. I would add, however, that Marian's detachment
works in deliberate counterpoint to Romney's notion of an embodied fem-
inine sensibility. For more on motherhood in *Aurora Leigh* see also Ficke,
"Crafting Social Criticism," 249–267.

63 Barbara Taylor and Marjorie Stone both note the centrality of Revelations
to socialist rhetoric. See Taylor, *Eve and the New Jerusalem*, 157–161 and
Stone, *Elizabeth Barrett Browning*, 181–182.

64 See Stone, *Elizabeth Barrett Browning*, 181–184 and Carpenter, "The Trouble
with Romola," 116.

65 Revelation, 12: 1.

2 "And talks to his own self, howe'er he please"

Robert Browning's Antisocial Speech and Mid-Victorian Reform

To a reader of Barrett Browning's emphatic, socially engaged poetry, Browning's work might look like its antithesis. His catalogue of wicked or morally compromised characters famously led Walter Bagehot to classify Browning as a "grotesque" writer, a peddler of "insane taste" whose poetry led readers to "gloat on carnage, to love blood...with a deep eager love."[1] Such an excessive, bloodthirsty aesthetic is at odds with Barrett Browning's appeal to a communal social body in *Aurora Leigh*. Furthermore, as one of his more recent critics has noticed, Browning "explodes aesthetic and philosophical assumptions about reciprocity and collective harmony."[2] Browning's address to his "British Public, ye who like me not," in *The Ring and the Book* (1868–1869) is an open admission of this antagonistic poetics, a poetics less focused than Barrett Browning's on viscerally engaging readers through formal appeals.[3] Browning himself was skeptical of the poet's ability to shape readers' political perceptions. Writing in 1853 to his longtime friend and collaborator, the French literary critic Joseph Milsand, Browning contrasts the respective degrees of influence among French and English poets:

> In your letter you bid me tell you something about the way of life of our literary men—we have none in your sense of the word. Ours are not your ways: it is the worse for us in many respects.... The whole life is led differently,—you all tend to influence politically, I think—with us, it would be absurd for the man who writes articles in the "Times" which are condensed into telegraphic messages from Kingdom to Kingdom, to try & obtain, on the strength of them, the secretaryship to the poorest embassy there. So a man learns his decreed place and curbs his desires accordingly—if he does not, nobody sympathises with him. So with us, those who are without a real vocation for literature as its own reward, keep very clear of it—the others take their love & labour into the quietest corner and live there as they like—and when people live so,—that is, not as others like & prescribe,—they generally lead praiseworthy lives.[4]

Browning describes the poet's political position as isolated and marginalized. While the French authors, in his estimation, "influence politically," authors across the Channel make their interventions from the sidelines. Browning's own dramatic monologues make good on his critique, as his frequently solitary and misunderstood speakers issue their most incisive criticisms of their society from isolated positions.

For their part, critics of Browning's dramatic monologues have read his political sympathies against this isolation, showing how the genre actually critiques the solipsism in which it trades. Tucker, for example, claims that "Each of Browning's speakers...utters a monomaniacal manifesto" that reveals the limitations of subjectivity and invokes "the counter-authority of communal norms" as a challenge to Mill's celebration of the inwardly directed lyric mode.[5] Armstrong likewise shows how Robert Browning's dramatic monologues reject Mill's understanding of poetry as a kind of "solipsist soliloquy," an argument taken up more recently by Saville in her work on Victorian soul-poetics.[6] Post-structuralist readings of *The Ring and the Book* have also emphasized how the poem challenges appeals to a single truth or authority, presenting "truth and language as interdependent, as conceptual themes interwoven through a dialectical process."[7] In all of these accounts, to read the dramatic monologue politically is to show how the dramatic monologue exposes and critiques the solipsism that it displays. Extending these claims, we might understand Browning's poetic excesses, his frequently jagged prosody, his thumping rhythms, and his startling diction, as something to be transcended. If we look through the formal difficulties and the isolation of the speakers, we recover a more benign democratic impulse.

Yet what if we were to take Browning at his word and read his poetry not as an exposure of solipsism and linguistic privacy, but as a paradoxical reinforcement of the barriers around the speaking self? What if we read his dramatic monologues not as works that expose their speakers' roles in invoking the *demos* but rather as acts of resistance toward that very prospect of harmony? Such an approach would necessarily beg the question of what such a poetics would be resisting, and in this chapter, I argue that the antisocial language of *The Ring and the Book* exposes the emergent Victorian political community as a social fiction, one then taking shape in the rise of the Liberal Party to power in 1859 and in the passage of the 1867 Reform Act.[8] Such an appeal to a mass consensus, Browning's poetry suggests, would be a dangerous fiction, perpetuating myths of communality belied by the ongoing exclusion of millions of colonial subjects, women, and working-class Britons from the electorate.[9]

For Browning, this illusion of harmony was a linguistic as well as a political issue, for the passage of the 1867 Act coincided with both popular and scholarly interest in language's relationship to national belonging. Looking back to Locke's characterization of language as a tool of "fellowship" for "sociable creature(s)," prominent philologists such as Müller emphasized the role of the community in shaping word forms, dialects, language-origins, and human-animal communication.[10] This interest in sociability would culminate in the massive collective project of the *NED,* with its worldwide network of volunteers who researched the English language. As many Victorian philologists themselves recognized, the concept of a shared language was central to the formation of political boundaries. "Nations and languages against dynasties and treatises," announced Müller in 1861, "this is what has remodelled, and will remodel still more, the map of Europe."[11]

In *The Ring and the Book,* Browning fuses this research with a cast of quarreling characters and a repeated motif of circular images—rings and coiled snakes—both to challenge consensus and to underline the latent authoritarianism and injustice that these language debates overlooked. Browning's resistance to the notion of a communal lexicon exposes these expressions of national harmony as fictions that continued to perpetuate injustice, calling attention to the despotisms inherent in the growth of imperial power and the ongoing influence of the aristocratic elite. Through sound patterns, circular imagery, and the juxtaposition of warring testimonies in *The Ring and the Book,* Browning dramatizes not communication but miscommunication, not sociability but isolation, in order to challenge the democratic pretenses of mid-Victorian philology.

Sociability and Mid-Victorian Philology

Browning's reading and social contacts frequently exposed him to current debates in the science of language. During his residence in Florence and afterward, he was an avid reader of the *Athenaeum,* which regularly reported on philology and lexicography; Hair has also demonstrated that Browning was deeply influenced both by Locke and by Johnson's *Dictionary.*[12] During his residence in London following Barrett Browning's death he had social engagements with *NED* co-founder Richard Chenevix Trench and, later in life, a tense friendship with Frederick J. Furnivall, the co-founder and second editor of the dictionary and the enthusiastic, if outspoken, champion of Browning's work through the London Browning Society.[13]

The founding of the Philological Society of London in 1842, the Society's widespread solicitation of volunteer readers in 1857, and its call for the *NED* in 1859 created widespread enthusiasm for etymology, and the creators of the *NED* regularly contrasted their own volunteer method with the seeming authoritarianism of the language academies in Italy and France. In *On Some Deficiencies in Our English Dictionaries* (1857), Trench insists that the gatherer of words is a historian and not a critic: "There is a constant confusion here in men's minds. They conceive of a Dictionary as though it had this function, to be a standard of the language; and the pretensions to be this which the French Dictionary of the Academy sets up, may have helped on this confusion. It is nothing of the kind."[14] Such stylistic policing could only be the work of "one self-made dictator, or forty."[15] Against this lexicographical dictatorship Trench upholds the people at large as the authorized compilers and recognized authorities on their national tongue. As he proudly declares, the dictionary project was to be a *"Lexicon totius Anglicitatis,"* a dictionary of all English that would marshal all words, both common and obsolete, into an authoritative national standard.[16] In his *Proposal for the Publication of a New English Dictionary* (1859), Trench urges all "Englishmen" to "come forward and write their own Dictionary for themselves" in a populist mode of collaboration.[17] Such democratic appeals to a mass readership helped secure philology's relationship to a nation-state circumscribed by its shared linguistic history.

Trench's sentiments reflect a broader history of connecting language to the democratic tribunal. Mid-century Victorian philologists found a basis for the relationship between language and sociability in the work of their Enlightenment predecessors. As we saw in Chapter 1, Locke's "Of Words" continued to be a foundational influence on nineteenth-century research into language: Müller, to take just one example, borrowed heavily from Locke in his popular lectures.[18] This emphasis on language's rootedness in the sociable community is also prevalent in the language-philosophy of the theologian and Dissenting clergyman Joseph Priestley, whose *Lectures on the Theory of Language and Universal Grammar* (1762) Browning owned.[19] Priestley's *Lectures* open, like Locke's "Of Words," with appeal to language's communal powers. Both spoken and written language are art forms "of unspeakable importance to mankind; as beings who, from the commencement to the close of this mortal life, can hardly subsist but as members of some particular community, and are, moreover, capable of the most extensive social connexions."[20] Unlike Locke, however, Priestley takes the relationship between language and sociability a step further by equating verbal complexity with a greater number of social contacts. This logic holds true for the animal kingdom as well as for human communities, who differ from animals only in their ability to modulate their voices in processes of articulation (127):

> The kind Author of nature hath given to every animal that is capable of any kind of society, a power of communicating his sensations and apprehensions, at least, to every other animal he is connected with: and this power is more or less extensive in proportion as the animal is fitted for a more perfect or imperfect state of society. An animal that hath little connection with, or dependence upon any others, either of his own or a different species, as he hath little to communicate, hath a power of communication proportionally small: but

> when the connexions of any animal are more numerous, and the dispositions and actions of others are of more consequence to him, it is requisite that, for his own advantage, he be furnished with a greater power of affecting them, by communicating his own ideas, apprehensions, and inclinations to them.
>
> (126)

Priestley links the number and quality of one's ideas to the complexity of one's social relations. Unlike Locke's autonomous, sensing individual who inwardly develops his thoughts and seeks to present them to others, Priestley's isolated animal has "little to communicate." Any individual's ability to speak or communicate is entirely bound up with his social existence (191–192). What holds true for the individual's language in Priestley also holds true for the greater political community to which he belongs. Like isolated individuals, isolated political communities are less likely to have innovative or changing forms of language, as exchange and traffic with other communities enlarges a society's stock of words.

Public announcements about the *NED* promoted the Eurocentric vision of linguistic abundance found in Priestley and, in turn, fed into the idea that so-called primitive languages were simpler and less complex than those of Western European societies. For example, Trench uses the suggestive image of Herodutus's Persian army conquering an island in order to explain the volunteer method. As he explains, Herodutus's Persian army had linked hands and moved slowly across their conquered territory in order to sniff out any remaining, hidden inhabitants. This martial strategy would also serve volunteer readers well as they took up arms for the dictionary: "this drawing as with a sweep-net over the whole surface of English literature, is that which we would fain see...being sure that it is only by such combined action, by such a joining of hand in hand...that we can hope the innumerable words which have escaped us hitherto will ever be brought within our net."[21] By converting volunteer readers to army members and likening their toil to that of the Persian Empire's territorial expansion, Trench weds the collaborative enterprise of the *Dictionary* with the aggressively imperial consolidation of the English tongue.[22] All the while, he appeals to a sense of shared fellowship and communal investment in the language.

There is, in Browning's correspondence, a tinge of patrician disdain for a democratic philology. In a letter to Isa Blagden about a volunteer reader who had contacted him seeking advice about some of the words in *The Ring and the Book*, Browning censures the reader's apparent unfamiliarity with standard literary works that contained the same vocabulary: "The archaic words being common in Shakspeare & Milton and the Bible...Now, what do you possibly imagine can exceed the conceit of a person who, with such an ignorance of the language, takes on herself to contribute to an ultimate and extraordinary Dictionary meant to supply the defects of its predecessors?"[23] His own syntax and vocabulary would resist the Philological Society's efforts to collate a national lexicon. As James A.H. Murray writes, Browning's unorthodox use of vocabulary posed endless challenges to the project: "Browning constantly used words without regard to their proper meaning. He has added greatly to the difficulties of the Dictionary."[24]

Browning's dramatic monologue "Respectability," from *Men and Women* (1855), enacts an opposition between isolated speakers and regulatory linguistic institutions. In this brief poem, a couple takes a romantic stroll through the streets of nighttime Paris and find themselves, at the end of the poem, standing before the formidable edifice of the Institut de France and its famed Academy.[25] The poem questions the value of sociability for political critique and exposes the stultifying effects of institutions that regulate language. In the third and final stanza, the two stop short before the Academy:

> I know! the world proscribes not love;
>   Allows my finger to caress
>   Your lips' contour and downiness,
> Provided it supply a glove.
> The world's good word!—the Institute!
>   Guizot receives Montalembert!
>   Eh? Down the court three lampions flare:
> Put forward your best foot!
>
> (17–24)

The speaker rejects the social world as a place of masquerade that truncates the sensory enjoyment and intimate privacy of the lover's caress and barricades the way to the woman's lips. Instead, the "world's good word!" interferes with its social regulations. Browning's juxtaposition of this "good word!" with the image of the woman's lips implies that these regulations will silence whatever verbal or nonverbal sentiments those lips would have expressed. The vague world of social respectability— up to now characterized in general terms like "men" and "women," and mostly defined by what it is not—takes on a sharp and palpable form in specific places and names: the Institut; the French statesman François Pierre Guillaume Guizot; and his one-time political opponent Charles Forbes René de Montalembert, whom Guizot publicly welcomed into the *Académie Française* in a ceremony that Browning attended in 1852.[26] The sight of the Academy abruptly truncates the sensory stroll and conjures up names associated with partisan squabbling. Much as Guizot receives his old political opponent Montalembert, so too do the lovers go forth and accept their old enemy, social convention, under the bright, flaring lamps of the Academy. Browning's disdain for the French

Academy in this poem reflects his broader distrust of such regulatory institutions, and of their role in perpetuate existing social hierarchies.

Browning's poetry resists this appeal to the language-community, turning instead to Chambers's *Vestiges*, a work associated with liberal reform.[27] In *Vestiges,* Chambers draws on ethnographical studies to explore the politically dissident potential of the isolated or provincial language-community, showing how a community's distance from metropolitan centers could give rise to new forms of language.[28] Chambers borrows heavily from the missionary Robert Moffat's account of the language of South African villagers, who, in contrast to the people who live in towns, live far from the social centers that help to regulate language through "festivals and ceremonies...songs...and constant intercourse."[29] Quoting from Moffat, Chambers goes on to compare these villagers to the unsupervised children of Manchester laborers:

> 'On such occasions [of distant travel], fathers and mothers, and all who can bear a burden, often set out for weeks at a time, and leave their children to the care of two or three infirm old people. The infant progeny, some of whom are beginning to lisp, while others can just master a whole sentence, and those still farther advanced, romping and playing together, the children of nature, through the live-long day, *become habituated to a language of their own.* The more voluble condescend to the less precocious, and thus, from this infant Babel, proceeds a dialect composed of a host of mongrel words and phrases, joined together without rule, and *in the course of a generation the entire character of the language is changed.*' I have been told, that in like manner the children of the Manchester factory workers, left for a great part of the day, in large assemblages, under the care of perhaps a single elderly person, and spending the time in amusements, are found to make a great deal of new language.[30]

In stark contrast to Priestley's representations of isolated communities as less complex, Chambers brings South African villagers' children together with the children of Manchester laborers in order to show how such language communities become the creative centers of new coinages. If Trench idealizes the democratic tribunal as a model for both language and political life, Chambers offers the relatively isolated social community as a viable source of new coinages and expressions.

"Caliban upon Setebos" (1864) dramatizes Chambers's remarks on the creative potential of isolated speech in its depiction of the half-human, half-animal creature of Shakespeare's *Tempest,* who snatches a few solitary moments in the middle of a hot day to sprawl out in his island cave and speak his mind aloud.[31] The poem's treatment of language is at one with its political message. As Armstrong has shown, "Caliban" challenges contemporary anthropological and philological hierarchies between primitive and civilized language as articulated by Romantics like Herder: "Partly a visceral imagining of a fantasy of 'primitive' consciousness, partly a rigorous unwinding of the contradictions of Victorian theories of race and language, 'Caliban' is a test case for the argument that the slave is incapable of reason and therefore without entitlement to recognition as a fully human being."[32] "Caliban" appeared shortly before Parliament began debating the 1867 Act, during which public discussion of domestic reform mingled with public alarm at the Morant Bay Rebellion, the Sepoy Rebellion, and at the Fenian uprisings in England and Ireland.[33]

Building on Armstrong's reading, I'd like to turn briefly to the poem's opening lines to show how Browning rejects the mid-century vogue for language and sociability, using antisocial speech to magnify the exclusions and marginalization of political subjects in the context of mid-century reform. In these initial lines, Browning refutes the widespread philological claim that isolation is a barrier to verbal complexity. Much as the children of Manchester laborers glean expressive power from their isolated locations in Chambers's account, Caliban gains expressive power in his temporary distance from the regulatory discourse of Prospero and Miranda. The poem takes place in a kind of double exile: the initial political usurpation that drove Prospero and Miranda away before the events of *The Tempest,* and the second, self-imposed exile of their servant Caliban in his island cave and at a distance from his sleeping captors. Caliban relishes his solitude:

[Will sprawl, now that the heat of day is best,
Flat on his belly in the pit's much mire,
With elbows wide, fists clenched to prop his chin.
And, while he kicks both feet in the cool slush,
And feels about his spine small eft-things course,
Run in and out each arm, and make him laugh:
And while above his head a pompion-plant,
Coating the cave-top as a brow its eye,
Creeps down to touch and tickle hair and beard,
And now a flower drops with a bee inside,
And now a fruit to snap at, catch and crunch,—
He looks out o'er yon sea which sunbeams cross
And recross till they weave a spider-web
(Meshes of fire, some great fish breaks at times)
And talks to his own self, howe'er he please,
Touching that other, whom his dam called God.

(1–16)

Browning's poetic form, sound patterns, and imagery all work to emphasize linguistic privacy through a series of figurative casings and wrappings. The poem's form, the dramatic monologue, is here wrapped inside of its distant precursor text, *The Tempest*; proceeding inward, we find that the typically first-person point-of-view is encased in a third-person perspective and that some of Caliban's lines are enfolded in square brackets, typographically sheltered one more remove from the auditor.

The natural world further underscores this sense of seclusion. The "pompion-plant, / Coating the cave-top" provides additional protection; the dropping flower encases and shelters the bee, the fruit bears, deep in its flesh, its potent and invisible seeds. Hard consonants, woven throughout these lines, mimic the "spider-web" of sunbeams Caliban glimpses in the distance and further suggest shelter and protection. He begins with a terminal c-sound in line five ("course"), crosses to an initial position in lines eight and nine ("Coating the cave-top," "Creeps"), returns to terminal c-sounds that parallel those of line eight ("catch and crunch"), and at last doubles back to the initial position in lines eighteen and twenty-one ("Could," "in confidence"). Like the sunbeams that "cross / And recross" over the water, Caliban's patterned c-sounds create a consonantal web around his words. The "small eft-things" that dart "in and out" each arm extend this weaving motion laterally, while the patterns of fauna, the pompion-plant, the flower, and lastly the "blossom" of his tongue, extend the pattern vertically. This web of isolation, *contra* Priestley, gives rise to Caliban's linguistic dexterity and freedom, including his bursting chain of fricatives ("feel," "flower," "fruit," "fire"), and his determination to relish his own isolation and verbal freedom ("And talks to his own self, howe'er he please"). In this dramatic monologue is not the developed, sociable community that fosters linguistic complexity but rather the isolated individual who articulates a series of complicated ideas about language, nature, the structures of power, and the assumptions of revealed religion.

Browning's departure from models of language and sociability in "Caliban upon Setebos" takes aim at a flattening tendency in Victorian philology, a tendency to overlook marginalized or dissident voices in the collective quest for a *lexicon totius Anglicitatis*. His work reveals how the emphasis on the development of the language-community that would culminate in the massive project of the great English lexicon too-readily bypasses or downplays the racial, ethnic, and social stratification that underlies mid-century philology. In Browning's hands the dramatic monologue shows how solitude, not communality, frees the speaker to issue his challenge to the social order. In *The Ring and the Book*, Browning further develops this poetics of isolation through a strategic reinterpretation of Locke's remarks on language and fellowship, showing how contemporary appeals to a national language-community overlook the injustices and exclusions of the reformed state.

These "filthy rags of speech": *The Ring and the Book*

The Ring and the Book showcases its antisocial poetics by depicting multiple speakers providing competing narratives of their experiences. A collection of dramatic monologues elevated, by length and scope, to epic status, *The Ring and the Book* refuses to present the liberal social body as a harmonious whole, rejecting communality by rejecting the very premise of the genre that Tucker describes as one of *"Consensus"* in *Epic: Britain's Heroic* Muse.[34] The epic, Tucker writes, tells "a sponsoring culture its own story, from a vantage whose privilege transpires through the successful articulation of a collective identity that links origins to destinies."[35] But Browning uses the epic genre instead to refuse the notion of a shared collective identity. Each book features a speaker connected to the 1698 triple murder case in which the grasping nobleman Count Guido Franceschini was accused of hiring a gang of men to attack his seventeen-year-old, pregnant wife Pompilia and her parents after Pompilia fled his abuse in the company of Giuseppe Caponsacchi, a disguised priest and her alleged lover. Based on the "Old Yellow Book," a source text Browning discovered by chance at a Florentine bookstall in 1860, *The Ring and the Book* turns this collection of legal documents and letters into a lively cross-section of different socio-linguistic registers in Rome, from the prattle of local gossips, the jargon of the counsel, and the verdict of Pope Innocent XII on to the conflicting testimonies of Guido, Caponsacchi, and Pompilia, who survives her wounds just long enough to tell her side of the story.

Despite its historical subject matter, *The Ring and the Book* demonstrates a number of recognizably Victorian concerns. Susan Brown writes that Pompilia's character and testimony incorporate debates about the Woman Question and about notions of sexual fallenness, while Tucker notes how the poem displays Browning's "constitutionally liberal suspicion of ordained power."[36] As *The Dublin Review* remarked in its 1869 review of the poem, Browning's tendency to portray priests as villainous characters perpetuates harmful, "fantastic," and anti-Catholic sentiments that, in turn, reveal contemporary English prejudices toward Ireland.[37]

Browning's stylistic excesses are also on full display in *The Ring and the Book*. Contemporary reviewers were quick to note the poem's wide-ranging linguistic experiments. An 1868 *Spectator* review of the work observed that the poem displayed a "close proximity of crabbed English," as well as "grammar so condensed as to be either grating or excessively obscure...very frequently his narrative...is couched in almost carefully eccentric English,—singular nouns with no article...plural adjectives accumulated on one substantive...new-coined combinations of nouns like 'ring-thing'" and "oddly interpolated ejaculations."[38] Another reviewer for the *Saturday Review* took issue with the wide dispersion of similes across the poem: "in the second part, to find Mr. Browning saying, 'Where was I with that angler simile?' in reference to a simile that had been well finished three pages before, is a little annoying."[39]

Not only does *The Ring and the Book* seem to revel in its own verbal dexterity, but it also showcases how language is embedded in the daily lives, prejudices, and perceptions of its broad social panorama of speakers. As Browning's narrator puts it, playfully, in the concluding lines, the central lesson of the poem is that "our human speech is naught, / Our human testimony false, our fame / And human estimation words and wind" (12:835–840). Yet *The Ring and the Book* is also more than a meditation on the relativism of truth or the instability of language. Browning staunchly refuses the appeal to a linguistic democracy, showing again and again how such appeals to language underwrite a false and impossible fiction of social harmony, and magnifying the conflicts, injustices, and lingering aristocratic influences that continue to shape the Victorian political community.

In order to do so, Browning re-interprets Locke's model of language as a tool of fellowship, suggesting instead that language is a tool of dissonance and estrangement. In "Of Words," Locke explains that the individual speaker uses words for ideas that he understands to exist in his own mind and, as a result, has no empirical verification that his chosen word will have the exact same meaning to others. For example, Locke explains that the word "gold" may prompt some speakers to think of a peacock's tail, others of a heavy, fusible substance, and so on. The same word can only ever be used to describe one's own idea of a thing, and all speakers, by necessity, must "suppose" their words to be signs of ideas for other speakers as well: "the knowing and the ignorant, the learned and the unlearned, use the words they speak (with any meaning) all alike. They, *in every man's mouth*, stand for the ideas he has, and which he would express by them" (364). He goes on to give examples of the various details that different speakers may come to associate with the word:

A child having taken notice of nothing in the metal he hears called gold, but the bright shining yellow colour, he applies the word gold only to his own idea of that colour, and nothing else; and therefore calls the same colour in a peacock's tail gold. Another that hath better observed, adds to shining yellow great weight: and then the sound gold, when he uses it, stands for a complex idea of a shining yellow and a very weighty substance. Another adds to those qualities fusibility: and then the word gold signifies to him a body, bright, yellow, fusible, and very heavy. Another adds malleability. Each of these uses equally the word gold, when they have occasion to express the idea which they have applied it to: but it is evident that each can apply it only to his own idea; nor can he make it stand as a sign of such a complex idea as he has not.

(364–365)

Language users enter into a kind of social contract, in that they imagine their own language to call forth similar ideas in the minds of others as well. In so doing, speakers take part in a shared fantasy of communication that temporarily suspends each speaker's own awareness that he alone can know the meaning of his own words. The groundwork of Locke's model of language and sociability is built on an intense linguistic privacy, an unbridgeable separation of individual minds. However, this isolation between speakers also gives rise to linguistic diversity and creativity, because the more different experiences speakers bring to the idea, the greater number of associations they have with the word "gold." Unlike Priestley's and Trench's sociable communities, Locke's isolated individuals paradoxically create different kinds of meanings and associations when they strive, but fail, to communicate. At the same time, Locke's emphasis on the language community is at one with his insistence that the creative language of the individual cannot be manipulated or dominated by political forces, as in his observation that even Augustus himself could not "arbitrarily appoint" any word's meaning "in the mouths and common language of his subjects" (366). The individual's liberty arises, in other words, from his singular ability to use words to stand for the ideas that he wishes them to stand for.

Browning incorporates these statements into the poem through the central framing trope of the ring. In Book 1, he explains how the craftsmen mix gold with alloy in order to shape the object:

> That trick is, the artificer melts up wax
> With honey, so to speak; he mingles gold
> With gold's alloy, and, duly tempering both,
> Effects a manageable mass, then works:
> But his work ended, once the thing a ring,
> Oh, there's repristination! Just a spirt
> O' the proper fiery acid o'er its face,
> And forth the alloy unfastened flies in fume;
> While, self-sufficient now, the shape remains,
> The rondure brave, the lilied loveliness,
> Gold as it was, is, shall be evermore:
> Prime nature with an added artistry—
> No carat lost, and you have gained a ring.
>
> What of it? 'T is a figure, a symbol, say;
> A thing's sign: now for the thing signified.

$$(18-32)$$

This passage has attracted much critical commentary, and scholars have persuasively shown how the ring reflects Browning's creative process.[40] However, these analyses miss Browning's striking reinvention of Locke's gold example as a poetic metaphor. In this passage, the elaborate process of ring-making approximates the equally complicated process of creating shared meaning out of language. Locke's imagined speaker is like the ring-maker fusing language with substance and presenting it to others, who take part in the shared fantasy of the word's meaning, much as here those who see the finished ring understand it as "Gold...evermore" and not as a substance filled with alloy. Strategically placed antitheses—wax and honey, gold and gold's alloy—oppose each other across enjambed lines and mimic the variety of meanings in Locke's account. The ring itself blends nature and artistry, reconciling these different meanings just as the word "gold" itself embodies different meanings. The signifier that is presented is not the original substance; all language is trickery and "device" (9), but trickery that results in a shared fantasy of meaning and understanding. This is not only evidence of language's difficulties: it is also evidence of the origins of the individual speaker's freedom to create meaning, to make the "thing signified" that liberates speech from arbitrary political and social imperatives.

This collation of competing, dissonant voices undermines Priestley's and Trench's vision of sociable language communities. Instead, the poet tells us, the Old Yellow Book reveals a group of characters wracked by endless legal disagreements:

> Thus wrangled, brangled, jangled they a month,
> —Only on paper, pleadings all in print,
> Nor ever was, except i' the brains of men,
> More noise by word of mouth than you hear now—
> Till the court cut all short with "Judged, your cause.
> Receive our sentence! Praise God!"
>
> (1:241–246)

A string of double-rhymed verbs in the first line stress the chaos and repetition of these disagreements as they carry on through the different mediums of print and casual gossip or "noise by word of mouth." There is no natural end to such discussions, the speaker suggests. In this case, they conclude only arbitrarily, in the internally rhymed moment when "the court cut all short." Abruptly, the court invokes legal and religious authority in order to put an end to the debate: "Judged, your cause. / Receive our sentence! Praise God!"

The poem's reflexive discussion of its source text also emphasizes competing and dissonant accounts of language through its description of both written and oral sources. Browning's speaker describes how the Old Yellow Book blends learned, literary language with the vernacular:

> Word for word,
> So ran the title-page: murder, or else
> Legitimate punishment of the other crime,

Accounted murder by mistake,—just that
And no more, in a Latin cramp enough
When the law had her eloquence to launch,
But interfilleted with Italian streaks
When testimony stooped to mother-tongue,—
That, was this old square yellow book about.

(1:132–140)

Through this antithesis between launching and stooping, between the Latin and the Italian vernacular, Browning emphasizes two poles of tension that set up the verbal range of the Old Yellow Book. In this, he channels one of the accounts of language and political history popularized by Müller's *Lectures* and quoted in the Introduction to this book. Once the church and state had consolidated their power, language hardened into an elite literary form that could only be destroyed, Müller asserted, through periodic social upheavals, in which "the popular, or, as they are called, the vulgar dialects, which had formed a sort of undercurrent, rise beneath the crystal surface of the literary language, and sweep away, like the waters in spring, the cumbrous formation of a bygone age."[41] However, while Müller describes this antithesis between vernaculars and elite languages as a stage in a complete revolutionary process, where the former overthrows the latter, Browning's Old Yellow Book preserves these two forms in a dynamic, never-ending process of collision, stressing dissent and disagreement in this unlikely community of speakers and capturing it through the structure of his own written language.

If language acts as a barrier between minds that paradoxically opens up new avenues of verbal creativity, it also raises misunderstandings that have life-or-death consequences, as the speaker of "Tertium Quid" explains in his account of the deal struck between Guido and the Comparinis. His lines initiate a lengthy comparison of language to a marketplace commodity and emphasize the wide gulf that lies between thought and speech:

There was a bargain mentally proposed
On each side, straight and plain and fair enough;
Mind knew its own mind: but when mind must speak,
The bargain have expression in plain terms,
There came the blunder incident to words,
And in the clumsy process, fair turned foul.
The straight backbone-thought of the crooked speech
Were just—"I Guido truck my name and rank
For so much money and youth and female charms."—
"We Pietro and Violante give our child
And wealth to you for a rise I' the world thereby."
Such naked truth while chambered in the brain

Shocks nowise: walk it forth by way of tongue,—
Out on the cynical unseemliness!

(4:508–521)

Like the minds of Locke's isolated speakers, the characters are relatively
safe and harmless in the separate chambers of their own intentions. The
internal repetition of "mind" in the third line plays upon multiple mean-
ings of "mind" as a reflective organ, as the seat of one's word choice,
and as the source of the more cautionary imperative of "minding" one's
tongue. The language here is curiously abstract and disembodied, with
the "mind" acting as a synecdochal substitution for the three different
speakers, coupled with a notable lack of pronominal specificity through-
out, in phrases like "There was" and "There came." The speaker gen-
eralizes from the quarrel between Guido, Pietro, and Violante to the
subject of communication as a universal quandary. Absent, at least ini-
tially, is any language of different sides, or even any language of full and
complete personhood. This larger generalization about language is most
striking in the fifth line, "There came the blunder incident to words,"
with its intertextual nod to Tennyson's notorious description of the dis-
placement of responsibility ("Some one had blundered") in "The Charge
of the Light Brigade."[42]

   In this blameless morass of talk, private reflection forms "The
straight backbone-thought of the crooked speech." This "straight
backbone-thought" gestures backward to the "straight" in the second
line where this widespread problem of language was first introduced,
the lines mimicking in syntax and repetition the same frustrating cir-
cuit between thought and language that they describe. The penultimate
line finally breaks this cyclical exchange, as alternating iambs ("walk,"
"forth," "way," "tongue") create the effect of a strolling forward
pace while also suggesting Pietro's and Violante's "walking forth" of
Pompilia into the arms of an abusive husband. In this cynical rational-
ization, mind, backbone, brain, and tongue all work at cross purposes,
expressing the impasse inevitable to any given community of speakers
and suggesting, in their corporeal language, the broken condition of the
body politic.

   The "Tertium Quid" speaker extends his weary critique of language
through an extension of the marketplace metaphor:

According to the words, each cheated each;
But in the inexpressive barter of thoughts,
Each did give and did take the thing designed,
The rank on this side and the cash on that—
Attained the object of the traffic, so.
The way of the world, the daily bargain struck
In the first market! Why sells Jack his ware?

"For the sake of serving an old customer."
Why does Jill buy it? "Simply not to break
A custom, pass the old stall the first time."
Why, you know where the gist is of the exchange:
Each sees a profit, throws the fine words in.

(4:527–538)

These lines work, in contrast to the ones earlier, to gradually fix and give order to meaning, setting up an orderly series of antitheses between words and thoughts, giving and taking, and rank ("this") and cash ("that"), and finally coming to rest and temporary closure upon an end-stopped proclamation: "Attained the object of the traffic, so." The speaker deploys a robust vocabulary of commodity exchange ("cheated," "barter," "cash," "bargain," "market") that seeks to naturalize these linguistic complications as an inevitable part of daily business in a monetized public sphere. He then shifts into a call-and-response structure, punctuated by midline caesuras, that further highlights the easy, give-and-take mutuality of this linguistic bargain through the imagined nursery-rhyme patter of "Jack" and "Jill." Here is where the antithesis breaks down, or rather collapses in upon itself. It collapses because the question-and-response structure merely enables him to mimic, via indirect speech, a conversation in fact entirely fabricated and which he stages for himself, as becomes apparent when his two noble interlocutors abandon him at the end of the book without giving any indication of having listened to these lengthy diatribes (4:1632–1640). Their eventual departure prompts a reaction in which the speaker re-enacts, in a truncated and unanswered fashion, the dilemma of communication he recounts: "I am of their mind: only, all this talk talked, / 'T was not for nothing that we talked, I hope?" (4:1635–36). The speaker falls prey to his own linguistic conundrum, repulsing others with his language, and with his sloppy and tactless negotiation of the split between thought and word. The "Tertium Quid" speaker's shamelessly opportunistic attempts at social climbing are but one of the many ways Browning magnifies class and rank tensions among the different speakers and, in so doing, emphasizes dissonance rather than harmony.

The poem's high-ranking characters do from time to time attempt to re-introduce social legibility into language by appealing to a hierarchy of speech registers that philologists like Müller often located in a fantasied, harmonious past or in a divine First Cause.[43] In Book 8, Guido's boastful counsel uses the heavenly origins of speech to legitimize his hierarchical vision of social life:

We must translate our motives like our speech,
Into the lower phase that suits the sense

> O' the limitedly apprehensive. Let
> Each level have its language! Heaven speaks first
> To the angel, then the angel tames the word
> Down to the ear of Tobit: he, in turn,
> Diminishes the message to his dog,
> And finally that dog finds how the flea
> (Which else, importunate, might check his speed)
> Shall learn its hunger must have holiday
> By application of his tongue or paw:
> So may varied sorts of language here,
> Each following each with pace to match the step,
> *Haud passibus aequis!*
>
> (8:1506–1519)

Like Müller, the counsel sees language as descending from a more perfect to a more degraded form, suggesting an Adamic trajectory of harmony and expulsion as a divine word becomes "tame[d]" in its transition from the angel down to the flea. However, this pattern of transcendence that ultimately fuels Müller's nostalgic construction of a lost linguistic paradise becomes, for Guido's counsel, a means of explicating a static social order in which more powerful forces continually reshape or "tame" meaning for those beneath them, in a fluid, top-down motion that is fundamentally aristocratic in nature. The imperative pronouncement, "Let / Each level have its language!" is reminiscent of biblical command and conjures the solemn air of a divine injunction. The enjambed lines that tame language down from the angel to the flea allow each level of language to spill into the next, naturalizing the social order through sonic cues and through the easy movement of the eye down the page. Instead of granting access to transcendence, this hierarchy of language registers merely fuels the counsel's class snobbery and his defense of traditional rank.

In the Pope's account, Browning pursues the question of whether any speaker can transcend the vagaries of communication in order to access a divine, harmonious language. The Pope acts as the mediator between earthly and heavenly speech, reflecting how best to cast a verdict on Guido in God's name, or how to "speak, act, in place of Him— / The Pope for Christ" (10:168–169). The Pope, like Müller and Trench, sets out from the assumption that all language is fallen:

> Expect nor question nor reply
> At what we figure as God's judgment-bar!
> None of this vile way by the barren words
> Which, more than any deed, characterize
> Man as made subject to a curse: no speech—

That still bursts o'er some lie which lurks inside,
As the split skin across the coppery snake,
And most denotes man!

(10:347–354)

"At what we figure at God's judgment-bar": these words nod toward
Barrett Browning's language of Eve in *A Drama of Exile*, in which words
and things are "what we name such"; here, too, Browning suggests that
the concepts that make up external reality could be illusions perpetuated
by the questionable act of naming.[44] Like Barrett Browning in *A Drama
of Exile*, Browning is concerned with the postlapsarian condition of lan-
guage after the "curse" which, in an arresting simile, transforms lan-
guage into a "split skin across the coppery snake," or a false, dead veneer
over a deceptive, living meaning. The Pope invokes Locke's ideas about
the separations among speakers:

But when man walks the garden of this world
For his own solace, and, unchecked by law,
Speaks or keeps silence as himself sees fit,
Without the least incumbency to lie,
–Why, can he tell you what a rose is like,
Or how the birds fly, and not slip to false
Though truth serve better? Man must tell his mate
Of you, me and himself, knowing he lies,
Knowing his fellow knows the same,—will think
"He lies, it is the method of a man!"
And yet will speak for answer "It is truth"
To him who shall rejoin "Again a lie!"
Therefore these filthy rags of speech, this coil
Of statement, comment, query and response,
Tatters all too contaminate for use,
Have no renewing: He, the Truth, is, too,
The Word.

(10:361–377)

The process of simple description of the material world—in Locke,
the description of gold, in the Pope's speech, that of roses and birds—
ignites the shared fantasy of comprehension, in which each speaker
speaks "knowing his fellow knows" the inevitable differences and
falsehoods that will creep into the exchange. Like the "Tertium
Quid" speaker, the Pope acknowledges that intent is irrelevant—the
universal "man" here cannot help but speak untruth—and gestures
toward the circular nature of communication in his evocative im-
age of the "coil / Of statement," an image that also recalls the lithe

curvature of the snake. The Pope concludes that these "filthy rags of speech" cannot be revitalized, and affirms that "He, the Truth, is, too / The Word."[45] The Pope sees no solution to the complications of earthly speech and so looks to heaven instead. Like Barrett Browning's speaker in *An Essay on Mind*, the Pope acknowledges what she calls the "imperfect government" of words.[46] Yet *The Ring and the Book* is less optimistic than *A Drama of Exile* about Christ's word descending to earth: solace remains in heaven, as earthly speech has "no renewing." This is problematic insofar as it forecloses earthly language as a vehicle for justice, and yet it is precisely language—in the form of the Pope's official response to Guido's appeal—which must mete out justice here.

In a social context in which all words are unmoored and torn from their divine substance, when all speech is falsehood, a refusal or resistance to yield to the cheat of language becomes the sole means of asserting truth. Of all the speakers in *The Ring and the Book*, Pompilia achieves the closest communion with a heavenly language and also with a type of divine silence that resembles Carlyle's career-long emphasis on a "silence which is better than any speech."[47] Pompilia's silence is a powerful indicator of her exploitation and abuse. Her mother, conducting her back home from the hasty marriage to Guido, urges her to keep quiet: "No one syllable / To Pietro! Girl-brides never breathe a word!" (7:459–460). Guido's marital abuse further imposes a regime of silence upon his young bride. Recounting Guido's jealous accusations about Caponsacchi, Pompilia describes how "I bore, this time, / More quietly than woman should perhaps; / Repeated the mere truth and held my tongue" (7:1033–1035). Much as Caliban clenches his teeth through his upper lip at the close of his dramatic monologue in order to self-censor, so too does Pompilia violently repress her own narrative. Guido's counsel wonders aloud why he revealed the secret of his wife's supposed infidelity: "Much rather should thy teeth bite out thy tongue, / Dumb lip consort with desecrated brow, / Silence become historiographer" (9:884–886). Pompilia's perpetual association with silence and muteness emphasizes her repeated exploitation and exposes her abusers' toxic imperatives of victim-blaming and censorship. Parallels with moments of self-censorship in "Caliban upon Setebos" suggest that Browning was drawing a broad and generalized comparison between European women and colonial subjects as unenfranchised and silenced members of the social body.

In this context, the Pope's pious appeal to heavenly speech is also a demonstration of his elite status, of his refusal to believe in justice even as he must dole it out, in stark comparison to Pompilia, who has no other recourse but to truth of her own account. Pompilia's testimony reveals a faith in communion with divine justice that is private and inward rather than social, and this privacy rescues language from its false and "filthy"

state as described by the Pope. Pompilia declares that God will sanction
her account even if no one else in Rome does:

> —why, what was all I said but truth
> Even when I found that such as are untrue
> Could only take the truth in through a lie?
> Now—I am speaking truth to the Truth's self:
> God will lend credit to my words this time.
>
> (7:1195–1199)

In these lines Pompilia underwrites the broader theme of isolation
throughout *The Ring and the Book* by showing how, in a social setting
beset with injustice and illegibility, justice and legibility are only avail-
able through private communion. The repetition of "true" and its vari-
ants throughout the first through fourth lines build to the personified
authority of "Truth's self," implying that it is possible to bridge the con-
nection between heavenly and earthly speech in the realm of private re-
flection. Indeed, Pompilia is the sole character who defies the Pope's and
the narrator's shared conviction that "truth seems reserved for heaven
not earth, / Plagued here by earth's prerogative of lies" (12:606–607).
She does so by understanding speech not as a social but rather a private
instrument.

That Browning was interested in creating analogues between this
community in seventeenth-century Italy and contemporary Britain is
apparent in his framing devices, which connect England to Italy with
the poet as mediator, using the oblique and "mediate" form of poetic
art to drawing parallels between the Florentine body politic and the
emergent Victorian social body (12:861). In the closing lines, Browning
fuses his own poetic art with that of his wife, alluding to the connec-
tion her own poetry forges between Italy and England.[48] Returning to
the image of the ring, crafted of lyric art and Lockean gold, Browning
concludes:

> And save the soul! If this intent save mine,—
> If the rough ore be rounded to a ring,
> Render all duty which good ring should do,
> And, failing grace, succeed in guardianship,—
> Might mine but lie outside thine, Lyric Love,
> Thy rare gold ring of verse (the poet praised)
> Linking our England to his Italy!
>
> (12:864–870)

The circular structure of the ring mimics the circular structure of
language itself, recalling the Tertium Quid speaker's reference to the
"chambered" brain and the Pope's imagery of the "coil," conjuring

the circular, fluid pathways between Italy and England, or between the historical past of the Old Yellow Book and the present of mid-century Britain, and reminding us of the looping traffic of meaning between Browning's reflections on language and Barrett Browning's meditations on the fallen tongue or "imperfect government" of speech. While Barrett Browning uses the forms of poetry to catalogue a lost language, connecting the divine and earthly world through the language of Christ, Browning, as a witness to the next major act of electoral reform, stresses the "wrangling, jangling" chaos of human communication as central to the emergence of the *demos*, harnessing the dramatic monologue to capture and juxtapose vital and necessary forms of dissent, and to illustrate the ongoing persistence of aristocratic rule.

The poem's staging of the battle between literary language and vernaculars, its depiction of language as a saleable commodity, its clashing testimonies between different characters, and its repeated emphasis on the circularity of communication may, at a first glance, seem only like the rejection of single truth that has become such a commonplace in studies of Browning. And, indeed, these formal traits do foreclose any appeal to an overarching, unifying meaning, stressing relativism and variation instead. Yet, for Browning, this ongoing verbal conflict goes beyond indicating the relativism of any given speaker in order to ensure the role of dissent in the linguistic and political community. Throughout *The Ring and the Book*, this division between thought, individual will, and meaning also opens up forms of resistance to the language of the public sphere, of gossip, and of the court and the state. This division also recasts meaning as private conviction, as seen in Pompilia's staunch adherence to the truth of her own account, and in her implicit challenge to the Pope's weary renunciation of speech. Browning refuses any easy consensus of the *demos* as imagined by Trench, showing how forms of mass consensus can perpetuate a dangerous and deadly collectivity—as in the growth of empire—as well as overlook those subjects still excluded from the political and social benefits of the reforming state. His poetry exposes this contradiction through its engagement with a poetics of the antisocial, one that refuses the fantasy that language can underwrite a united polity. Instead, Browning uses the form of the dramatic monologue, here elevated into an epic collocation, in order to reintroduce an oppositional stance into human communication, making visible and audible the conflicts that the newly reformed social body silences or denies.

The mid-century emphasis on language and sociability was not the only development in philology to preoccupy politically engaged poets writing in response to electoral reform in 1867. Developments in philology and evolutionary biology sparked renewed interests in age-old questions about human-animal communication in scientific works by

Lyell and Darwin, philological studies by Trench, Müller, and Wedgwood, and anthropological research by Edward Tylor. Inevitably, these debates became linked to the Victorian imperial enterprise, predicated as it was on a Eurocentric hierarchy of primitive and civilized speech that Tennyson's poetry both reflects and disrupts. The next chapter shows how research on the human-animal language boundary informs the Victorian poetic engagement with colonial sovereignty in Tennyson's work.

Notes

1 Bagehot, "Wordsworth, Tennyson, and Browning," 56–61.
2 Christopher Lane, *Hatred and Civility*, 136–137.
3 Browning, *The Ring and the Book*, eds. Richard D. Altick and Thomas J. Collins (Peterborough: Broadview, 2001), 1: 410. Hereafter citations will be given by book and line number in parentheses within the text.
4 Robert Browning to Joseph Milsand, 16 June 1853, in Kelley and Hudson, *The Brownings' Correspondence*, 19: 127.
5 See Tucker, "Dramatic Monologue and the Overhearing of Lyric," 228.
6 Armstrong, *Victorian Poetry*, 142; Saville, *Victorian Soul-Talk*, 135. See also Langbaum's discussion of readerly sympathy and judgment in *The Poetry of Experience*, 75–108. Hughes discusses how "the speaker of Browning's monologues typically faces outward"; see *The Manyfacèd Glass: Tennyson's Dramatic Monologues*, 18. More recently, Cornelia Pearsall pursues a similar argument in her work on Tennyson by claiming that the dramatic monologue seeks to "effect social and political transformations by inciting personal ones"; see Pearsall, *Tennyson's Rapture*, 10.
7 E. Warwick Slinn, "Language and Truth in *The Ring and the Book*," 118. On the poem's relativism see Langbaum, *The Poetry of Experience*, 109–136. Other deconstructive readings of the poem include W. David Shaw, "Browning's Murder Mystery: *The Ring and the Book* and Modern Theory," and L.M. Findlay, "Taking the Measure of *Différance*: Deconstruction and *The Ring and the Book*." On Pompilia's complicated relationship to truth see William Walker, "*Pompilia* and Pompilia," 47–63. For challenges to relativist readings see John Killham, "Browning's 'Modernity,' *The Ring and the Book*, and Relativism," 153–176 and Armstrong, "*The Ring and the Book*: The Uses of Prolixity," 178–179. See also Patricia Rigg's contention that Browning resists reclaiming any notion of absolute truth while showing that "the process of representing the telling of truth can be reclaimed" in *Robert Browning's Romantic Irony in The Ring and the Book*, 22.
8 On the advent of the Liberal Party see Jonathan Parry, *The Rise and Fall of Liberal Government in Victorian Britain*. Saville discusses the influence of liberal and republican thought on Browning's 1860s poetry in *Soul-Talk*, 136–139.
9 As critics have shown, mid-century reform did not substantially improve the plight of many working-class people, it did not mount a fierce challenge to the landed aristocratic tradition, and it ultimately preserved the exclusion of women from the electorate. On the relatively modest effects of reform see Hoppen, *The Mid-Victorian Generation*, 254–271 and Evans, *The Forging of the Modern State*, 443–447. Catherine Hall has demonstrated how the Act also worked within the empire to reconstitute the polity among racial lines, sorting out which colonial subjects of Britain and its empire

were entitled to political autonomy. The Second Reform Act, the Canadian settlement (1867) and the Jamaica Act (1866) all worked to "formally differentiat[e] black Jamaicans from white British, white Canadians or white Australians...from brown Indians...[and] Anglo-Saxons from Celts." The "'white settlers' in Australia, Canada, the Cape and New Zealand were granted forms of self-government which were rejected as totally out of the question in India and Jamaica because the majority population was not white." See "The nation within and without," 182–183. See also Hall's *Civilizing Subjects*. For the restructuring of the franchise in mid-century Ireland see Hoppen, *Elections, Politics, and Society in Ireland*, 31–32.

10 Locke, *Essay*, 361.

11 Müller, *Lectures*, 12.

12 For Browning's regular reading in the *Athenaeum* see, for example, Robert Browning to Henry Fothergill Chorley, 11 March 1850, in Kelley and Hudson, *The Brownings' Correspondence*, 16: 72. The *Athenaeum* reported periodically on the progress of the *NED*, including on the number of volunteer readers; see Mugglestone, *Lost for Words*, 16–17, 21–22, 30, and 76. See also Hair, *Robert Browning's Language*, 8–58. Hair's study has greatly influenced my own work on Browning. I differ from Hair primarily in stressing the political dimensions of Browning's interest in philology; Hair's emphasis is on Browning's understanding of the meaning of language in the context of his dissenting religious background (3–7).

13 Browning accepted an invitation to call on Trench and his wife in May 1862; see Robert Browning to Trench, Frances Mary and Trench, Richard Chenevix, 28 May 1862, in Baylor University's digital collection, *The Browning Letters*, For the correspondence between Browning and Furnivall see Peterson, ed., *Browning's Trumpeter*.

14 Trench, *On some Deficiencies*, 4–5.

15 Ibid., 5.

16 Ibid., 52.

17 Trench, *Proposal*, 8. For general histories of the OED see Winchester, *The Meaning of Everything*, and Mugglestone, *Lost for Words*.

18 See, for example, Müller's *Lectures*, 14, 29–30, and 341–342.

19 According to the Armstrong Browning Library's catalogue, Browning had at one point owned and inscribed a copy of Priestley's *A Course of Lectures on the Theory of Language and Universal Grammar*. Priestley continued to influence the Victorians by way of his metaphysical ideas, which shaped the utilitarian thinking of Mill and Jeremy Bentham. See Canovan, "The Un-Benthamite Utilitarianism of Joseph Priestley," 435–450.

20 Priestley, *English Grammar*, 121. All citations will be to this edition and will follow the quotation in parentheses within the text.

21 Trench, *On Some Deficiencies*, 57.

22 On the OED as an imperial production see Willinsky, *Empire of Words*.

23 Robert Browning to Isa Blagden, 30 December 1870, in *Dearest Isa*, 353.

24 Qtd. in K.M. Elisabeth Murray, *Caught in the Web of Words*, 235.

25 All citations to "Respectability" are taken from Browning, *The Complete Works*, 5: 257, and will be given in parentheses within the text.

26 John Berkey, Ashby Bland Crowder, Jr., Susan Crowl, et al. provide background on this ceremony in their notes to "Respectability"; see Vol. 5 of the *Complete Works*, 376–377.

27 For the politics of *Vestiges* see James A. Secord's "Introduction" to Robert Chambers's *Vestiges of the Natural History of Creation*, ix–xlv. In all likelihood Browning knew this widely discussed title, if not firsthand, then

through discussions with Elizabeth Barrett Browning, who in 1845 described
Vestiges as "one of the most melancholy books in the world"; five years later,
when the Brownings were settled in Casa Guidi, Mary Russell Mitford was
still debating the authorship of the book in a letter to Barrett Browning.
See Elizabeth Barrett Browning to Julia Martin, 25 January 1845, in Kelley
and Hudson, *The Brownings' Correspondence*, 10: 41 and Mary Russell
Mitford to Elizabeth Barrett Browning, 25 March 1850, in Kelley and Hud-
son, *The Brownings' Correspondence*, 16: 86. I discuss Barrett Browning's
response to *Vestiges* in Chapter 1.

28 See Secord's "Introduction" to Chambers's *Vestiges*, ix–xlv.
29 Chambers, *Vestiges*, 317.
30 Ibid., 317–318.
31 All citations are to "Caliban upon Setebos," *The Complete Works*, 6:
   259–270 and will be given in parentheses within the text.
32 Armstrong, "Browning's 'Caliban' and Primitive Language," 77. Beer has
   shown how Caliban is a liminal creature somewhere between brute and
   man, a "missing link" that troubled the elaborate racial taxonomies of
   mid-Victorian philology and evolutionary science. See Beer, "Forging the
   Missing Link," 138–139. See also her reading of the poem as a Darwinian
   challenge to anthropocentrism in "Darwin's Reading and the Fictions of
   Development," 578–582.
33 See Hall, "The Nation within and without," 179–182.
34 Tucker, *Epic*, 13.
35 Ibid.
36 See Brown, "'Pompilia': The Woman (in) Question," 15–37. Brown notes that
   the poem's emphasis on social institutions such as the family, the church, and
   the state makes *The Ring and the Book* feel more contemporary than other
   Victorian historical works that are more oriented toward pastoral modes and
   that foreground the difference between the past and the present; see p. 18. For
   Tucker's analysis of Browning and narrative authority see *Epic*, 439.
37 "The Ring and the Book," *The Dublin Review*, 48.
38 Unsigned review of *The Ring and the Book*, *Spectator*, 775.
39 "The Ring and the Book," *Saturday Review*, 833.
40 On the ring figure as it relates to Browning's creative process see, for exam-
   ple, Paul A. Cundiff, "The Clarity of Browning's Ring Metaphor," 1276–
   1282, George Wasserman, "The Meaning of Browning's Ring-Figure,"
   420–426, Mary Rose Sullivan, *Browning's Voices*, 9–11, and Hair, *Brown-
   ing's Experiments with Genre*, 118–121. Tucker reads the ring metaphor as
   a historicist negation of "pristine or virginal presence" (11); on this reading,
   both book and ring reveal the collaborative inventions that have created
   them. See "Representation and Repristination," 67–86. For a more general
   reading of *The Ring and the Book* as an exercise in "critical-creative read-
   ing" see Buckler, *Poetry and Truth*, 24. *Sordello* (1840) anticipates this im-
   agery of language and workmanship: see, for example, how the poet "slow
   re-wrought / That Language,—welding words into the crude / Mass from the
   new speech around him" (2: 574–576). On language-issues in *Sordello* see,
   for example, Peter Allan Dale, "'Paracelsus and Sordello': Trying the Stuff
   of Language," 359–369.
41 Müller, *Lectures*, 61–62.
42 See "The Charge of the Light Brigade" and the notes in Ricks, *Poems*, 2:
   510–513.
43 As Müller declared in his *Lectures*, ancient man was thought to live in a
   "primitive and perfect state" in which "the creative faculty" gave to each

idea, "as it thrilled for the first time through the brain, a phonetic expression" (370–371). Abberley reads this nostalgic strain of Victorian philology as a form of "language vitalism" that mythologizes "verbal purity" in *English Fiction*, 91.

44 Barrett Browning, *A Drama of Exile*, 959.

45 Richard D. Altick and James F. Loucks, in their chapter on the Pope's speech, show how "the gift of speech, however susceptible it is to human misuse... nevertheless comes from God." See *Browning's Roman Murder Story*, 129.

46 Barrett Browning, *An Essay on Mind*, 2: 659.

47 Carlyle, *The French Revolution*, 2: 29. Pompilia's account has attracted much feminist scholarship. For a book-length study that recovers Browning's poem as a challenge to Victorian patriarchy see Ann P. Brady's *Pompilia: A Feminist Reading of Robert Browning's The Ring and the Book*. Kay Austin analyzes Pompilia's spirituality and argues for her centrality to the poem in "Pompilia: 'Saint and Martyr Both,'" 287–301. Candace Ward reads the poem as caught in an ideological struggle between a problematic idealization of women and the violently sexist views of Guido; see "'Damning Herself Praiseworthily,'" 1–14.

48 See Altick's and Collins's gloss of these lines in n.2, p. 763 of the *Broadview* edition.

3 The "yelp of the beast"

Alfred Tennyson's Animal Language, Victorian Empire, and the End of Politics

In the brief, enigmatic dialogue poem "By an Evolutionist" (1889), Tennyson brings beast and man together in a single body. In so doing, he recasts the human-animal language boundary as a metaphor for political governance. The speaker pictures himself as a human core in an animal casing, or the "soul of a man" temporarily lodged in the "house of a brute."[1] If he is in fact an animal, the speaker reasons, why shouldn't he forget the state of his soul and take pleasure in sensory delights, enjoying his wine, women, and hounds (8)? A second speaker, Old Age, responds by sternly recalling man's place in the evolutionary hierarchy, and his superior role as the only creature who possesses articulate speech:

> I.
> If my body come from brutes, tho' somewhat finer than their
>   own,
> I am heir, and this my kingdom. Shall the royal voice be mute?
> No, but if the rebel subject seek to drag me from the throne,
> Hold the sceptre, Human Soul, and rule thy province of the
>   brute.
>
> II.
> I have climb'd to the snows of Age, and I gaze at a field in the
>   Past.
> Where I sank with the body at times in the sloughs of a low
>   desire,
> But I hear no yelp of the beast, and the Man is quiet at last,
> As he stands on the heights of his life with a glimpse of a height that
>   is higher.
>
> (13–20)

In a sweeping eight-beat line roomy enough to enfold species history into a single quatrain, section I sets up an antithesis between modern civilization and the evolutionary past. An alternating pattern of alliteration links the initial *h* and *s* sounds in the last line of the stanza ("Hold the sceptre, Human Soul"), urging a personified soul to assert dominance over the "rebel subject," while the heavy downbeat of the trochees lend this command a solemn finality.[2] The passage from brute to man is not only an act of violent self-mastery, of learning to quell the "wild beast," the poem implies, but also a means of seizing political control through the use of language.

Yet the diction, meter, and sound patterns of these lines also undermine this antithesis between the human king and the rebel brute. In the first quoted line earlier, alliteration links man and animal in the conditional phrase "If my body come from brutes," and the qualified comparative adjective, "somewhat finer," hesitates in its proclamation of absolute superiority. The speaker seeks to re-assert control with a firm declarative statement that ends in a midline caesura ("I am heir, and this my kingdom"), only to undermine himself with the tentative query, "Shall the royal voice be mute?" In the second quatrain a chain of slouching anapests places stress on the alliterated words "sank" and "sloughs," both of which suggest a regression and defeat only partially compensated for by the internal repetition of "height" in the last line. In "By an Evolutionist," the confident language of liberal modernity is always at risk of collapsing into the wild but tantalizing "yelp" of the animal. This chapter gives a new reading of Tennyson's poetry that analyzes how his work dissolves the human-animal language boundary to expose the political contradictions of empire.

Critics have long recognized Tennyson's role as a quintessential Victorian poet of science, tracing his engagement with geology, astronomy, and evolutionary biology.[3] Hair, Armstrong, and Michele Geric have further considered the influence of Victorian language-theory on Tennyson's work.[4] Scholarship on Tennyson's politics has been equally rich, revealing how his poetry reflects broader cultural anxieties about the governance of Britain's far-flung empire.[5] Yet none of these accounts show how Tennyson's depiction of British rule overseas arises directly from his reading in human-animal language debates and from the ambivalent notions of sovereignty they express. In this chapter, I argue that *Maud* (1855), *Idylls of the King* (1859–1885), and "By an Evolutionist" incorporate contemporary scientists' claims about civilized human language to underwrite their fantasies of Britain as a coherent, stable, liberal republic. But Tennyson's poetry also uses animal language and its associations with primordial lawlessness to expose the ongoing class tensions and colonial unrest that persisted under a reforming and expanding empire. By constructing the habitats of the metropolitan underclass and the unenfranchised colonies as lawless primal spaces filled with animal cries, Tennyson's poetry imagines these sites as necessary outlets for the failures of political reform.

This chapter begins with an analysis of *Maud*, showing how Tennyson's mid-century monodrama draws on human-animal language accounts by Lyell, Trench, and Chambers to challenge the brutality of the class system in post-Reform Britain. Collapsing metropole and colony through its geographic reversals and poetic compressions, *Maud* looks abroad in search of an outlet for the roiling class antagonisms expressed in the poem's characterization of the landed elite as growling, wolfish beasts. Post-Darwinian controversies about human-animal language inform the following two sections. I show how *Idylls of the King* reflects Tennyson's close attention to a series of widely followed debates between Darwin and Müller on the human-animal language boundary, and I trace these debates to Tennyson's little-known support for the imperial federation movement of the 1870s–1890s that sought to establish unified political representation for Britain's overseas territories. Tennyson's epic enacts a fantasy of imperial federation through its presentation of language, testing emergent democratic ideals in the colonies before reincorporating these ideals into an imaginary vision of a reformed Britain.

An analysis of human-animal language in Tennyson's poetry deepens our understanding of the intersections between literature, politics, and science, extends the existing literature and science scholarship on Tennyson, and sheds fresh light on literary representations of liberal empire and its contradictions. Ultimately, Tennyson's poetry does not transcend the racial hierarchies that structure the study of language in the Victorian period. The slippery lines of demarcation that divide so-called brutal and civilized tongues do invite readers to recognize the tenuous ideological construction of the empire, and the impossibility of reconciling Britain's reformist outlook to its atrocities against its working classes and its colonial subjects. In *Maud* and the *Idylls*, what Alice Meynell called the "excessive ease" of Tennyson's style is constantly disrupted by the anarchic presence of the animal.[6] Through sound patterns, metonymic substitutions, and lupine and canine imagery, Tennyson subtly challenges the use of philology and evolutionary science as a model for British imperial sovereignty.

Human-Animal Language in *Maud*

If "By an Evolutionist" brings together humans and animals in a single speaker, *Maud* takes a wider scope by presenting the class system in Britain as a microcosm of the animal kingdom. The despairing, unnamed speaker of Tennyson's monodrama tells, in three parts, the story of his disastrous love for the young, aristocratic Maud, from their secret walks together on through his murder of her brother, his subsequent ravings in the madhouse, and his final resolution to go to "the Black and the Baltic deep" and fight "the blood-red blossom" of battle during the tense, nationalistic fervor of the Crimean War.[7] *Maud*'s speaker uses the human-animal language boundary to mount a fierce attack on the British class system, still dominated in the post-Reform era by the landed privilege of the men at the Hall. It does so by reversing the depictions of the poor as a brutish underclass, portraying the aristocracy instead as a herd of speaking, wolfish beasts. In so doing, the poem resists the idea of evolutionary perfectibility as a model for liberal progress.[8]

In *Maud*, the animal presence works to express the glaring inequalities between the speaker and the landed men at the Hall, and reveals, in turn, how the human-animal language boundary helped Victorian poets grapple with ongoing social unrest in their age of reform. Scholars have long recognized how the equation of European languages with civilization works to maintain rigid racial and social hierarchies.[9] More recently, however, Ferguson and Abberley have questioned the stability of this equation in Victorian scientific and literary texts. Ferguson shows how late-Victorian popular fiction finds in the notion of the "brutal tongue" the "imaginative potential to either reinforce or transform existing social or species hierarchies," while Abberley observes that philology can both set up and break down boundaries between speakers.[10] I argue that *Maud* does even more than this. Through the form of the monodrama, Tennyson's speaker not only acknowledges the slipperiness of the human-animal language boundary and the social order it underwrites but also reverses the terms of the hierarchy itself. The poem transforms the landholding aristocracy into articulate monsters and wolves, and makes the fantasied wildness of colonial spaces into outlets for the ongoing injustices of Britain's class system.

Maud's animals reflect Tennyson's copious reading in geology and human-animal language research. Lyell's *Principles of Geology* (1830–1833) revived the old question of the orangutan's proximity to the human earlier explored by James Burnett, Lord Monboddo in his *On the Origin and Progress of Language* (1773–1792).[11] Lyell, paraphrasing the naturalist Jean-Baptiste Lamarck, presents the orangutan as "the last grand step in the progressive scheme, whereby the orang-outang... is made slowly to attain the attributes and dignity of man."[12] In Lamarck's early evolutionary model, as orang-outangs came to dominate other species and to live in more and more complex social communities, they had a greater range of ideas to express, which, in turn, led the animals to "habitual exercise of their tongue, throat, and lips" that modified these organs "until they became fitted for the faculty of speech."[13] Lyell dismisses Lamarck by insisting that such speculations about man's prehistory are founded on scanty and incomplete evidence, much of it from "foreign" and "barbarous" countries.[14] Trench's *On the Study of Words* (1851), known to Tennyson, also takes issue with the idea that "the primitive condition of man was the savage one, and the savage himself the seed out of which in due time the civilized man was unfolded; whereas, in fact, so far from being this living seed, he might more justly be considered a dead withered leaf."[15] Instead, Trench looks to Adam's naming-process in Genesis as the origin story for human speech. The fact that every primitive society has language, Trench argues, is sufficient evidence that language could not have been a skill acquired through development and modification alone.

What appears to many Victorian observers as "rude" or undeveloped language, on this model, belongs to so-called lower races as well as to the British underclasses whose primitive living conditions are seen as barriers to evolutionary and linguistic advancement. As Chambers explains in *Vestiges*, "leisure and abundance" rather than "mean and engrossing toils" work to produce the courtesy of "the upper classes of almost all civilized countries."[16] Consequently, societies that are "dense and refined" possess more uniform languages (315). By contrast, as we saw in Chapter 2, unregulated, unsupervised communities, such as those made up of the children of Manchester factory laborers, create an "infant Babel" of "mongrel words and phrases, joined together without rule" (317). Chamber's telling use of the word "mongrel" links such proletarian speech-communities to a primordial past, and to the confused, indistinct human-animal relations of man's evolutionary prehistory.

By the time he composed and published *Maud*, Tennyson had already read and absorbed the work of Lyell, Trench, and Chambers. *The Princess* (1847) incorporates several references to primordial man and his relationship to contemporary European civilization. The opening lines to Tennyson's blank verse medley describe a temporal jumble of objects, including "Huge Ammonites, and the first bones of Time" scattered together with "objects of every clime and age" on Sir Walter Vivien's lawns, filled with students of the local Mechanic's Institute ("Prologue" 15–16). The setting brings together the civilized upper classes, the proletarian students of the Institute, and the relics of primeval and colonial man. Lady Psyche's description of early humankind later in the poem reinforces this juxtaposition of civilized and savage society, showing how primal society persists both abroad, in the colonies, and among the "lowest" classes at home:

> This world was once a fluid haze of light,
> Till towards the centre set the starry tides,
> And eddied into suns, that wheeling cast
> The planets: then the monster, then the man;
> Tattooed or woaded, winter-clad in skins,
> Raw from the prime, and crushing down his mate;
> As yet we find in barbarous isles, and here
> Among the lowest.

(2:101–108)

An introductory phrase in the fourth line prepares the reader's ear for the evolutionary arrival of dinosaurs, followed by the arrival of humans: "then the monster, then the man." This parallel structure implies that monsters and men are comparable, even alike. They both arrive in a close time frame, one abruptly collapsed into one half-line after the more sweeping, three-line account of deep planetary history. Lady Psyche locates the ongoing existence of primitivism both in the colonies or "barbarous isles" and in the "lowest" classes who dwell nearby, or "here," while her adverbial "yet" emphasizes the persistence of otherwise ancient primal behaviors among these modern-day groups. Her lines anticipate the nightmarish vision of evolutionary history in stanza LVI of *In Memoriam* (1850), where "Dragons of the prime" destroy each other (22), where a violent Nature "shriek[s]" (16), and where the "spirit does but mean the breath" rather than the divine aspiration of God giving language to the world (7). Like the scientists whose work he avidly read, Tennyson imagines primitive culture as a site of violence and unholy, passionate speech. This primal habitat promises both danger and allure: it is a place that serves as a discomfiting reminder of man's evolutionary prehistory and as a place where social tensions can be ventilated and released, as in "Locksley Hall" (1842) where the advancing mob is "a lion creeping nigher" (135).[17] Animal proximity stands for the proximity of social disorder and chaos.

The speaker of *Maud* extends this imagery by using animal language to symbolize class antagonisms. Describing his father's failed financial speculation and subsequent suicide, he laments how "the poor are hovelled and hustled together, / each sex, like swine" in a passage reminiscent of Burke's vision of the "swinish multitude" of the French Revolution (1:33–34). Questioning the relationship between evolutionary and social progress, he predicts that man's money-lust and self-interest will eventually topple him from his crowning place in the animal kingdom:

> A monstrous eft was of old the Lord and Master of Earth,
> For him did his high sun flame, and his river billowing ran,
> And he felt himself in his force to be Nature's crowning race.
> As nine months go to the shaping an infant ripe for his birth,
> So many a million of ages have gone to the making of man:
> He now is first, but is he the last? is he not too base?
>
> (1:131–137)

In a poetic compression reminiscent of Lady Psyche's evolutionary lesson in *The Princess*, the speaker compares beasts to men. Alliterated m-words reiterate the "monster/man" distinction of *The Princess* in the first line, where the stress falls on the initial syllables of "monstrous" and "Master," while the capitalized "Lord" portends the later arrival of Maud's suitor, the "new-made lord" (1:332). The deferred verbs of the second line suggest the great eft's dominion, as the deferral allows the speaker to place the preposition and object pronoun "For him" at the beginning of the line, syntactically enacting the closing query, "He now is first." An end-stopped phrase lends temporary authority to the eft's belief in his mastery: "he felt himself in his force to be Nature's crowning race."

Yet the simile that opens the fourth line begins to question this mastery, likening nine months of gestation to the millions of years of evolutionary prehistory that precede man's arrival as a species. This temporal comparison suggests that the "monstrous eft" resembles the "infant ripe," a resemblance that undermines the eft's domineering power and apparent permanence. The query that follows the caesura of the final line, "is he not too base?" ends with a spondee that end-rhymes with "race" in the third line, suggesting that baseness and corruption are inherent vices of the "crowning race" of the planet. The speaker diminishes mankind's evolutionary achievement by recalling the extinction of the "monstrous eft" or dinosaur and finding some bitter solace in the fact that advanced man's exploitative ways will eventually negate his million years of prehistory. Evolutionary perfectibility, in the speaker's despairing view, is no indicator of social progress.

Accordingly, the speaker presents the most advanced social class in the poem not as a "crowning race" but rather as a herd of untamed animals. In so doing, he reverses contemporary depictions of the poor as a swinish underclass by revealing instead the rapacious brutality of the landed elite, anticipating Matthew Arnold's dubbing the aristocracy "Barbarians" in *Culture and Anarchy* (1869).[18] Maud's father, absent throughout the poem, is a "gray old wolf and a lean" (1:471) off in a "wilderness, full of wolves" where he gathers bones and howls (2:292–294). Maud's protective, class-prejudiced brother is an "o'ergrown whelp" (2:293) and her wealthy suitor a "padded shape" (1:358) with a "rabbit mouth" (1:360). Interestingly, her suitor's fortune comes from a family mining business whose growth, the speaker suggests, resembles the slow evolution of primordial man:

> Was not one of the two at her side
> This new-made lord, whose splendour plucks
> The slavish hat from the villager's head?
> Whose old grandfather has lately died,
> Gone to a blacker pit, for whom
> Grimy nakedness dragging his trucks
> And laying his trams in a poisoned gloom
> Wrought, till he crept from a gutted mine
> Master of half a servile shire,

And left his coal all turned into gold
To a grandson, first of his noble line,
Rich in the grace all women desire,
Strong in the power that all men adore,
And simper and set their voices lower,
And soften as if to a girl...

(1:331–345)

The suitor's economic ascent re-enacts the evolutionary trajectory of the "monstrous eft" passage, even reproducing its diction of mastery and lordship. The image of the coal workers, described collectively in a state of "Grimy nakedness," echoes the image of men "Raw from the prime" in *The Princess*, while the upright carriage of the grandson, the "new-made lord," re-enacts the progression into bipedalism and rehearses stereotypes about civilized upper classes and uncivilized laborers. This new-made lord, in turn, is the "first" of the noble line, which reiterates the previously unanswered question, "He now is first, but is he the last? is he not too base?" (1:131–137). By encapsulating man's evolutionary trajectory in just fifteen rapid lines that depict the contrast between the savage and the gentleman, the speaker depicts class mobility as a fundamentally debased and primal struggle only barely disguised by the newfound "grace" of the arrogant suitor. The sound patterns reinforce this sense of unjust mastery. Alliterated sibilants throughout hint at treachery and subservience ("slavish," "servile," "simper," "set"), while the assonance and juxtaposition of "coal" and "gold" in the tenth line emphasize the rapid and wickedly alchemical transformation of the one into the other. This new vocabulary of economic domination leads to a debasement of language as the adoring men "soften" their voices into girls' voices and, in so doing, embody emasculated regression rather than triumphant evolutionary progress.

Expanded manuscript versions of the poem further expose the animality of class conflict by comparing Maud's love for the speaker to a debased hunting expedition. In earlier versions of lines 1:73–76, the speaker revises the romantic trope of the hunt in the sonnet tradition, imagining his beloved as "One of the monkeys who mimic wisdom," a woman who undermines language by making romantic terms of endearment "bite" their recipients (525nb).[19] He uses this trope to describe class exploitation:

Well, I was half-afraid but I shall not die for her sake,
Not be her 'savage' and 'O the monster'! their delicate ways!
Their finical interlarding of French and the giggle and shrug!
Taken with Maud – not so – for what could she prove but a
    curse.

Being so hard, she has hardly a decent regard for her pug.
Thanks! there is fatter game on the moor; she will let me
    alone;
Thanks, for the Devil best knows whether woman or man be
    the worse.
I will bury myself in my books and the Devil may pipe to his
    own.

(525nb).

In this rather misogynistic presentation of Maud as a predatory hunt-ress, the speaker communicates his awareness of the social and eco-nomic disparities between them: he is a "savage" suitor somewhere on the level of the pet pug that Maud neglects in the fifth line, where the internal rhyme of "hard," "hardly," and "regard" emphasize her intrac-tability. Inevitably, he reasons, Maud will seek out "fatter game" to kill, presumably a member of her own social class. The distinctions between the speaker and his cruel beloved are apparent in their relationship to language as well as in their animal-human dynamic: while Maud and her family lace their words with "finical" and showy French phrases, the speaker's series of interjections in the second, third, and sixth lines sug-gest the supposed emotional qualities of animal expression. Maud and her family are the refined (if frivolous) connoisseurs of highly evolved European languages, and he is the "monster" who expresses himself in passionate exclamations.

The speaker's passionate exclamations in these excised lines hint at the theory of the expressive cry believed to prevail among early societies. In his *Lectures on Rhetoric and Belles Lettres* (1783), Blair describes how language evolved from cries and gestures meant to communicate emotions:

> If we should suppose a period before any words were invented or known, it is clear, that men could have no other method of commu-nicating to others what they felt, than by the cries of passion, accom-panied with such motions and gestures as were farther expressive of passion. For these are the only signs which nature teaches all men, and which are understood by all. One who saw another going into some place where he himself had been frightened, or exposed to danger, and who sought to warn his neighbor of the danger, could contrive no other way of doing so, than by uttering those cries, and making those gestures, which are the signs of fear: just as two men, at this day, would endeavor to make themselves be understood by each other, who should be thrown together on a desolate island, ignorant of each other's Language. Those exclamations, therefore, which by Grammarians are called Interjections, uttered in a strong

and passionate manner, were, beyond doubt, the first elements or beginnings of Speech.[20]

In Blair's account, emotions related to imminent danger helped give rise to the need to communicate that danger to others, and language was born of these early, passionate utterances. Such theories of early language-formation were familiar to many eighteenth-century thinkers, and tended to collapse the human-animal language boundary by showing how nonhuman animals also possessed the capacity to utter passionate cries. As Aarsleff writes, in Condillac's work these *cris naturels* are not unique to humans since animals use them as well; rather, man's unique reasoning capabilities eventually foster the development of artificial signs from these natural ones.[21] Hair writes that Tennyson was familiar with the *cris naturels* not only from accounts by Blair and Lord Monboddo but also from Lucretius, whose *De Rerum Natura* compares human cries to the inarticulate, creaturely sounds found in nature.[22]

Even as Tennyson equates animal language with ideas of brutishness, he also embraces these *cris naturels* as authentic and necessary sources of human expression. Blair's account offers a precedent for this view. Blair writes that even after language had developed further, this "antient manner of Speech still subsisted among many nations" and gave rise to further communications through significant actions and gestures, inflections of voice and tone, and the "smooth and musical sounds" that form the "Prosody of a Language."[23] Thus emerged, in turn, the arts of declamation and theater, with their "musical and gesticulating pronunciation."[24] These *cris naturels*, then, were not only crude utterances but forms of language that gave rise to art. The inarticulate cry in this sense of human expression is central to Tennyson's description of the crying infant in *In Memoriam*:

> Behold, we know not anything;
>   I can but trust that good shall fall
>   At last—far off—at last, to all,
> And every winter change to spring.
>
> So runs my dream: but what am I?
>   An infant crying in the night:
>   An infant crying for the light:
> And with no language but a cry.

(LIV.13–20)

Significantly, Tennyson grants this infant cry the status of language, and affirms its centrality to human experience. Christopher Ricks notes the derivation of "infant" from the Latin *infans*, or "unable to speak," and yet the child's cry is still a clear communication of a feeling, even without articulate speech.[25] As Hair writes, Tennyson's poetry both acknowledges and reimagines accounts of the *cris naturels*: in his work language "has a wholly natural origin – it begins as a function of our physical makeup – but Tennyson takes a quite different view of this primal cry, hearing in it the expression of a mysterious, spiritual, and unique self."[26] We might extend Hair's analysis to account for the dual position of the speaker in these lines, who is infant and poet simultaneously. The speaker is at once the infant uttering his *cri naturel* and the poet shaping language into the expressive form of the elegy, or the "Short swallow-flights of song" that comprise the individual stanzas (XLVII.15). Tennyson merges the story of language-origins with what Blair calls the "musical sounds" of art. The *cris naturels* continue to survive into the developed language from which Tennyson shapes his "swallow-flights of song," and the passionate cry retains its importance as a form of expression. This elevation of the *cris naturels* is also evident in *Maud*, which opens with a striking instance of an expressive cry, the "shrill-edged shriek of a mother" that follows upon the father's suicide (1:16). There was "*love* in the / passionate shriek," the speaker insists, thereby affirming the cry as a crucial and necessary articulation of inner feeling (1:56–57). The *cris naturels*, then, are both animal and human, at once expressive of basic needs and of a selfhood communicated through language and art.

At key moments in *Maud*, Tennyson explores the *cris naturels* as utterances that break down the human-animal language barrier and, by extension, the social class divide. Maud herself suggests the possibility that the class rift between the two families can be healed through romantic union. The speaker is attracted to the sound of her "wild voice" singing a "passionate ballad," in a passage that recalls Blair's remarks on the musicality of speech (1:174, 1:165). Moreover, Maud's association with the birds in the garden establishes a powerful correspondence between human and creaturely language:

> Birds in the high Hall-garden
>   When twilight was falling,
> Maud, Maud, Maud, Maud,
>   They were crying and calling.

(1:412–415)

The speaker substitutes Maud's name for the sound of the birds' cries, suggesting a natural connection between human and animal expression further expressed in the variation six stanzas later, where the birds are communicating to Maud directly, or "crying and calling to her" (1:437). The speaker also joins in this *cri naturel*, finding his own humanity affirmed in this chorus: "I to cry out on pride / Who have won her favor!" (1:429). The birds in the garden supply an alternative setting to the Hall and the hill throughout the poem, suggesting that nature, by way of the passionate cry, both blesses and sanctifies a union that is unacceptable to civilized society. Tennyson extends this blessing through the cries of the flora:

> There has fallen a splendid tear
>   From the passion-flower at the gate.
> She is coming, my dove, my dear;
>   She is coming, my life, my fate;
> The red rose cries, 'She is near, she is near;'
>   And the white rose weeps, 'She is late;'
> The larkspur listens, 'I hear, I hear;'
>   And the lily whispers, 'I wait.'
>
> (1:908–915)

This description of Maud as a "dove" recalls the crying birds in the earlier passage, while the series of present-tense verbs—"weeps," "listens," "whispers"—both intensify and echo the range of emotions already expressed in the birds' passionate cries. The speaker intersperses the cries of the flora with his own mounting desire—"She is coming"—in a rhythm that further emphasizes the correspondence between humans and nature. He also speaks to the lily and the rose directly, in lines reminiscent of the birds crying and calling to Maud (1:868–887). Throughout the courtship passages, the *cris naturels* offer a different account of human-animal language, one that emphasizes the passionate relation between himself and Maud rather than the brutish behavior of Maud's social circle.

The speaker further exonerates Maud from her family's brutality by separating out the male and female lines of descent. Maud's goodness comes from her mother's side rather than from her wolfish paternity:

> And fair without, faithful within,
> Maud to him is nothing akin:
> Some peculiar mystic grace
> Made her only the child of her mother,
> And heaped the whole inherited sin
> On that huge scapegoat of the race,
> All, all upon the brother.
>
> (1:480–486)

The speaker excludes Maud from the language of brutality that characterizes her family by showing how her femininity elevates her above her aristocratic male relatives. Elsewhere she is the first woman in Christianity, an Eve before the fall in the cedar forests of Lebanon:

There is none like her, none.
Nor will be when our summers have deceased.
O, art thou sighing for Lebanon
In the long breeze that streams to thy delicious East,
Sighing for Lebanon,
Dark cedar, though thy limbs have here increased,
Upon a pastoral slope as fair,
And looking to the South, and fed
With honeyed rain and delicate air,
And haunted by the starry head
Of her whose gentle will has changed my fate,
And made my life a perfumed altar-flame;
And over whom thy darkness must have spread
With such delight as theirs of old, thy great
Forefathers of the thornless garden, there
Shadowing the snow-limbed Eve from whom she
         came.

(1:611–626)

The speaker further removes Maud from the history of evolutionary descent by linking her to an arboreal history instead, tracing her origins to a "Dark cedar" that he lovingly apostrophizes. Instead of brutes and wolves, the speaker places Maud in a setting characterized by pastoral simplicity and growth. The "limbs" of the displaced cedar blend with the "snow-limbed" Eve, implying connection and organic harmony. Eve and her descendant Maud gracefully occupy a "thornless garden" that precedes the later fall and division of society into classes. By aligning Maud with a fantasy of aboriginal feminine virtue, the speaker elevates her above the wolfish struggles of the town's reigning patriarchs.

Because the rigid, long-naturalized class divisions of the poem do not create an ideological universe in which revolution or wholesale transformation is even possible, or where the scenes of communion in the garden can be transferred to other settings, the speaker sets his sights abroad, fantasizing about the approval his and Maud's love will gain from the subjects of the empire. In the song "Go not, happy day," he imagines the moment "When the happy Yes / Falters from her lips" (579–580) and resounds across the globe:

Pass and blush the news
    Over glowing ships;

Over blowing seas
Over seas at rest,
Pass the happy news,
Blush it through the West;
Till the red man dance
By his red cedar tree,
And the red man's babe
Leap, beyond the sea.
Blush from West to East,
Blush from East to West,
Till the West is East,
Blush it through the West.
Rosy is the West,
Rosy is the South,
Roses are her cheeks,
And a rose her mouth.

(1:581–598)

The speaker blends the geography of empire with the physical features of Maud's face, imagining how the news of their love will collapse West and East and prompt the "red man" to celebrate by a cedar tree that further links him with Maud's aboriginality in the previous passage. If their union cannot be recognized at home, the speaker seems to reason, it will be recognized and celebrated by subjects abroad who, like Maud / Eve, are romantically located in pastoral, classless, and ante-political settings. Fast-paced trochees, assonance, and rhyme ("Over glowing," "Over blowing") hasten the tempo and imply the rapid spread of the news overseas. The anaphora of the eleventh, twelfth, and thirteenth lines continues this pace, but these lines also include an antimetabole that reverses the direction of the news and begins to collapse the opposition between West and East: "Blush from West to East, / Blush from East to West, / Till the West is East." The West and the South are both rose-colored at once, a resemblance that further illustrates the breakdown of geographical boundaries.

In the last two quoted lines, metonymic metaphors dissolve Maud's body into blushing parts and blend them with this geography of empire. Tennyson accomplishes this blending by linking these metonymic metaphors with the adjectival "rosy" in the preceding lines: "Roses are her cheeks, / And a rose her mouth." As Anne McClintock reminds us, such metropolitan depictions of empire often trade in abstracted images of the female body as "a geometry of sexuality held captive under the technology of imperial form."[27] Tennyson's metonymic disassembly of Maud's body seems to be a variation on this trope. Yet these lines do more than set up a boundary between center and margin: they illustrate the chauvinistic and metropolitan appropriation of empire while also breaking down the distinction between metropole and colony, imagining the blushing lands of the West, East, and South not as places to conquer but as sites of fantasied escape that absorb the forbidden sensuality of Maud's features.

The end of the courtship with Maud also brings the end of the egalitarian potential extended by the *cris naturels*. In keeping with the speaker's description of domestic class politics as submerged and disguised, Tennyson elides the scene of the speaker's slaying of Maud's brother, leaving a narrative gap in between the passage where he awaits Maud in the garden and the passage where the speaker sits "stunned and still" and rues the murder (2:2). The beginning of Book 2 dramatically foregrounds the central *cri naturel* of the poem, Maud's "passionate cry, / A cry for a brother's blood" (2:33–34). Maud's cry echoes the "shrill-edged shriek of a mother" that opens the poem and, in so doing, further suggests the correspondence between feminine virtue and suffering and a benign representation of the primordial. Indeed, the speaker understands that the cry "will ring in my heart and my ears, till I die, till I die" (2:35) much as the mother's shriek creates a "shock" on his "heart" in the opening stanzas (1:14). Later, the speaker remembers that one of the rings on the slain brother's hands was of "his mother's hair" (2:118), a lingering image that affirms the humanity of the man the speaker calls, parenthetically, a "poor worm" (2:118). Maud's passionate cry punctuates their separation and symbolizes the loss of the moments in the garden. This loss also truncates the potential communion produced by the *cris naturels* of the birds and flora.

The poem marks this transition by amplifying the theme of brutal language. The mutually constitutive relationship between a rigid British class system and the fantasy of a primordial empire intensifies in the madhouse lines that follow the murder, in which Maud's ghost urges the speaker on to a more open warfare abroad that contrasts sharply with the more hidden and "underhand" struggle at home (1:28). Now even more acutely aware in his captivity of the association between the underclass and animals, and between hereditary madness and brutality, the speaker imagines lowly beasts broadcasting his most private statements to the world at large:

> Nothing but idiot gabble!
> For the prophecy given of old
> And then not understood,
> Has come to pass as foretold;
> Not let any man think for the public good,
> But babble, merely for babble.
> For I never whispered a private affair
> Within the hearing of cat or mouse,

No, not to myself in the closet alone,
But I heard it shouted at once from the top of the house;
Everything came to be known.

(2:279–290)

The speaker again refers to animals and brutish language in order to characterize the class system as irredeemable. Any reformation of the "public good" is impossible in a realm where supposedly civilized speech is mere "idiot gabble"; even the mice are in league against him. As Tucker notes, this section demonstrates the speaker's awareness of "a breakdown between public and private discourses—a breakdown that unleashes a semiotic bedlam from which he seeks protection."[28] These lines also echo a passage early in the poem, where, living alone after the death of his mother, the speaker hears "the shrieking rush of the wainscot mouse, / And my own sad name in corners cried" (1:260–261). Likewise, the "British vermin," the rat, "lies and listens mute / In an ancient mansion's crannies and holes" (2:298–299). Much as social and economic inequality creates a submerged and "underhand" atmosphere in domestic English spaces, so too do the smallest creatures act as spies and betrayers, magnifying the speaker's suffering through their animal cries. Implicit in this domestic setting is a kind of devolution to a primal habitat, one that mirrors the family's financial collapse and that populates the house with vermin. In a reversal of the sympathetic cries of the birds and flora, these vermin amplify and distort the speaker's expressive speech.

Maud's unsettling final lines revisit the human-animal boundary by conjuring a vision of primal violence abroad that finally acts as an outlet for the intractable class tensions at home. Maud's ghost urges the speaker on to do battle in the Crimea, in an open act of warfare that will bring an apocalyptic end to the "iron tyranny" of social and economic oppression (3:20). Summoning a picture of Mars glowing "like a ruddy shield on the Lion's breast" (3:14), the speaker looks forward to a coming age when "The glory of manhood stand on his ancient height, / Nor Britain's one sole God be the millionaire: / No more shall commerce be all in all" (3:21–23). In these lines the speaker reverses the image of man's evolutionary decline he imagined in Part One, where the degradations of social and economic exploitation usher in the dinosaur-like extinction of human life. Instead, he takes solace in this redemptive vision of military violence and in the glory he will gain from fighting in the war. "I have felt with my native land, I am one with my kind" (3:58), he explains, imagining how the battle will usher in an age of plenty where the "herd" will "increase" (3:25).

With this animal imagery, *Maud* overturns accounts of brutal language by Chambers, Lyell, and other Victorian scientists. While these thinkers relegated animal speech to the lower classes, *Maud* characterizes the language of the aristocracy as barbaric. It is only abroad, in the thick of a contemporary military battle recast as a heroic primordial struggle, that the speaker imagines a return to the "ancient height" of man, and to his martial language or "battle cry" (3:35). At the same time, this brutality still festers back at home in the woods and in the Hall, in the desperate struggles of the underclasses, and in the aristocracy's lawless accumulation and hoarding of wealth. In the *Idylls*, Tennyson attempts to resolve this crisis by depicting the colonies as testing-grounds for a more democratic social order in the metropole, linking both through a romantic vision of imperial federation. In so doing, he uses the fluid lines of demarcation between human and animal language as imaginary, symbolic pathways into a more comprehensive political reform.

Imperial Federation and the Human-Animal Language Boundary

If *Maud* uses the human-animal language boundary to expose the irresolvable crisis of Victorian class relations, the *Idylls of the King* write the animal theme even larger by depicting the advent and decline of empire as a cycle of evolution from, and degeneration into, brutes. Appearing in installments from 1859–1885, Tennyson's twelve-book epic uses a range of source texts (including Sir Thomas Malory's *Morte d'Arthur*, French romances, and Celtic folklore), to tell the story of King Arthur's Round Table, a tale full of violent battles with heathens, sexual intrigue, and roaming, marauding animals.[29] The poem begins with Arthur conquering the wilderness, narrates his knights' various quests and adventures, and concludes by describing how Arthur's realm "Reels back into the beast" and collapses ("The Passing of Arthur" 26).

Tennyson's epic features many recognizably Victorian updates of the Arthurian legend. The repentant adulteress Guinevere is a type of the Victorian "fallen woman," while the constant rebellions against Arthur and his knights would have reminded many readers of the 1857 Sepoy Rebellion (after which the British government ruled India directly), and the 1865 Morant Bay Rebellion, brutally and violently suppressed by Governor John Eyre, to whose defense fund Tennyson contributed.[30] Tennyson's lush descriptions of the handsome young knights aiding each other in battle also recall the homosocial relations of empire, in which Victorian men sought escape from the pressures of conventional domesticity alongside other bachelors in the colonies.[31] A concluding commemorative poem to Queen Victoria celebrates the empire's expansion and assures the reader that the British Empire will avoid the fate of Arthur's Round Table. And Tennyson himself updates the legend in a working note where he describes the Round Table as a symbol of "liberal institutions," perhaps alluding to the liberal Victorian state and its enfranchisement of middle-class and, eventually, working-class men.[32]

Critics have long recognized how Arthur's court and its battles with the inhabitants of the surrounding wilderness represent Britain's struggles to govern its far-flung empire. Tennyson's presentation of the court as a godly center surrounded by droves of violent heathen openly expresses the poem's strain of imperialist jingoism. As Patrick Brantlinger observes, Arthur's enemies in the *Idylls* are generally unspecified and carry the generic designations of heathens or pagans, at one point located "overseas," although they are sometimes identified as Saxons or Germans and, in "Guinevere," as Celts.[33] Matthew Reynolds traces Tennyson's concerns about the growth of the Fenians in Ireland and his opposition to Home Rule, showing how anti-Irish prejudice shapes his presentation of the character Balin as an easily angered Celtic savage.[34] Linda Hughes also describes how the antecedent texts of Geoffrey and Malory depict Arthur engaged in battle with African kings while Tennyson's Arthur, by contrast, does battle with "peoples generically typed as 'heathen.'"[35]

While these imperialist overtones of the *Idylls* are well known, none of the aforementioned accounts discuss Tennyson's interest in the growing movement for imperial federation that took shape in the mid- to late-Victorian period, even though these debates about the political status of the so-called dependent colonies were crucial in shaping his thinking about the empire during the composition of the *Idylls*.[36] Politicians had raised the idea of a more formal system of representation for the colonies at Westminster earlier in the century: in 1848, for example, the radical Sir William Molesworth argued for the financial advantages of allowing the colonies to oversee their own affairs.[37] However, anxieties about colonial rebellion and the possible dissolution of the empire that followed in the wake of the Sepoy Rebellion and the Morant Bay Rebellion reignited the topic and fueled an energetic, if ultimately unsuccessful, movement for imperial federation that began in the 1870s and reached its peak in the 1880–1890s, when the Imperial Federation League campaigned to present various schemes for a united empire with some form of political representation for the colonies.[38]

One ideologically powerful aspect of the imperial federalist movement was its promise to alleviating ongoing social unrest and inequality among the reformed polity, with advocates like Sir Charles Dilke viewing the colonies as a testing-ground for new political ideas which could then be incorporated back into the metropole.[39] As Duncan Bell explains, in the minds of many imperial federalists, the "democratic nature of the colonial empire...might help to catalyze change at home. Democracy would finally be released from the shackles imposed on it by an aristocratic political system and the residues of feudalism."[40] This vision of a benevolent confederation collapsed stark distinctions between colony and metropole, imagining the colonies as sites of regeneration for a British social body long ruined by the persistent legacy of aristocratic rule and landed privilege that Tennyson had criticized in *Maud.*

Tennyson embraced the fantasy of imperial federation as a possible solution both to domestic poverty and to the uncertain political status of Britain's overseas possessions. "How strange England cannot see her true policy lies in a close union with our colonies!" Tennyson declared in 1871.[41] The following years would find him penning a letter in support of an "intimate union" between Britain and its empire that would result from the "heightening of individuality to each member"; he was also reading arguments in favor of imperial federation in *Fraser's*.[42] One such piece, "More on Great Britain Confederated," which appeared in August 1871, promised that confederation would helped to solve the ongoing problem of pauperism in England and prevent anarchic organizations of international workers from banding together in revolt. Imperial federation would have "magical" effects, creating "boundless pathways" which would enable Irish emigrants to return home and share the wealth they had earned abroad.[43] Ireland, consequently, would become the "most prosperous country on the face of the earth" and Britain would maintain its military power in the face of challenges from Germany and America.[44] Through federation, the article proclaimed, Britain would consolidate its overseas empire and eliminate the vestiges of aristocratic privilege that continued to haunt the social body.

Tennyson's epic incorporates these ideas about imperial federation through the lens of human-animal language research. The *Idylls* span the period of intense scientific and philological investigations into man's prehistory that included the publication of Darwin's *On the Origin of Species* (1859) and *The Descent of Man* (1871), Lyell's and Wedgwood's writings on primitive language, Müller's *Lectures*, and Müller's rebuttals to Darwin. These years also found Tennyson reading John Lubbock's *Prehistoric Times* (1865), breakfasting with Müller at Farringford, and visiting with the philologist Joseph Ernest Renan.[45] The century-long project of British electoral reform had an ongoing and uneasy connection to the status of Britain's overseas holdings and to the status of so-called primitive languages. As Catherine Hall has shown, the parliamentary debates that ushered in the Second Reform Act of 1867 worked to reconstitute the British social body in the context of the Fenian uprisings, the Hyde Park demonstrations, and the 1865 Morant Bay rebellion, ultimately leading the Parliament to accord greater political agency along racial lines: "Beyond the nation yet within the empire, 'white settlers' in Australia, Canada, the Cape and New Zealand were granted forms of self-government which were rejected as out of the question in India or Jamaica because the majority of the population was not white."[46] Widespread anxieties about colonial rebellion and the perceived unfitness of non-white subjects for self-government fueled hazy but powerful lines of demarcation between settler colonies in Australia, New Zealand, and Canada and the so-called dependent territories of India, Africa, and the

West Indies.[47] Such distinctions were routinely underwritten by philological distinctions between the primitive and the civilized. "Comparing the grammars and dictionaries of races at various grades of civilization," wrote Edward Tylor in *Primitive Culture* (1871), "it appears that, in the great art of speech, the educated man at this day substantially uses the language of the savage, only expanded and improved."[48]

The publication of Darwin's *On the Origin of Species*, along with an expanding fossil record and the institutional ascendancy of evolutionary biology, ethnography, and anthropology, ignited these speculations about man's linguistic past. While the excavation of human flint tools and animal bones at Brixham Cave in 1858 provided ample evidence of man's antiquity, *The Origin* would explicitly draw a parallel between the evolution of man and the evolution of language.[49] "If we possessed a perfect pedigree of mankind," Darwin wrote, "a genealogical arrangement of the races of man would offer the best classification of the various languages now spoken throughout the world."[50] As Stephen Alter has documented, Darwin drew heavily on philological research in his notebooks as he developed his ideas about common descent, drawing on philology's groupings of languages into families to formulate his "Tree of Life" that connected living and extinct species to a shared ancestor.[51] The German linguist August Schleicher further made the link between evolution and philology explicit in his *Darwinism Tested by the Science of Language* (1869), urging naturalists to focus more on the development of language, or to "the observation and application of linguistic varieties in their significance for the natural history of man."[52] For Schleicher, as for many other Victorian scientists and laymen, understanding the history of language was a key aspect of understanding man's developmental history more broadly.

Darwin's *The Descent of Man* further dissolved the human-animal language boundary by rejecting the claim that understanding articulate speech alone was a uniquely human capacity. "The habitual use of articulate language is...peculiar to man" Darwin wrote, "but he uses, in common with the lower animals, inarticulate cries to express his meaning, aided by the gestures and the movements of the muscles of the face."[53] Dogs and human infants could comprehend words and brief sentences without being able to speak words of their own (107). For Darwin, man was distinguished from animals only because he had an "almost infinitely larger power of associating together the most diversified sounds and ideas; and this obviously depends on the high development of his mental powers" (108). Even this facility of a complex association of ideas, however, did not necessarily distinguish humans from animals in clear-cut or definitive ways. Darwin used the example of animals dreaming as evidence that animals did possess some ability to connect ideas mentally even without articulate language: "a long succession of vivid and connected ideas may pass through the mind without the aid of any form of language, as we may infer from the movements of dogs during their dreams. We have, also, seen that animals are able to reason to a certain extent, manifestly without the aid of language" (110). Moreover, primeval man's development of his language-faculties owed much to the example of the animals in his habitat: "I cannot doubt that language owes its origin to the imitation and modification of various natural sounds, the voices of other animals, and man's own instinctive cries" (109). This vision of the natural world as a training ground for the development of human language collapsed the distance between man and beast by placing man directly under the influence of his gesturing, communicating animal companions.

In his *Lectures*, Müller refuted Darwin by claiming language as the definitive boundary between man and beast. "Now, however much the frontiers of the animal kingdom have been pushed forward, so that at one time the line of demarcation between animal and man seemed to depend on a mere fold in the brain," Müller declared, "there is *one* barrier which no one has yet ventured to touch—the barrier of language."[54] In a series of "Lectures on Mr. Darwin's Philosophy of Language," given at the Royal Institution in 1873 and published in *Fraser's* the same year, Müller revisited the topic of animal and human communication, insisting that language was not a fluid boundary between species, but rather the "primeval and never-ending autobiography" of a uniquely rational mankind.[55] A wistful glimpse backward into this never-ending autobiography could offer disillusioned Victorians a utopian portrait of life before the formation of modern political systems. Müller imagined the earliest primeval languages as infinitely creative, free from the stifling effects of modern nations and confederations:

> whatever the origin of language, its first tendency must have been towards an unbounded variety. To this there was, however, a natural check, which prepared from the very beginning the growth of national and literary languages. The language of the father became the language of a family; the language of a family that of a clan.... The same circumstances which give rise to the formal language of a clan, as distinguished from the dialects of families, produce, on a larger scale, the languages of a confederation of clans, of nascent colonies, of rising nationalities.[56]

Müller differed vastly from both Lyell and Trench, who saw the development of the English language as having reached a high state of achievement by the nineteenth century—an achievement commemorated in the ongoing, and widely publicized, preparations for the *NED*. Instead, Müller reversed the developmental trajectories of Darwin and Lyell, looking back to primeval languages as the creative productions of egalitarian, aboriginal utopias that eventually give way to the restrictive, power-laden, and patriarchal formations of national and colonial tongues. The history of language acted as a connecting link between civilized Western man and his primordial, ante-political past, located in a time when men roamed freely with animals and when human speech was in the earliest, most liberating stages of development. Articulate language may have been a sign of a higher civilization for Victorians like Müller, but it also marked the loss of imagined forms of human communality free from the restrictive social divisions of modernity.

In the *Idylls*, Tennyson uses this vision of a utopian linguistic past to explore imperial federation as a political model that can at once exorcize and rehabilitate the lingering feudal aristocracy. Conscious of the inequality that persisted in spite of liberal reform measures and yet wary of revolutionary outbreak in any form, Tennyson looks to colonial territories as fantasy primal spaces that offer forms of expression and democratic participation denied to Arthur's knights, servants, and women. That is, the beastly yells and language that surround the linguistic and political community of Arthur's court work, as in *Maud*, to ventilate the social conflicts repressed in Arthur's polity. But the surrounding wilderness, with its primal language, also serves as a place of greater inclusion for characters such as the savage Balin and the gossiping Vivien, both of whom are persistently associated with barbaric and unholy speech. Through their circular structure and their use of the epic wild man, the *Idylls* set up and repeatedly dissolve the boundary between human and animal language in order to explore a romantic vision of imperial federation in which the barbaric outside acts as a testing-site for ideals of democracy that, in the concluding, commemorative verses "To the Queen," are reincorporated into a reformed liberal state.

Human-Animal Language in *Idylls of the King*

The *Idylls* embrace a long epic tradition of depicting relationships between humans and nonhuman animals. In an often-quoted passage from the frame poem, first published separately as "The Epic" in 1842, Tennyson compares epic poetry to an extinct animal:

> 'Why take the style of those heroic times?
> For nature brings not back the Mastodon,
> Nor we those times; and why should any man
> Remodel models?'

("The Epic" 35–38)

In a reflexive gesture, the speaker likens the poem itself to a relic of evolutionary history, reading human achievement and oral tradition alongside cycles of animal growth and extinction. Simon Dentith observes that such "epic primitivism" reveals Tennyson's awareness of the "anachronism" of writing epics in the nineteenth century, while Tucker notes that this frame tale works to disavow epic at the same time that it prefaces the "stately archaism" of the "Morte d'Arthur."[57] The poem also signals its epic affiliations through its appeal to classical and ancient examples of the wild man and the nonhuman monster, both of which play key roles throughout the cycle. Figures of primordial monstrosity in the epic tradition are abundant, from *Gilgamesh's* Enkidu to Homer's Cyclops, but Tennyson would have needed to look no further than the story of Grendel in *Beowulf*, portions of which he had translated privately and which would go on to influence "The Epic" and "Morte d'Arthur" (1842).[58] By surrounding Arthur's realm with prowling wolves and monsters, the poem enacts and then breaks down the barriers between men and beasts. In so doing, it looks to the realm of the beast as a habitat where wayward subjects can ventilate and express their rage at the court before they are re-absorbed within its parameters.

The opening lines of "The Coming of Arthur" further develop this animal imagery. Before Arthur's arrival, Cameliard was a land of unbridled animality, "Wherein the beast was ever more and more, / But man was less and less" (11–12). In this realm of confused species relations, humans and other mammals mingle freely:

> ...wild dog, and wolf and boar and bear
> Came night and day, and rooted in the fields,
> And wallowed in the gardens of the King.
> And ever and anon the wolf would steal
> The children and devour, but now and then,
> Her own brood lost or dead, lent her fierce teat
> To human sucklings; and the children, housed
> In her foul den, there at their meat would growl,
> And mock their foster-mother on four feet,
> Till, straightened, they grew up to wolf-like men,
> Worse than the wolves.
>
> ("The Coming of Arthur" 26–33)

Alliteration and assonance in the first line bring the different nonhuman animals into relationship with one another while the end-stopped third line suggests a momentary barrier between the wolves and dogs and the human boundary they seek to cross. The next eleven lines stage a metamorphosis from devouring to nursing, mingling humans and animals in one domestic family. Language indexes this shift as the growling and mocking "human sucklings" begin their slow transformation into "wolf-like men." While Darwin asserts that humans learned communication from imitating their natural environment, Tennyson shows this imitation taking place within that most sacred of bonds, that of the mother and child.[59]

Throughout the *Idylls* Tennyson blends his reading in human-animal language research with anecdotal observations gleaned from watching his own pets. His son's annotations to "Gareth and Lynette" give a note or letter by Tennyson that describes a scuffle between his dogs:

> When we lived in Kent we had two large dogs, one a large white one, an uneducated ruffian always chained to an apple tree, the other a larger black one and much more of a gentleman. One day when I was passing with this last too near the tree, the white one seized hold of him and tore his ear. Then followed a duel. I separated them with some difficulty and then took my dark friend on a walk of some six miles. All the way out and half the way back he growled and swore to himself about every five minutes.[60]

This playful passage blends the language of class—the ruffian and the gentleman—with the language of animality, reading human social organization into the animal kingdom. Tennyson anthropomorphizes his own family pet in the memorable image of the dog who "growled and swore to himself."

In "Gareth and Lynette," however, Tennyson flips the anthropomorphic transformation by assigning the behavior not to a dog but to a human. Kay watches jealously as his kitchen-hand and social subordinate, Gareth, departs for a knightly quest in splendid armor:

> So Gareth past with joy; but as the cur
> Pluckt from the cur he fights with, ere his cause
> Be cooled by fighting, follows, being named,
> His owner, but remembers all, and growls
> Remembering, so Sir Kay beside the door
> Muttered in scorn of Gareth whom he used
> To harry and hustle.

> (686–692)

The six-line epic simile intervenes between Sir Kay and his nemesis, re-enacting the beastly struggle in the context of rank: Kay's anger stems from the unexpected social ascent of a subordinate worker he is fully accustomed to "harry and hustle." The cur who "growls / Remembering" recalls the growling wolves on their "four feet" from "The Coming of Arthur" and again uses animal communication to index the shift to the human, as the canine grumble of the epic simile changes into the muttering of Sir Kay.

The poem builds upon this connection between brutality and social status in "Geraint and Enid," where Edyrn credits his elevation in status with his ability to suppress his animal impulses. Once beset with violent impulses and endless quests for revenge, Edyrn describes how a period of rest in Arthur's civilizing court has helped transform him from an animal to a man:

> first as sullen as a beast new-caged,
> And waiting to be treated like a wolf,
> Because I knew my deeds were known, I found,
> Instead of scornful pity or pure scorn,
> Such fine reserve and noble reticence,
> Manners so kind, yet stately, such a grace
> Of tenderest courtesy, that I began
> To glance behind me at my former life,
> And find that it had been the wolf's indeed:
> And oft I talked with Dubric, the high saint,
> Who, with the mild heat of holy oratory,
> Subdued me somewhat to that gentleness,
> Which, when it weds with manhood, makes a man.
>
> (855–867)

Lupine and human behaviors appear as stages in the same life span, with the blurry antimetabole of beastly emotions ("scornful pity or pure scorn") presented as a stage in Edyrn's "former life." This reform of manners accompanies a reform of language, as the "mild heat" of Dubric's words subdues Edyrn's wolfish speech. This manly gentility, so different from the "simper" of the men's voices in *Maud*, elevates language as a vehicle of biological and spiritual transformation.

This constant presence of the animal threatens the stability of the court and its governing language. Reynolds writes that Arthur's court is a center of linguistic security, a "realm of semantic, etymological, and rhythmical solidity within a world of linguistic chaos."[61] Yet this security is always tenuous and contested. As Vivien explains,

>   this rhyme
> Is like the fair pearl-necklace of the Queen,
> That burst in dancing, and the pearls were spilt;
> Some lost, some stolen, some as relics kept.
> But nevermore the same two sister pearls
> Ran down the silken thread to kiss each other
> On her white neck – so is it with this rhyme:
> It lives dispersedly in many hands,
> And every minstrel sings it differently;

Yet there is one true line, the pearl of pearls:
"Man dreams of Fame while woman wakes to love."
                              ("Merlin and Vivien" 448–458)

The device of the epic simile does present the court as a centralized lin-
guistic order, with meaning radiating outward from the Queen's person,
metonymically eroticized in the image of the necklace around her "white
neck." Yet the language of this court is also scattered throughout the
realm in the contrasting metonymic dispersal of the "many hands" who
speak and sing the language differently. The spilt pearls kept as "relics"
suggest the eventual death and memorialization of the court, anticipat-
ing the relic of Excalibur in the epic's closing lines, while the adage that
"woman wakes to love" slyly alludes to Guinevere's infidelity. Vivien's
invocation of the "one true line," too, is ironic, as Vivien's language of
rumor functions throughout the *Idylls* as the dark other of the court's
sanctified speech. Her slander works to tear apart the linguistic unity
Arthur and his men have established as she

                                        let her tongue
Rage like a fire among the noblest names,
Polluting, and imputing her whole self,
Defaming and defacing, till she left
Not even Lancelot brace, nor Galahad clean.
                              ("Merlin and Vivien" 798–803)

These lines enact a dramatic shift from pearls to fire, from the erotic
metonym of the Queen's neck to the blazing metonym of Vivien's tongue.
A string of present participles in the second and third lines accelerate her
rumors' destruction, culminating in a vision of language in ruins.
    Visual symbols of evolutionary perfectibility continue the pretense of
courtly civilization. The zones of sculpture that adorn the hall set out
four key stages in human existence, from the animal to the human:

And four great zones of sculpture, set betwixt
With many a mystic symbol, gird the hall:
And in the lowest beasts are slaying men,
And in the second men are slaying beasts,
And on the third are warriors, perfect men,
And on the fourth are men with growing wings,
And over all one statue in the mold
Of Arthur...

                              ("The Holy Grail" 232–239)

Of this passage Hallam Tennyson records that "The four zones represent
human progress: the savage state of society; the state where man lords

it over the beast; the full development of man; the progress towards spiritual ideals."[62] The tidy antimetabole of the lines, "And in the lowest beasts are slaying men, / And in the second men are slaying beasts" implies the fluid boundary between the human and the brute in primordial times, before the emergence of "warriors" or "perfect men." The zones, swelling toward the crowned figure of Arthur, create a narrative of evolutionary anthropocentrism that places the development of man as a crowning achievement of nature. At the same time, it reminds the reader of the potentially recursive form of Arthur's polity, born from a wilderness and, hence, at any moment, ready to collapse back into a wilderness.

"Balin and Balan" effects this collapse through the uneasy transfer of power from the court to the wilds outside. Published in 1885, "Balin and Balan" borrows very little from Malory, and is composed mostly of Tennyson's original material.[63] It is also one of the books that engages most heavily with the human-animal language theme. If Edyrn's story perpetuates the myth of middle-class self-making as a real possibility in Arthur's royal court, "Balin and Balan" undermines this myth by suggesting that those born into a state of racial otherness—here coded as unregenerate savagery—are prevented from taking part in a reformist ideology of self-help and social elevation won through hard work and class mobility. At the same time, "Balin and Balan" expresses Tennyson's romanticized vision of imperial federation in which dissent is ventilated in the colony.

Balin's associations with animal language place him firmly within the terrain of a primordial wilderness. Exiled from Arthur's court for his fits of temper, Balin is a "Savage among the savage woods" (479) who tries to achieve the courtesies of Lancelot but who cannot will himself into civilization and self-mastery. While Lancelot's courtesies are "Born with the blood, not learnable, divine, / Beyond *my* reach" (170–172), Balin's temperament is the product of a hereditary madness:

> My father hath begotten me in his wrath.
> I suffer from things before me, know,
> Learn nothing; am not worthy to be knight;
> A churl, a clown!
>
> (278–281)

Balin believes he is destined to repeat his father's madness in his acts of violence, much as the speaker in *Maud* wonders if his own ravings descend from his patrimony. By introducing the figures of two brothers, one born wild, the other able to reform his behavior, Tennyson destabilizes the evolutionary hierarchy and illustrates how a politics of self-making fails subjects who are born into states of social and racial otherness.

"Balin and Balan" also incorporates Müller's distinction between the language of affect and the language of abstraction as it pertained to human-animal communication. In his "Lectures on Mr. Darwin's Philosophy of Language," given at the Royal Institution in 1873 and published in *Fraser's* the same year, Müller distinguishes between what he terms "Emotional" and "Rational" language. In the second of his "Lectures," he defines emotional language as "showing by outward signs what we feel" in connection to memories of pleasure and pain, whereas rational language is "the faculty of forming and handling general concepts" through articulate language.[64] All beings share emotional language, whereas only man can discuss abstract concepts: "Interjections, for instance...are emotional language, and they are used by beasts as well as by men, particularly by a man in a passion, or on a low scale of civilisation. But there is no language, even among the lowest savages, in which the vast majority of words is not rational" (676–77). Drawing on well-worn cultural stereotypes of non-European races as quick to anger, Müller stops short of linking speakers of "low civilization" to brutes, maintaining the existence of rational and abstract concepts as unique to man only.

"Balin and Balan" challenges this assertion. Unlike Edyrn, who reforms his wolfish behavior into human spiritual dignity, Balin declines from courtesy to beastliness and, in so doing, unravels the neat stages of progression presented in the statue garden, where men slay beasts before they turn into warriors. Instead, Balin's ability to pass from the woods to the court suggests the porousness of the boundaries of Arthur's court, across which the elements of animality cross and re-cross. When he overhears Vivien's toxic gossip about Guinevere's infidelity, Balin forgets the self-restraint he has desperately tried to learn from Arthur's men and lapses into an animal rage:

> He ground his teeth together, sprang with a yell,
> Tore from the branch, and cast on earth, the shield,
> Drove his mailed heel athwart the royal crown,
> Stampt all into defacement, hurled it from him
> Among the forest weeds, and cursed the tale,
> The told-of, and the teller.
>   That weird yell,
> Unearthlier than all shriek of bird or beast,
> Thrilled through the woods.

(530–537)

A series of strong transitive verbs ("ground," "sprang," "Tore," "cast," "Drove," "Stampt," "hurled"), in parallel structures throughout and divided by medial caesuras in the first, second, and fourth lines, collectively work to intensify Balin's relentless sense of anger. The destruction of the courtly relics, the shield and the crown, speaks further to the impermanence and unjustness of the political order they represent. His "weird yell" outdoes the language of birds and beasts in its strange wildness, but Tennyson's diction—the sonic image of the noise that "Thrilled" through the wilderness—also suggests an enticing, collective, and cathartic release from the courtly hierarchy, recalling the *cris naturels* of the garden in *Maud*. As the "brother beast" both to his more civilized brother and to the animals outside, Balin is both primitive and coeval, collapsing distinctions between the human and the animal and the civilized and the savage. His tragic death in the woods—both slaying and being slain by his own brother—acts as a powerful reminder of the violent presence of those subjects who are subject to Arthur's laws but who take no substantial part in governance. By sending Balin to his final death in the primal wilderness, the *Idylls* present revolutionary outbreak as a dangerous force that must be banished beyond the realm in order to benefit and protect those who are inside. The woods act as a primal space through which to ventilate, express, and ultimately contain the lawless unrest of those subjects still left unenfranchised by the project of reform.

"Balin and Balan" anticipates the collapse of the social order in "The Passing of Arthur," which returns to the primordial wilderness that existed before Arthur's reign. The final battle takes place in a coastal landscape where "fragments of forgotten peoples dwelt" and where the mists make it impossible to determine social and political ranks and relationships (84):

> and even on Arthur fell
> Confusion, since he saw not whom he fought.
> For friend and foe were shadows in the mist,
> And friend slew friend not knowing whom he slew.
>
> (98–101)

Much as Balan slays his own brother in the wilderness, the men slay each other without regard to their normal relationships of solidarity and affiliation, collapsing the social order in their violence. The brotherly relationship in the earlier fight stands in as a proxy for the larger tensions of the realm, artificially split between court and wilderness and only tenuously unified through a political system in which the majority of its subjects are disenfranchised.

As if to reassure the reader that such primitive scenes of lawlessness are long vanished, the commemorative "To the Queen" concludes that such times of "war" and "wantonness" are over by looking to Britain's gradualist agenda for change (44):

> –if our slowly-grown
> And crowned Republic's crowning common-sense,
> That saved her many times, not fail – their fears

Are morning shadows huger than the shapes
That cast them, not those gloomier which forego
The darkness of that battle in the West,
Where all of high and holy dies away.

(60–66)

Tennyson's political modifiers, the "slowly-grown," "common-sense" attributes of the modern Republic, insist that a liberal sensibility of gradualism and rational debate will forestall the paradoxes and injustices that destabilized Arthur's fictional realm. Yet this modern Republic is still "crowned" in ways that recall its feudal inheritance, and its status and power are still built on a vision of martial valor, or the "roar" of the battle at Waterloo that left England powerful enough to lord over the "silent cry" of the many subjects of its empire (20, 10). These lines recall the "monstrous eft" of *Maud* who, believing himself part of the "crowning race," nevertheless stares down his inexorable decline. Like "By an Evolutionist," "To the Queen" invokes a vision of rebel subjects put down by more powerful voices, and yet these more powerful voices gain their force from the same cries that the court disavows. The old order that perishes in the last battle of the West acts as an imaginary outlet that will redeem Britain from its "lust for gold" and from the groaning figure of "Labour" (54–55). England's "slowly grown" republic looks to overseas violence and primal habitats as places both to acknowledge and to confine ongoing social unrest. These primal spaces act as confederated lands that can ventilate and test out unstable ideals of democracy and self-making while preserving the vestiges of feudal authority in the metropole.

Throughout this chapter, I have argued that Tennyson's use of the human-animal language boundary mounts a challenge to the liberal belief in the growth of the British Empire as an outcome of scientific and evolutionary progress. Sound patterns, repetitions, poetic compression, metonyms, and the epic trope of the wild man continuously upset the poem's imperial mission. Balin's climactic "weird yell" reminds us of the role human-animal language debates played in the story of evolution. In many prominent philological studies and debates, the boundary between man and beast shifted again and again as scientists, authors, and lay readers contemplated the supposed difference between higher and lower beings, and, by extension, between who was best suited to rule and who was best suited to be ruled. Tennyson's poem takes part in this dehumanizing vision of human subjects as half-beasts, almost reassuring itself and its readers, in the closing dedication to Queen Victoria, that such violent thinking is a mere footnote in the grand future of the imperial realm. Yet the *Idylls* also expose the human costs of thinking in this way. In so doing, they subtly challenge the use of the human-animal kingdom as a model for political domination. For all of its overt patriotism, Tennyson's epic also undermines a vision of liberal empire as an orderly seat of governance, surrounded by subjects who yield to its rational and benevolent language, a language built on false distinctions between the brutal and the evolved, the emotional and the rational, between those unsuited to sovereignty and those destined to rule. In the *Idylls,* as in *Maud,* these false distinctions circulate, and ultimately collapse, under the disruptive sign of the speaking animal.

While Tennyson's work looks to the possibility of colonial federation as a means of further securing and reforming the polity, Hardy's poetry looks to the provincial settings and dialectal language of Wessex to register his ambivalence toward the Third Reform Act. The 1884–1885 Reform and Redistribution Acts would, in effect, extend their geographic reach beyond the urban, working-class electorate in order to enfranchise rural laboring men. Their passage coincided with the release of the first fascicle of the *NED,* which had, over the previous twenty years, sparked widespread debates in philological and public circles about the role of rural dialects in relationship to the national community. Presented to the public with a "Preface" that explained how dialectal words moved slowly into the mainstream lexicon, the *NED* and the Third Reform Act both suggested that the provinces were becoming incorporated within the broader parameters of the nation. However, Hardy's Wessex poetry resists this notion of the provincial districts as safe havens from industrial capitalism and global war and, in so doing, works to localize parts of Britain at a moment of intense national consolidation.

Notes

1 "By an Evolutionist." *The Poems of Tennyson,* ed. Christopher Ricks (Berkeley: University of California Press, 1987), 3: 202. All Tennyson poems in this chapter are cited to Ricks' three-volume edition and will be given by line number in parentheses within the text. Citations to the *Idylls* will be given by book title as well.

2 My thanks go to Sarah Perrier for her insights on the complex meter of this poem.

3 There is a vast literature on Tennyson's relationship to the Victorian sciences. See, for example, Dean, *Tennyson and Geology,* Henchman, "The Globe we Groan in," 29–45, and Holmes, *Darwin's Bards,* 59–74 and 229–256. Holmes also provides a helpful overview of Tennyson's critical reception as a poet of science in "The Poet of Science," 655–678. Matthew Margini reads the *Idylls* and its many animal references as a posthumanist challenge to man's evolutionary achievement; what I am stressing is that the poem's human-animal boundaries are relentlessly constructed along the axis of articulate language. See "The Beast with the Broken Lance," 171–192. For a formalist reading that stresses how the poem's animals symbolize a dramatic fall from civilization into brute sensuality see Edward Engelberg, "The Beast Image in *Idylls of the King,*" 287–292.

4 Hair provides a helpful and in-depth study of Tennyson's familiarity with the language-theories of Trench and Whewell; the human-animal language boundary, however, does not figure into his analysis. See *Tennyson's Language*. On the intersection of geology and language-theory in Tennyson's work see Armstrong's *Victorian Poetry: Poetry, Poetics, and Politics*, 247–278 and Geric, "Tennyson's *Maud* (1855) and the 'unmeaning of names': Geology, Language Theory, and Dialogics," 37–62. Geric explores this intersection at greater length in her monograph, *Tennyson and Geology: Poetry and Poetics*. For a recent analysis of the speaking animal in children's literature see Jessica Straley, *Evolution and Imagination in Victorian Children's Literature*.

5 See, for example, Brantlinger, *Victorian Literature and Postcolonial Studies*, Kiernan, "Tennyson, King Arthur, and Imperialism," and Sherwood, *Tennyson and the Fabrication of Englishness*.

6 Meynell, "Some Thoughts of a Reader of Tennyson," 7.

7 For general histories of the Crimean War see, for example, Ponting, *The Crimean War* and Rath, *The Crimean War in Imperial Context*. Stefanie Markovits reads Maud's ballad as a figurative erasure and silencing of Tennyson's "The Charge of the Light Brigade," the other of his two Crimean War poems. See *The Crimean War in the British Imagination*, 148–167.

8 As a dramatic poem from the perspective of a troubled speaker, *Maud* does not, of course, necessarily represent the political views of Tennyson himself. However, the poem's figurative use of animal language does allow the reader license to interrogate the class system.

9 For language's relationship to race in the nineteenth century see Olender, *The Languages of Paradise* and Alter, *Darwinism and the Linguistic Image*.

10 Ferguson, *Language, Science and Popular Fiction*, 2, Abberley, "Race and Species Essentialism," 45. For an account of the human-animal language boundary in the history of science see Radick, *The Simian Tongue*.

11 Beer discusses Lord Monboddo's elaboration of the orangutan theory and its legacy to the Victorians in *Open Fields*, 98–99.

12 Lyell, *Principles of Geology*, 2: 15.

13 Ibid., 2: 17.

14 Ibid., 2: 22.

15 Trench, *On the Study of Words*, 15–16.

16 Chambers, *Vestiges*, ed. James Secord (Chicago: University of Chicago Press, 1994), 303–304. Hereafter all citations in this chapter are to this edition of *Vestiges* and will be given in parentheses within the text.

17 See Purton and Page's discussion of Tennyson and democracy in the *Palgrave Literary Dictionary*, 59–60.

18 Arnold, *Culture and Anarchy*, 76.

19 These earlier draft lines are not numbered in Ricks and are given in his notes to *Maud* in *Poems*, 2: 525. I cite them by page number and by the letter of the note.

20 Blair, *Lectures on Rhetoric and Belles Lettres*, 56. See also Rousseau, *Essay on the Origin of Languages*, 5–74.

21 Aarsleff, "The Tradition of Condillac," in *From Locke to Saussure*, 146–209.

22 Hair, *Tennyson's Language*, 125–126.

23 Blair, *Lectures on Rhetoric and Belles Lettres*, 58–59.

24 Ibid., 59.

25 See Ricks's note to line 18 in *Poems*, 2: 370. See also Hair's discussion of these lines in *Tennyson's Language*, 124–125.

26 Hair, *Tennyson's Language*, 126.

27 McClintock, *Imperial Leather*, 4.

28 Tucker, *Tennyson and the Doom of Romanticism*, 427.
29 See Ricks, *Poems*, 3: 667 for source notes. These are based on Hallam Tennyson's notes on his father. See also David Staines, *Tennyson's Camelot*.
30 Hallam Tennyson, *Alfred Lord Tennyson*, 2: 40–41.
31 See John Tosh, *A Man's Place: Masculinity and the Middle-Class Home in Victorian England*.
32 See Hallam Tennyson, *Memoir*, 2: 123 and Ricks's headnote in *Poems*, 3: 668.
33 Brantlinger, *Victorian Literature and Postcolonial Studies*, 117. See also Brantlinger's discussion of Tennyson's "Ulysses" in *Rule of Darkness*, 35–37, Kiernan, "Tennyson, King Arthur, and Imperialism," 126–148, and Sherwood, *Tennyson and the Fabrication of Englishness*.
34 Reynolds, *Realms of Verse 1830–1870*, 258–265. For Tennyson's views of Ireland in his late poetry, including "Locksley Hall Sixty Years After," see Bevis, "Tennyson, Ireland, and 'The Powers of Speech,'" 345–364.
35 Hughes, "Come Again, and Thrice as Fair," 60. There is a large body of excellent scholarship on Tennyson's relationship to classical philology and textual studies. As McKelvy and LaPorte have both demonstrated, the *Idylls'* use of the Arthurian legend replicates the fascination with textual recovery and emendation inspired by the Higher Criticism. Taking its cue from debates about the authorship and composition of the Homeric epics, the Higher Criticism posited the Bible as a variable, shifting text with gaps and revisions like any other text. See McKelvy, "Much Better Burnt: Reading Arthur's Return by the Light of Troy," 31–50 and LaPorte, *Victorian Poets and the Changing Bible*, 67–110. Sherwood locates the inspiration for the *Idylls* in Victorian Anglo-Saxonism in her *Tennyson and the Fabrication of Englishness*, 103–136. In "The Epic" (1842), the frame tale precursor to the *Idylls*, Tennyson introduces the Arthurian legend as a textual relic with "faint Homeric echoes" (39), and the *Idylls* themselves draw heavily on early texts such as Sir Thomas Malory's *Le Morte d'Arthur* (1485) and the medieval Welsh stories that make up the *Mabinogion*. Tennyson's source materials are detailed in David Staines, *Tennyson's Camelot*. Tennyson's Arthurian legends attempt to construct, from these diverse materials, what Tucker has called a "national dreamwork" of cultural identity based in the textual past in his *Tennyson and the Doom of Romanticism*, 391. What I am emphasizing is that contemporary scientific debates about primal man and language-origins were equally important to the *Idylls*, and that these debates look beyond conceptions of a national past rooted in a reconstructed Arthurian tradition to an evolutionary history not recoverable by a textual record. See also Annmarie Drury's *Translation as Transformation in Victorian Poetry*, 57–99 on Tennyson's "troubled" adaptation of the Welsh story he encountered in Guest's *Mabinogion* (58).
36 Sherwood does acknowledge Tennyson's interest in imperial federation but does not discuss it at length. See *Tennyson and the Fabrication of Englishness*, 165.
37 See Evans, *The Forging of the Modern State*, 427–428.
38 Bell, *The Idea of Greater Britain*, 12. See also Burgess, "Imperial Federation," 60–80.
39 Bell, *The Idea of Greater Britain*, 55.
40 Ibid., 55–56.
41 Hallam Tennyson, *Memoir*, 2: 101.
42 Ibid, p. 223, n. 1 and 2: 109.
43 "More on Great Britain Confederated," 249.

44 Ibid., p. 249.
45 For Tennyson's acquaintance with Darwin and his ideas see Hallam Tennyson, *Alfred Lord Tennyson*, 2: 57–58; for his reading of Lubbock see 2: 32; for his acquaintance with Müller see 1: 460 and also 1: 384.
46 Catherine Hall, "The Nation within and without," 183.
47 Bell, "Empire and Imperialism," 872–873. Bell observes that the difference between colonial dependencies and colonial dominions was often slippery and hard to discern.
48 Tylor, *Primitive Culture*, 145.
49 Van Riper discusses the Brixham Cave excavation in *Men among the Mammoths*.
50 Darwin, *On the Origin of Species*, 370.
51 Alter, *Darwinism and the Linguistic Image*, 20.
52 Schleicher, *Darwinism Tested by the Science of Language*, 17–18.
53 Darwin, *The Descent of Man*, eds. James Moore and Adrian Desmond (New York: Penguin, 2004), 107. Hereafter all citations will be to this edition and will be given in parentheses within the text.
54 Müller, *Lectures*, 13.
55 Müller, "Lectures on Mr. Darwin's Philosophy of Language," May 1873, 529.
56 Müller, *Lectures*, 54–55.
57 Dentith, *Epic and Empire*, 76 and Tucker, *Epic*, 319.
58 See McKelvy, "Much Better Burnt," 40–43 for *Beowulf's* influence on Tennyson's use of the trope of the "fire-damaged epic text" (42).
59 Tennyson's late-Victorian readers were quick to link his work to anthropological research on supposed cases of children raised by wolves. Both Harold Littledale's *Essays on Lord Tennyson's Idylls of the King* (1893) and Hallam Tennyson's edited Eversley Edition of the *Idylls* (1908), for example, direct readers to what Littledale calls the "indubitable case" of a child raised by wolves in India described in the *Journal of the Anthropological Society of Bombay*. Both Littledale and Hallam Tennyson refer to the first volume of the *Journal of the Anthropological Society of Bombay*, but I am unable to find any references to children raised by wolves in this volume. See Tennyson, *Idylls of the King*, edited by Arthur Hallam, 455, n.5, and Littledale, *Essays on Lord Tennyson's Idylls of the King*, 65, n.2. Littledale also cites the legends of wolf children in texts from Greek, Roman, French, English, Teutonic, Norman, and Breton traditions.
60 See Tennyson, *Idylls of the King*, edited by Arthur Hallam, 463n.
61 Reynolds, *Realms of Verse*, 269.
62 Tennyson, *Idylls of the King*, ed. by Arthur Hallam, 493n287.
63 See the headnote to "Balin and Balan" in Ricks's *Poems*, 3: 787.
64 Müller, "Lectures on Mr. Darwin's Philosophy of Language," June 1873, 674–675.

4   To "obliterate his local colour"

Thomas Hardy's "Provincial" Poetry and the Reform Act of 1884

So far, this book has studied how poets blended new ideas about language with the materials of poetic form to negotiate the major reforms of 1832 and 1867. In this last chapter, I demonstrate how Hardy's *Wessex Poems* (1898) and *Poems of the Past and Present* (1901) challenge the metropolitan appropriation of rural speechways into a unified vision of the nation that followed the passage of the 1884 Reform Act. Drawing on philological and popular accounts of rural speechways and the newly enfranchised figure of "Hodge," Hardy's poetry insists on the distinct local rootedness of dialects and challenges a contemporary body of research, by Philological Society members Murray, Frederick Elworthy, and others, that tended to romanticize rural language and trace the flow of regionalisms from the rural margins to the metropolitan mainstream. As Taylor has shown, Hardy's knowledge of so-called provincial language was wide-ranging, encompassing editorial work on William Barnes's dialect poetry, personal correspondence with Murray, and eloquent defenses of his rendering of dialect in the periodical press and in his prefaces to his novels.[1] However, his poetry also works to maintain distinctions between town and country and between rural and metropolitan speechways, at once providing a glimpse into dialectal language and showing the disastrous consequences of its absorption into a national tongue. Through private depictions of lovers' speech, exchanges between dialect-speakers and engaged listeners, and through images of speaking phantoms, Hardy's poetry challenges contemporary appeals to the coherent nation-state, an entity that, in the late-Victorian period, was imagined to be both politically and linguistically circumscribed.

Hardy's use of diction also challenges accounts of rural speech that emphasized its supposed quaintness and authenticity. Elworthy, for example, maintained that it was possible to retrieve a singular, nostalgic, national past through the study of dialects. By contrast, Hardy uses language in his poems to depict multiple, complicated pasts, to reveal histories always in excess of the single word or the simple meaning. As Taylor writes, "Hardy's poems allegorize the search for an origin which by the nature of language can never be found."[2] This is because his work is "controlled by a past which he cannot know and his words derive from ancient words whose meaning he cannot penetrate."[3] Hardy is well aware that words bear their histories, but his attention to both the past and present meanings of words allows him to undermine Elworthy's idea that the past is stable, consistent, and available for nostalgic retrieval.

Hardy's resistance to the Philological Society's image of a nationally unified whole anticipates later critical efforts to "provincialize" Europe, in that his poetry invites an understanding of nation-states like Victorian Britain as imaginary constructions rather than integrated totalities.[4] While the Philological Society's *NED* project was by no means an exclusively insular or nationalist production, it did promote a vision of a linguistically unified nation bolstered by the generative influences of the provinces.[5] Hardy's poetry resists philology's incorporation of rural regions into a unified vision of the polity. Instead, he shows how the provinces have their own distinct habits and relationships to language, and how these provinces, therefore, cannot act as sanctuaries for a national identity he felt was becoming increasingly treacherous as part of a larger quest to expand and defend Britain's overseas empire. His poetry thus registers the impossible contradiction of reconciling democratic reform to the declining rural districts and to the theater of global military conflict in the late-Victorian and Edwardian periods.

Dialectology and the Third Reform Act

In late-Victorian Britain, the subject of regional dialects and the imagined dissolution of the boundary between town and country converged in a single year, 1884, which saw both the passage of the Third Reform Act and the release of the first fascicle of the *NED*, later the *OED* (1888–1928). Both of these events worked to incorporate the rural districts into the national community: while the *NED* included many so-called provincial and dialectal words, the Representation of the People Act of 1884 and the Redistribution Act of 1885 enfranchised rural male laborers by extending the vote to all rate-paying male householders in the boroughs and the counties.[6] The Third Reform Act was a decided shift away from the elite notion of one's fitness for the franchise and toward a general understanding of voting as a natural right for those who were recognized as citizens.[7] It was also, in Martin Pugh's formulation, a symptom of "the changing orientation of politics from the local to the national level, and from community to class" that continued the effacement of local allegiance that the decline of agricultural prices after 1875 had already started.[8] The philological interest in rural speechways and regionalisms came to prominence just as allegiances to local and rural politics were on the decline. Hardy was at the forefront of this transformation; as Taylor has demonstrated, Hardy consulted the *OED* frequently and had his own poems and novels quoted 1,436 times.[9] *Wessex Poems* and *Poems of the Past and Present* appeared in the aftermath of a political shift that saw a more general recognition of rural male laborers' right to the franchise, a shift symbolically paralleled in the dictionary's inclusion of non-standard dialectal words and phrases in the national lexicon.

Hardy's resistance to this vision of a linguistically unified national community stems from his skepticism that electoral reform would ever bring material gains for the rural working classes. As he argues throughout "The Dorsetshire Labourer" (1883), agricultural workers would gain greater benefits from maintaining their historical ties to the land, not through any scheme that would contribute to the dissolution of the town-country divide. Responding to *Contemporary Review* editor Percy Bunting's request for an article about the rural electorate in October 1883, Hardy observes that "there seems very little to say about them as voters—the franchise being a subject to which the labourers as a body have (as far as I see) given no thought at all."[10] This general sense of rural detachment from parliamentary politics exists because the rural laborer's real concern is the instability of his lodging, his precarious employment, and his estrangement from the land, rather than his participation in the national franchise: "It is obvious that there is no remedy for this growing dis-association with localities—this complete reversal of the old condition of things—but some system by which he could have a personal interest in a particular piece of land."[11] In Hardy's view, the improvement of the conditions of working laborers is only possible through an intensification of locality and renewed ties to agriculture and place, ties symbolically preserved by the maintenance of traditional speechways. Where the Philological Society envisioned a salutary dissolution of the boundary between town and country, Hardy saw a disastrous appropriation of rural life into the urbanizing, metropolitan nation.

Hardy develops this claim further in his short speech "Dorset in London," (1908), published in the yearbook of *The Society of Dorset Men in London*. In this piece, he observes that country accents had grown fashionable. The last fifty years, he asserts, had seen an "almost total disregard of provincialism" in metropolitan social circles.[12] While in previous times a rural visitor to London would do his best to disguise his rural accent or "obliterate his local colour" in an effort to fit in with fellow Londoners, now the city had become a "a huge menagerie, and at what are called the best houses visitors hear with no surprise twangs and burrs and idioms from every point on the compass."[13] The end result of this assimilation, Hardy comically predicts, will be a reversal of the century-long migration from country to town. Instead, London cosmopolites will descend upon the shires in search of new dialects:

> Who knows that country accents and words may not some day be affected by smart society men in Town, like the newest pattern in waistcoats, and members of fashionable clubs go down to the shires

with week-end tickets, to get a little private practice? Unless, on the other hand, all local differences become obliterated before that date by the amalgamating effect of perpetual intercourse arising out of endless facilities for travel.[14]

Hardy describes a reverse migration of metropolitan "society men" to the regional shires. Such class tourism contributes to the flattening-out of regional distinctiveness through the "perpetual intercourse" that Hardy describes as a by-product of global traffic. Hardy's wry prediction takes aim at perceptions of rural areas as sources of regeneration and authenticity for world-weary city dwellers.

As Hardy himself notes, the previous decades had seen the study of non-standard speech rise to a topic of serious scholarly and even popular attention. While a steady market for prescriptive grammar manuals and pronunciation guides for those wishing to speak and pronounce English with a metropolitan accent continued to flourish throughout the period, the founding of the English Dialect Society in 1873, and the publication of Alexander J. Ellis's *The Existing Phonology of English Dialects* (1889) and Joseph Wright's six-volume *English Dialect Dictionary (EDD)* (1898–1905) helped assure that non-standard speech was the ongoing subject of scholarly and popular attention.[15] The Philological Society's plans for the *NED*, too, had explicitly broadcast the Society's commitment to provincial language. Over a series of meetings from 1859 to 1860 the *NED's* planners, among them Trench, Furnivall, and Herbert Coleridge, declared their aims to publish "every word in the language for which sufficient authority, whether printed or oral, can be adduced."[16] This would include "Provincial" and "Local" words "where their existence can be vouched for" by evidence.[17]

In practice, this inclusion of provincial vocabulary often, of course, resulted in a nostalgic presentation of the rural districts as sites of verbal authenticity and havens untouched by the displacements of modernity. As K.M. Peyt writes, most dialectologists of the period "assumed that the only worthy object of study is 'genuine' or 'pure' dialect—in other words, forms of speech which are a regular development from some earlier stage of the language, as far as possible unaffected by the corrupting influence of Standard English."[18] For example, Derwent Coleridge challenges the necessity for printed records as authorities for the dictionary, arguing that these would displace the authentic oral forms of provincial speech, "with what force will you shut the door against the genuine independent remains...of the ancient spoken language of the country, still heard, in spite of railroads and national schools, in our remoter and more secluded hamlets."[19]

Dialects, for Coleridge, are not the corrupted versions of a Standard English but rather the fragments of a genuine and authentic language of the past, one in danger of vanishing under the regulatory influence of the national schools.

Extending this presentation of rural authenticity, Elworthy's "Dialect of West Somerset," which appeared in the 1875–1876 *Transactions of the Philological Society,* looks to a rural peasantry unaffected by modern life. Like Coleridge, Elworthy imagines the rural districts as anti-modern spaces, assuring his listeners that "railways, telegraphs, machinery, and steam" had yet to eradicate the last dialectal traces of "Briton, Saxon, and Dane."[20] What is interesting about Elworthy's account is the way he describes the role of the philological researcher, the lexicographical tourist who, like Hardy's London urbanites, travels to the provinces in search of authentic vocabulary. The traveling philologist, Elworthy explained, must be patient and must lay aside his metropolitan airs if he wants access to the genuine language of the provinces:

> practical information is hard to get, except by those who are actually living amongst the people and with whom they feel at home. The peasantry, who are the true repositories of verbal treasures, are shy, and not easily drawn out by any one they look upon as a *jin•l-mun.* Any attempt from a stranger, or even the *paa•sn* (unless he mixes much with them), to extract information from a real native, is at once to cause Hodge to become like his namesake, and to effectually shut himself up in an impenetrable shell of company manners, and awkward mimicry of what he supposes to be *jin•l-vŏaks wai ŏa spai•kin.*[21]

Elworthy describes the peasantry as a bashful, living archive of antiquated language, and observes that only a tactful insider may access the hidden "verbal repository" of the genuine peasant or "real native." To present before this community with one's metropolitan or upper-class identity on display is to invite artifice and suspicion rather than the genuine and full-hearted effusions of the living Hodge. While Elworthy does not explicitly identify himself as a careful insider here, his comfort with using and reproducing dialectical renderings of "gentleman" shows his easy familiarity with the language of West Somerset and his comfort transitioning in and out of this rural community. The careful, embedded observer will glimpse, in Hodge's language, a connection "with the times when our British forefathers were elbowed back by the prolific Saxon, and lorded over by the proud Norman."[22] Here the provinces become the repository of lost arts of trade and language alike, knowable only to the open-minded and patient visitor.

The first fascicles and volumes of the *NED* likewise broke down the distinction between dialects, colloquialisms, and mainstream literary language, even suggesting that dialects and colloquialisms were the ultimate source of standard, literary English. In his 1888 "Preface" to Volume 1 ("A and B") of the *NED*, Murray writes that

> The unwritten dialects, and, to some extent, even slang, and colloquial speech, approach in character to language in its natural state, aiming only at being expressive, and treating memory and precedent as ministers, not as masters. In the local dialects, then, in slang, and in colloquial use, new vocables and new expressions may at any time be abruptly brought forth to serve the needs of the moment, in accordance with feelings of inherent natural fitness, of imitative suggestiveness, or of subtle instinctive analogy with groups of words or parts of words already familiar. Some of these, sooner or later, pass from conversational, into epistolary, journalistic, and finally into general literary use, or from the colloquy of the novel into the literary composition of the novelist, and are registered in the dictionary as 'new words', the origin of which is searched for as vainly in the 'word-hoard' of Old English speech, or even the fullest vocabulary of Indo-European roots, as in a school manual of Latin and Greek roots and affixes.[23]

Murray shows how provincial words begin as spontaneous, vernacular utterances and gradually make their way into the received national standard. This shift from the rural or colloquial margins to the written mainstream effaces geographical and linguistic boundaries between the country and the town. The remoter districts are sites of verbal creativity, points of origin for free expression that slowly, through letter-writers, journalists, and authors, become part of the mainstream lexicon.

Hardy's dialogue poem, "The Ruined Maid," satirizes these generalized oppositions between the polished metropolitan center and the unsullied provinces.[24] Composed in 1866 and later published as part of *Poems of the Past and Present*, "The Ruined Maid" stages a conversation between a world-weary city prostitute, "'Melia" and her unnamed former friend from the country who chances to meet her in town. The rustic friend, in awe of her former companion's dress and language, enthusiastically catalogues the ruined maid's new trappings of gentility:

"O 'Melia, my dear, this does everything crown!
Who could have supposed I should meet you in Town?
And whence such fair garments, such prosperi-ty?" —
"O didn't you know I'd been ruined?" said she.

— "You left us in tatters, without shoes or socks,
Tired of digging potatoes, and spudding up docks;

And now you've gay bracelets and bright feathers three!" —
"Yes: that's how we dress when we're ruined," said she.

— "At home in the barton you said thee' and thou,'
And thik oon,' and theäs oon,' and t'other'; but now
Your talking quite fits 'ee for high compa-ny!" —
"Some polish is gained with one's ruin," said she.

(1–12)

The reader is placed in the position of an eavesdropper, perhaps any passing listener who could be lingering on the streets of this town. The poem's structure, almost entirely in dialogue except for the attributions ("said she"), gives the impression of spontaneous, immediate conversation. Hardy's singsong anapests refuse gravitas or moral judgment while emphasizing the friend's innocent enthusiasm in potential spondees ("gay bracelets") that verbally and metrically enhance the effects of these bright accessories. The country friend continues:

— "Your hands were like paws then, your face blue and bleak
But now I'm bewitched by your delicate cheek,
And your little gloves fit as on any la-dy!" —
"We never do work when we're ruined," said she.

— "You used to call home-life a hag-ridden dream,
And you'd sigh, and you'd sock; but at present you seem
To know not of megrims or melancho-ly!" —
"True. One's pretty lively when ruined," said she.

— "I wish I had feathers, a fine sweeping gown,
And a delicate face, and could strut about Town!" —
"My dear — a raw country girl, such as you be,
Cannot quite expect that. You ain't ruined," said she.

(13–24)

The poem reaches its comic climax with the rustic's innocent desire to be "ruined" herself in the final lines, where she longs, too, to have the gown and trappings of her fallen companion. With an amusing display of contempt, the ruined maid rebukes her friend: such a "raw country girl" from the barton could never trade places with her, because she "ain't ruined." In the context of the opposition between the two of these women, it seems that the colloquial "ain't" is here associated with the country, and it is tempting to read 'Melia's use of the colloquial "ain't" as evidence of her unconscious lapse into the habits and language of the rustic peasant girl she has left behind. However, with Hardy's wry vision of language-gentrifying cosmopolites in mind, we might read 'Melia's use of "ain't" as further evidence of her metropolitan affectations. Much as she performs her new city identity through bracelets, feathers, and standard, polished language, so too does she perform her new status before her rustic friend by appropriating her colloquialisms. This performance also suggests the impossibility of recovering an authentic national past through an appreciation of its dialectal words and usages. 'Melia's "ain't" has migrated from past to present, where it takes on a new and different meaning, social context, and linguistic effect. *Wessex Poems* extends this analysis of the town-country divide, resisting the incorporation of the provinces as a part of national heritage, and arguing for the distinctiveness of rural districts against the threat of their incorporation into a linguistically unified vision of the nation.

Provincial Language, Lovers' Dilemmas, and War in *Wessex Poems*

Wessex Poems, Hardy's first published volume of poetry, challenges simplified perceptions of provincial spaces through two recurring themes: the complications and moral dilemmas of lovers' speech and the traumatic memories of war rendered in Wessex dialect. Throughout the volume, Hardy strove for dialectical authenticity. As he explains in his "Preface," whenever "an ancient and legitimate word still current in the district, for which there was no close equivalent in received English, suggested itself, it has been made use of, on what seemed good grounds" (5). Accordingly, several of the poems are titled as vernacular "Songs," bear the parenthetical epigraph "Wessex Dialect," or feature speakers who freely use dialectal words and phrases. However, his poems about thwarted lovers' language refute accounts like Elworthy's and Murray's that understand rural language as straightforward and authentic, existing in a "natural state" before it takes on the elaborate artifices of literary language. Hardy's thematic emphasis on lovers' speech shifts language out of the sphere of public, national expression and relocates it to the fraught, private space between lovers instead. These lyric songs feature moments of dialogue, generally take place in decaying settings, and end with little sense of resolution or justice, often contemplating instead the deceptiveness of speech and its association with a bleak, decaying nature. They also stress the willful invention of the past, refusing the nostalgia that characterized many of the Philological Society's representations of rural life and speechways. Hardy extends this negation of nostalgia through a second repeated device, that of the sympathetic interlocutor who listens to soldiers' stories in these communities. Through this device, Hardy shows how the trauma of war lingers in the countryside, and exposes how the rural districts are co-opted into the service of national war efforts even as they remain estranged and detached from the political causes of war. Together, the lyrics about lovers' speech and the device of the sympathetic interlocutor insist on the distinctive identity of the Wessex provinces and resist their linguistic and political incorporation into the militant form of the nation.

"Neutral Tones" introduces the problem of lovers' utterance as deception. The poem's title plays on the meaning of "tones," suggesting both tones of speech and the muted color palette of the winter pond and the barren ash trees that the lovers contemplate as they talk. The speaker extends this correspondence between language and nature by likening words to fallen leaves:

> We stood by a pond that winter day,
> And the sun was white as though chidden of God,
> And a few leaves lay on the starving sod;
> —They had fallen from an ash, and were gray.
>
> Your eyes on me were as eyes that rove
> Over tedious riddles of years ago;
> And some words played between us to and fro
> On which lost the more by our love.
>
> (1–8)

Parallel placement and structure in the third lines of each quatrain suggest the similarity between dead leaves and dead words. Both "few leaves" and "words played" can be scanned as spondees, which establish their metrical resemblance. Both lines also contain past participles, "lay" and "played," that rhyme with each other, and the image of words playing between the pair visually recalls the image of leaves playing to and fro as they fall from the ash tree. This correspondence between leaves and words rehearses the familiar characterization of rural language as an outgrowth of nature, but it also challenges this characterization by depicting nature as exhausted and plundered, no longer the site of spontaneous, rustic utterance. Hardy continues this correspondence by evoking the shape and curve of the mouth:

> The smile on your mouth was the deadest thing
> Alive enough to have strength to die;
> And a grin of bitterness swept thereby
> Like an ominous bird a-wing....
>
> Since then, keen lessons that love deceives,
> And wrings with wrong, have shaped to me

Your face, and the God-curst sun, and a tree,
And a pond edged with grayish leaves.

(8–16)

The speaker fixates on the paradoxical smile of the beloved as a site of both vitality and decay, its curved shape mimicking the curve of the white sun and the winter pond. This shape persists in the speaker's memory long into the haunted present ("Since then") and endlessly evokes that old wasted terrain.

Hardy's use of diction underlines this imagery of a withered past. Wright's *EDD* defines the adjective "keen" as "eager" and "hungry," particularly for the hunt, as in a "Keen killer" or an "eager shooter of game."[25] This meaning gestures back to the "ominous bird a-wing" of the previous line and suggests that the lover's smile is like a predatory animal. At the same time, Hardy was surely aware of the meaning of "keen" as a verb, in the sense given by the *EDD* of a dirge or a wailing for the dead. The poem itself is a kind of keening, or a lamentation for a bygone romance. In the next line, "wrings" evokes the sense of pressing, squeezing, or drying out, all definitions supplied by the *NED* and illustrated with quotes from recipes; here, the verb indicates the preservation of something that has lived beyond its prime, like the relationship between these two lovers.[26] Language is kin to nature, but only a dying nature; there is a past, but it is Gothic rather than nostalgic; the lover's grin is an avatar of deception rather than a symbol of homespun charm or honesty, or a gateway to Elworthy's "verbal treasures."

"Her Dilemma" repeats this quandary, but from a third-person perspective that offers a glimpse into the minds of both of the lovers, and in an interior church setting that replicates, with some variation, the decay of the ash and the winter pond. A dying man and his lover sit in a "sunless church" with "mildewed walls, uneven paving-stones, / And wasted carvings" as the "dull monotones" of the clock beat around them (1–4). He takes her hand and begs her to tell him she loves him. This, in turn, elicits her private reflections on language and deception:

She would have given the world to breathe 'yes' truly,
So much his life seemed hanging on her mind,
And hence she lied, her heart persuaded thoroughly
'Twas worth her soul to be a moment kind.

But the sad need thereof, his nearing death,
So mocked humanity that she shamed to prize
A world conditioned thus, or care for breath
Where Nature such dilemmas could devise.

(9–16)

The poem is written in a kind of loose ballad measure, in quatrains rhyming *abcb* and *dede*, but Hardy's irregular meter, consisting of a mixture of iambs and dactyls, disrupts the smooth procession of the form.[27] The metrics of the poem are like the "uneven paving-stones" that surround the lovers, jagged and irregular rather than smooth, and suggestive of the complicated linguistic dilemma the woman herself faces. The first quatrain expresses her quandary by parceling her self, her speaking body, into three parts: the mind that reasons, the heart that feels and empathizes, and the soul that this lie will compromise. These stanzas doubly evoke the idea of spirit as breath and thus of breath as a natural extension of a divine impulse to speech, as in Barrett Browning's Adam in *A Drama of Exile*, who describes "God breathing through my breath."[28] Yet here this double evocation, the verb "to breathe" and the noun "breath," suggests a sundering of divine spirit and human utterance. "Breath" rhymes with "death," recalling the correspondence between the curve of the lover's grin and the shore of the winter pond in "Neutral Tones." The lover cannot "breathe yes truly" or "care for breath" because there is no Romantic or Herderian correspondence between the two. Instead, there is only a wily force personified and apotheosized as "Nature" in the final line, fashioning moral quandaries and interfering in the human world like a scheming deity in an epic poem. Far from being the spontaneous, natural utterance of Murray, language here is a vehicle for well-intentioned and deeply considered, if impossibly complex, deceptions.

Unrequited love is also the subject of a four-part lyric series, "She, to Him," whose very title foregrounds the absence of reciprocal communication. Together, these four lyrics establish a progression similar to the progression of a sonnet sequence, advancing through the wearying stages of a one-sided love affair. Yet the speaker's initial meditations on love's brevity quickly transform into a morbid preoccupation with the inadequacies and injustices of human speech and, in so doing, turn the rhetorical occasion of the love poem into a meditation on the shortcomings of words themselves. For example, in the second lyric, the female speaker imagines that one day, when she is dead, her beloved will encounter "Some other's feature, accent" that will carry him back to what she "used to say" and remind him of his "love's decline" (2–4). The speaker imagines the distorted, false sentimentality this unexpected memory will trigger in her lover:

> Then you may pause awhile and think, 'Poor jade!'
> And yield a sigh to me—as ample due,
> Not as the tittle of a debt unpaid
> To one who could resign her all to you—
>
> And thus reflecting, you will never see
> That your thin thought, in two small words conveyed,

Was no such fleeting phantom-thought to me,
But the Whole Life wherein my part was played;
And you among its fitful masquerade
A Thought—as I in your life seem to be!

(5–14)

The speaker anticipates his paltry remembrance of her, which is
largely unarticulated in language but rather expressed in a brief sigh
that operates as one half of the antithesis that divides the two lovers,
the antithesis between "yield a sigh" and "resign her all" in the first
quatrain. Both "yield" and "resign" imply sacrifice, but to different
degrees: the beloved relinquishes only a sigh while she submits her
whole being. This inequality continues in the second stanza, as his
"two small words" come to encompass her "Whole Life" in a similar
fashion. Hardy also signals this antithesis through his use of capitals:
the beloved's "thin thought" becomes her personified "Thought," an
edict for her to live by. The poem foregrounds the distortion and un-
evenness of language, expressed in a mathematical and verbal inequal-
ity between lovers. "She, to Him II" differs from "Neutral Tones"
in its presentation of time: it shows the anticipatory construction of
a past that has not happened yet and, in so doing, emphasizes the
created nature of nostalgia. Language is part of this distortion, with
single words or phrases wholly inadequate to measure or express the
completeness of experience: two sharply different interpretations of
the past converge as the speaker reflects on that single word, "jade."
Like Elworthy, Hardy understands there is a past available in words,
but insists that this past meaning cannot be a guarantor of authenticity
in the present because of the shifting nature of language, meaning, and
context.

   "My Cicely" likewise emphasizes the willful construction of the
past, but with a deliberate invocation of the Wordsworthian "real lan-
guage of men" that equates nostalgia with the deliberate distortion
of some accounts and the elevation of others. "My Cicely" explicitly
invokes Wordsworth's "Strange fits of passion I have known" in the
name of its beloved ("Cicely" slant-rhymes with "Lucy"), its temporal
setting ("17—," perhaps looking backward to the publication of *Lyr-
ical Ballads*), and in its imagined scenarios of the horse ride and the
fantasy of the beloved's death. Single lines, too, compress and recall
Wordsworth's poem: the "passion the planets had scowled on" in the
fifth quatrain (17) suggests both the "passion" of Wordsworth's title
and his speaker's startling vision of the dropping "planet" ("Strange
fits of passion" 24).[29] Yet in Hardy's variation the beloved has been
falsely declared dead and is, in fact, still living, working as a prosti-
tute in a stage-hostel after a disastrous marriage. Hardy extends the
long horse-ride of Wordsworth's poem, past "bleak hill-graves" and

creaking gibbets (31), to have his speaker unwittingly hear the fallen language of his beloved:

> For riding down hither I'd halted
>   Awhile at the Lions,
> And her—her whose name had once opened
>   My heart as a key—
>
> I'd looked on, unknowing, and witnessed
>   Her jests with the tapsters,
> Her liquor-fired face, her thick accents
>   In naming her fee.
>
>   (77–84)

The lover "cried" upon hearing this, again invoking "Strange fits," but while Wordsworth's speaker "cried" to think that Lucy might be dead, Hardy's speaker "cried" to think that the beloved still lives, albeit in a "lapse[d]" condition (86, 71).

Hardy's diction further stresses drastic and ironic variations of meaning from the past to the present. "Fee" here carries the primary definition of a price or charge for services, but the *NED* also gives older meanings from feudal law, where "fee" means "an estate in land" or "fief" held "on condition of homage and service to a superior lord." With this word, Hardy emphasizes conditions of economic exploitation while revealing the sharp and ironic difference between his contemporary moment and the feudal past. Just as the ruminative woman of "Her Dilemma" bears silent witness to an impossible moral quandary, the lover of "My Cicely" listens in despair to his former sweetheart's "thick accents" and decides to engage in a willful reinvention of history. As he gallops away from the stage-hostel, he imaginatively recreates the tragic fall he has just witnessed:

> A feeling stirred in me and strengthened
>   That *she* was not my Love,
> But she of the garth, who lay rapt in
>   Her long reverie.
>
> And thence till to-day I persuade me
>   That this was the true one;
> That Death stole intact her young dearness
>   And innocency.
>
>   (101–108)

The lover convinces himself that the actual love of his youth is indeed the woman in the grave and not the woman he has seen at the Lions, deliberately sketching out a vision of pastoral innocence and tragedy that requires him to "shun the West Highway" forever so that he will not have this "choice vision" disturbed again (117–118). The speaker distorts and alters the story of his beloved much in the same way his author, Hardy, distorts and alters the precursor poem. To revisit the rural past from a distance is to open up the possibility of its disruption in the realm of fantasy. The reader may begin the poem expecting Wordsworth's fond, silent Lucy and get instead the "liquor-fired face" and "thick accents" of the fallen Cicely. This substitution threatens to exchange one caricature for another, replacing the rustic and voiceless Lucy with the bawdy humor of Hardy's variation. Yet, like "Neutral Tones," the poem also foregrounds the emotional dangers of assuming a simplified narrative of the past, and counters Elworthy's nostalgia.

Like the poems about lovers' speech, poems that feature silent or sympathetic listeners also challenge accounts of the simple pleasures of rural speechways. In "Valenciennes," "San Sebastian," "Leipzig," and "The Peasant's Confession," speakers recount traumatic bombings and war crimes at great length to silent listeners who do not interject or otherwise interfere with the procession of these grim stories. This simple device appears politicized when we remember that the figure of the sympathetic listener, the silent and trustworthy visitor to the country, appears frequently not only in accounts like Elworthy's but also in newspaper accounts of the Third Reform Act. Stories about verbal exchanges with the "Hodge" archetype appeared frequently in the periodical press, often stressing the authentic, man-to-man interactions that were necessary in order to understand the rural laborer and his new political significance as a member of the newly reformed electorate. According to a December 1885 article in *Blackwood's*, "Establishments and Disestablishment," the newly enfranchised "household-suffrager," the "labourer, artisan, or mill-hand" might sound "slow of speech" but his political views are astute: "Touch him on class feelings and interests, and he is as obstinate and tenacious as any duke. Reason with him, and put things fairly before him, talk in plain straightforward language which he can understand, and does not suspect of flummery,—you will find him shrewd and fair in judgment."[30] Such straightforward communication with Hodge would soon reveal that his political sympathies were more in line with those of gentlemen rather than those of his enemies, the posturing members of the middle class.[31] In a manner that resembles Elworthy's emphasis on the authenticity of personal acquaintance, the *Blackwood's* writer shows how personal interactions with laboring communities can provide a useful political analysis of Hodge, if the visitor only knows what kind of language to use.

In an 1889 piece for *Time*, "Canvassing the Rustics," Lucy Birkbeck Hill describes her work distributing political pamphlets in the countryside in similar terms: "No one who has not had village election work to do can appreciate the character of the rustic voter. City people think him a boor. They cannot conceive how a man, living on fat bacon and wearing hobnailed boots, can feel his heart stirred by patriotism.... He is Hodge,—the clodhopper—a creature without an aspiration."[32] Yet in these districts, she insists, one would find all extremes of political behavior, from enthusiastic political engagement to complete detachment: "Here [is] an ardent politician who thinks his newly given vote his proudest possession, and there [is] a fellow who finds a three-mile walk excuse enough for ignoring it altogether."[33] Hill is eager to disabuse readers of their notions that Hodge was verbally backward and slow-witted, telling stories about working men outwitting the squires who attempted to sway their political opinions: "Practice makes [Hodge] quick at evading questions, especially if they come from a parson or a landowner," she writes: "A little lad, the son of the squire's head gardener, was once asked about his father's political views. 'Which is your father, my boy,' said the parson to him, 'a Liberal or a Conservative?' 'Oh please sir,' said the small boy, 'Father isn't either a Liberal or a conservatory. He's a greenhouse.'"[34] As with the *Blackwood's* writer, Hill's insider access to these stories stems from her ability to make herself welcome as an outsider to these communities, and from her ability to suspend her judgments about rural life and speech.

Readers often associated Hardy's own poetry and prose writings with this insider view of the rural districts. The dialectal words and provincial settings of *Wessex Poems*, writes an *Academy* reviewer in 1899, make the volume read like a "versified guidebook."[35] Actual travel guides of Hardy's Wessex encouraged readers to soak in the district's regionalisms. Bertram Windle's *The Wessex of Thomas Hardy* (1902), for example, urges Dorsetshire-bound travelers to study the dialect poetry of the Dorset clergyman William Barnes, while Hermann Lea's *Thomas Hardy's Wessex* (1913) includes a romantic description of a walk toward Salisbury Cathedral on market-day, with its "old-world atmosphere" intensified by the "snatches of dialect" visitors heard as they moved through the crowds.[36] Hardy was familiar with stories about "Hodge" in the periodical press, having employed this figure himself in his piece "The Dorsetshire Labourer." Hardy invites his genteel readers to visit Hodge in his rural home, where they would learn how

the language, instead of being a vile corruption of cultivated speech, was a tongue with a grammatical inflection rarely disregarded by his entertainer, though his entertainer's children would occasionally make a sad hash of their talk. Having attended the National School they would mix the printed tongue as taught therein with the unwritten, dying, Wessex English that they had learnt of their parents,

the result of this transitional state of theirs being a composite lan-
guage without rule or harmony.[37]

Like Elworthy and the *Blackwood's* writer, Hardy adopts an insider per-
spective that attempts to disabuse city readers of their notions about
Hodge and his language in a political moment where rural laborers were
joining the national electorate.

Accordingly, many verses in *Wessex Poems* repeat this scenario of the
rural speaker or the tale-telling Hodge. However, rather than stressing
a new sense of belonging in the national community, or a sharp anal-
ysis of contemporary politics, Hardy's speakers often look to the past,
and to the traumatic memories of the Napoleonic wars, to emphasize
the lingering trauma of those wars on rural soldiers and the remoteness
of that geopolitical conflict from the lived experience of its provincial
veterans. In "Valenciennes," for example, the speaker remembers the
1793 Siege of Valenciennes, an Allied victory, as a key battle, the first
Revolution-era conflict where "French and English spilled each other's
gore" (10). The larger significance of this battle, or its ultimate purpose,
he confesses, is lost on him:

> 'Twas said that we'd no business there
> A-topperén the French for disagreën;
> However, that's not my affair—
> We were at Valencieën.
>
> (13–16)

For this Wessex speaker, the greater significance of this battle is
the indelible mark it has left both on his memory and his hearing.
Shelled near his ears in the fight, the soldier recalls how the battle
forever obliterated the sensory pleasures he once took in his pastoral
surroundings:

> 'Twer true. No voice o'friend or foe
> Can reach me now, or any livèn beën;
> And little have I power to know
> Since then at Valencieën!
>
> I never hear the zummer hums
> O'bees; and don' know when the cuckoo comes;
> But night and day I hear the bombs
> We threw at Valencieën.
>
> (41–44)

In these lines provincial charm fades under the traumatic memory of
the battle as the Wessex landscape is indelibly shattered by phantom

explosions. Concluding that heaven is "the on'y Town I care to be in…" the soldier wonders if in heaven, too, the enemy will "bomb the walls" (54–55). The natural sounds of bees and cuckoos are muted by these lingering blasts. In addition to the various feasts and fair-days associated with the cuckoo bird, the *EDD* gives for the verb form of "cuckoo" the meaning "To harp on one subject, to say the same thing over and over again like a cuckoo or parrot," a meaning which suggests that the speaker may be repeating this story of his trauma again and again to listeners in fits of psychic disturbance. The verb form also gestures toward the repetition of the poem's refrain in the fourth line of each stanza. "Valenciennes" traces the international to the regional, showing how battle trauma leaves its mark on the countryside. This is no romantic haven from global warfare; rather, the haunting memories of previous military conflicts continue to shape and torment the minds of its retired peasant soldiers.

These poems show how the horrors of international tragedy continue to haunt rural life, undermining the idea that districts like Wessex could provide respite for global military conflict. Hardy's *Wessex Poems* also warns of the threats and dislocations that larger geopolitical conflicts have already unleashed upon the countryside. In *Poems of the Past and Present*, he further demonstrates how the geopolitical conflicts of late-century Victorian Britain threaten to hasten the rootlessness of contemporary life and to exploit a vision of national belonging that seeks to uproot rural soldiers from their ties to the land.

Rootless Speech and Wandering Bodies in *Poems of the Past and Present*

While *Wessex Poems* features speakers deeply rooted in rural life, Hardy's second published volume, *Poems of the Past and Present*, focuses more intensely on the sense of rootlessness produced by the "endless propensity for travel" and the obliteration of "local differences" that he later envisioned in "Dorset in London." Published in the wake of two trips to Europe and in the aftermath of the Boer War, *Poems of the Past and Present* features war poems, poems of "pilgrimage," and miscellaneous verses, the latter ranging from short narratives, vignettes, and lyrics of Wessex life on to a poem about the Higher Criticism and a poem about the medieval legend of the Lost Pyx. While the greater variation in subject matter of the poems in Hardy's second volume somewhat downplays the emphasis on rural life that is so apparent in *Wessex Poems*, *Poems of the Past and Present* is nevertheless deeply concerned with the role of provincial language and identity on the world stage. If *Wessex Poems* foregrounds an intense sense of locality, speechways, and memory rooted in a provincial landscape, *Poems of the Past and Present* takes on more speculative and geographically more wide-ranging locations and themes in order to represent once-localized identities uprooted and erased by the dislocations of international warfare. Countering Elworthy's and others' nostalgic images of a language uprooted by modernity, Hardy shows how his Wessex landscape is already frighteningly, desperately modern in its embeddedness in violent geopolitical conflict, and illustrates the dangers of the destruction of locality he believed would harm the working-class, rural electorate. In "V.R. 1819–1901: A Reverie," "God-Forgotten," and "The Bridge of Lodi," he represents this dislocation through the motif of lost words, snapped threads, and forgotten songs, while, in the "War Poems" sequence, he does so through images of drifting phantoms and soldiers' spirits. These poems carry to the most startling extreme the dissolution described by Murray, in which individual words travel to the metropolis for legitimization and absorption. In *Poems of the Past and Present*, this movement creates an evacuation of the province, leaving behind rootless forms of expression and soldiers' ghosts.

Hardy signals this linguistic crisis in the first lines of the opening poem of the volume, "V.R. 1819–1901: A Reverie," at once an elegy for Queen Victoria and a curious meditation on the divine origins of language. The speaker opens with an appeal to the political tradition of associating hereditary monarchy with divine appointment, but also imagines this moment as one of immediate separation between divinity and the earliest "mortal[s]" (7). "The mightiest moments pass uncalendered," the speaker begins,

> And when the Absolute
> In backward Time pronounced the deedful word
> Whereby all life is stirred:
> 'Let one be born and throned whose mould shall constitute
> The norm of every royal-reckoned attribute,'
> No mortal knew or heard.
>
> (1–7)

Recognizably akin to the God of Genesis who created man on the sixth day, Hardy's rechristened "Absolute" gives the command or "deedful word" to create the sovereign, but this great act goes unnoticed. Hardy uses "mould" primarily in the sense of a "form" or model, but the *EDD* also gives "the earth for a grave," which suggests the poem's reflections on death. Hardy intensifies the poem's sense of estrangement from the divine-origins story of language by substituting the "Absolute" for "God."

This separation between divine origins and earthly language is more pronounced in "God-Forgotten," a poem that extends this motif of separation by staging a conversation between the "Lord Most High" and an unnamed speaker "Sent thither by the sons of earth, to win / Some answer to their cry" (3–4). God, however, has no recollection of the earth nor the people he has created, and so the speaker gently reminds him: "— 'O Lord, forgive me when I say / Thou spakest the word that made it all.' —" (9–10). Unanswered questions compound this sense of a breakdown in communication, as God several times interrogates the speaker and then continues on without waiting for an answer (5–6, 15–16). Hardy continues this idea through the trope of snapping threads:

> 'Dark, then, its life! For not a cry
> Of aught it bears do I now hear;
> Of its own act the threads were snapt whereby
> Its plaints had reached mine ear.
>
> 'It used to ask for gifts of good,
> Till came its severance, self-entailed,
> When sudden silence on that side ensued,
> And has till now prevailed.
>
> 'All other orbs have kept in touch;
> Their voices reach me speedily:
> Thy people took upon them overmuch
> In sundering them from me!
>
> (21–32)

In the second quatrain, a cluster of hissing sibilants ("severance," "self-entailed," "sudden silence," "side," "ensued") heightens the sense of treachery. The *NED* gives for "severance" legal definitions that involve the separation of two parties "joined in a writ," while "entail" pertains to estate law and the "rule of descent" established for an estate. God's use of this legal vocabulary adds to his curt and businesslike tone, while the idea of "entail" as a rule of descent also indicates how this original separation will come to shape generations to come. At the same time, "entail" as "with reference to embroidery" enhances the image of snapped and broken threads in the previous stanza. God concludes that he will send intermediaries or "Messengers!" to earth as a compromise, in a gesture that only compounds the poem's tone of loss and resignation (43).

"The Bridge of Lodi" both takes up and revises this theme of separation by depicting a famous setting evacuated, over time, of an oral tradition that memorialized it. While "A Reverie" and "God-Forgotten" show how language's ties to the divine have been sundered, "The Bridge of Lodi" illustrates how language and history have been wrenched apart. "The Bridge of Lodi" is the second-to-last of the poems in the "Poems of Pilgrimage" section, and takes place on the eponymous bridge where

Napoleon's Italian army fought the Austrians in 1796. In Spring of 1887, however, the time Hardy gives at the outset of the poem, few of the residents and passerby remember this battle. The speaker opens by describing the "strange delight" the song "The Bridge of Lodi" has always brought to him (4), and the way its "forward-footing tune" conjures images of mingling armies and crushed columns in his imagination (6). The speaker projects the romance of the song and of his imagination onto the passing women of Lodi:

> Any ancient crone I'd toady
>   Like a lass in young-eyed prime,
> Could she tell some tale of Lodi
>   At that mighty moving time.
>
> So, I ask the wives of Lodi
>   For traditions of that day;
> But alas! not anybody
>   Seems to know of such a fray.
>
> And they heed but transitory
>   Marketings in cheese and meat,
> Till I judge that Lodi's story
>   Is extinct in Lodi's street.
>
> (25–36)

The speaker's hunt for stories of Lodi in the recollections of older women conflates past and present, and sexual pursuit with a nostalgic desire for folklore. The solitary male traveler seeks an oral tradition that is gendered and embodied as feminine, suggestive of the feminization of the nation in poems by Barrett Browning and other contemporaries.[38] This organic oral history, now displaced by capitalist exchange, goes "extinct." Hardy's use of "fray" carries the primary definition of "battle" or "fight" but the *NED* also supplies the definition "a war of words," which here suggests the conflict the speaker feels as he searches for folklore and is met with silence and rejection. Like the speaker of "My Cicely," the solitary traveler resolves to preserve the illusion of the organic past, sitting and singing "That long-loved, romantic thing" although none of the passing strangers acknowledge or recognize this performance (66). The romance of the song is only internal; the bridge itself seems evacuated of its past, the distinctiveness of this locality blotted out by the busy transactions of the marketplace.

This loss of place is especially apparent in "War Poems," the first grouping of *Poems of the Past and Present*, which makes clear Hardy's awareness that the greater political and linguistic inclusion of the rural male electorate came at a time when Britain was consolidating its military forces for the Boer War and as the enlistment of young men in colonial conflicts was wreaking havoc on rural families. "It seems a justification of the extremest pessimism that at the end of the 19th Centy we settle an argument by the Sword, just as they wd. have done in the 19th centy B.C.," he laments in an 1899 letter to Florence Henniker; elsewhere, he declares, "I am happy to say that not a single one [of my 'War Effusions'] is Jingo or Imperial—a fatal defect according to the judgment of the British majority at present."[39] Throughout his poetry, Hardy shows how international conflicts register in the drifting, phantom images of soldier's bodies and in passages where a distinct sense of place dissolves on the stage of the global war theater. "War Poems" consists of eleven poems that examine this theme from a variety of perspectives. In "Embarcation" an unidentified speaker stands at Southampton Docks and watches families take leave of departing soldiers; in "The Going of the Battery" a group of Casterbridge wives, speaking in the first-person plural, mourn their dead husbands; in "The Souls of the Slain" dead soldiers return home as ghosts only to find their loved ones remember them for "old homely acts" rather than great deeds of valor (69).

Hardy understood this condition of wandering to be emblematic of the rootlessness of modernity. In a letter to the *Daily Chronicle* defending his depiction of an agonized phantom in "A Christmas Ghost-Story," he explains his aims to represent a soldier's spirit that was "neither British nor Boer, but a composite, typical phantom" not located in any one geographic place:

> One's modern fancy of a disembodied spirit—unless intentionally humorous—is that of an entity which has passed into a tenuous, impartial, sexless, fitful form of existence, to which bodily courage is a contradiction in terms. Having no physical frame to defend or sacrifice, how can he show either courage or fear? His views are no longer local; nations are all one to him; his country is not bounded by seas, but is co-extensive with the globe itself, if it does not even include all the inhabited planets of the sky. He has put off the substance, and has put on, in part at any rate, the essence of the Universal.[40]

Hardy's gloomy phantom is the symbol of the obliteration of local differences he had imagined in "Dorset in London." No longer local, he is a rootless ghost traversing an earth whose geographical boundaries mean nothing to him, a symptom of the geopolitical amalgamation of regions into a homogenous mass.

As if to challenge this dislocation, the first three pieces in "War Poems" bear the location and year of their gestation—Southampton

Docks, 1899—thereby insisting on their rootedness in place and time. "Embarcation" and "Departure" are further linked as companion poems through their loose sonnet structure and through a shared aural pattern of tramping soldiers' footsteps. Unlike "The Bridge of Lodi," the Southampton Docks do still bear traces of their military history in the speaker's opening allusions to "Vespasian's legions," "Cerdic with his Saxons," and "Henry's army" (1–3). Yet this is not the romanticized stuff of song but rather the "selfsame bloody mode / Which this late age of thought, and pact, and code / Still fails to mend" in lines that echo Hardy's letter to Henniker (6–8). The second part of the eighth line, "Now deckward tramp the bands," initiates an aural pattern that later extends into the companion poem, "Departure," which begins just after the soldiers have sailed:

> While the far farewell music thins and fails,
> And the broad bottoms rip the bearing brine –
> All smalling slowly to the gray sea-line –
> And each significant red smoke-shaft pales,
>
> Keen sense of severance everywhere prevails,
> Which shapes the late long tramp of mounting men
> To seeming words that ask and ask again:
> How long, O striving Teutons, Slavs, and Gaels
> Must your wroth reasonings trade on lives like these,
> That are as puppets in a playing hand?
>
> (1–10)

The first quatrain is filled with sharp sonic cues, alliterated patterns of fricatives ("far farewell"), plosives ("broad bottoms"), and sibilants ("smalling slowly"). Together, these sound patterns build a mood of rich vitality and activity that contrasts sharply with the "sense of severance" that settles over the crowd as the ships disappear. The rare use of "smalling" as a transitive verb for which the *NED* gives the synonyms "to lessen, reduce" speaks to the gradual vanishing of the ships but also the reduction or lessening of the men from this town as their lives vanish in battles fought abroad. "Severance" here echoes the "severance" of "God-forgotten" and recalls that motif of snapped threads whereby language and meaning become sundered from the divine realm.

Hardy's use of "wroth," too, is suggestive. The *NED* gives meanings of "wroth" that range from "rage, or fury" to, when used with animals, "a violent or fierce nature." Reason, on the other hand, is a faculty of thinking and reflection the *NED* maintains is "usually regarded as characteristic of mankind, but sometimes also attributed in a certain degree to the lower animals"; the ability to reason, of course, was claimed as the dividing line between humans and animals by Müller in his responses to Darwin's writings on language. "Wroth reasonings," then, are paradoxical, suggesting both animal fury and detached contemplation, with each undermining and contradicting the other, and calling attention to the violent urges and intentions that underwrite the decision of the "playing hand" to send these men to war. The noisy, tramping bands of "Embarcation" become here the "late long tramp" of memory; this sound, in turn, transforms into a collective, unexpressed question about the foolishness and inevitability of war. While the soldiers' bodies disappear, their metonymic, tramping feed fading on the horizon, we are left with a lingering, disembodied language of protest, and a sense of the men's disappearance from a rooted, familiar place into a theater of crisis.

This image of vanishing, uprooted bodies continues throughout "War Poems." Hardy utilizes similar formal strategies in "A Christmas Ghost-Story" as he does in "Departure." The form is loosely that of a sonnet (or, at twelve lines, a sonnet manqué), and the fading body of a soldier, like the disappearing men in "Departure," again gives way to a meditation on the purposelessness of war:

> South of the Line, inland from far Durban,
> A mouldering soldier lies – your countryman.
> Awry and doubled up are his gray bones,
> And on the breeze his puzzled phantom moans
> Nightly to clear Canopus: 'I would know
> By whom and when the All-Earth-gladdening Law
> Of peace, brought in by that Man Crucified,
> Was ruled to be inept, and set aside?
> And what of logic or of truth appears
> In tacking "Anno Domini" to the years?
> Near twenty-hundred liveried thus have hied,
> But tarries yet the Cause for which He died.'
>
> (1–12)

With the dactylic "mouldering" in the second line, Hardy creates a sonic echo that resembles the echoing feet of the tramping soldiers of the opening verses, as the dactyls that follow ("countryman," "Canopus," "gladdening") recall the images of the man's decomposing form. As we saw in "V.R. 1819–1901," the word "mould" suggests a form or model. Hardy's description of the "mouldering soldier" here thus suggests not only a decaying soldier but a decaying soldier whose body will serve as a symbolic cast or mold for the countless other soldiers and civilians who will follow him to the grave. The closing image of "twenty-hundred liveried" conjures the *NED*'s definition of "livery" in its obsolete form as "a liveried retainer or servant," and thus equates soldiery with servitude to an elite. Like "Departure," the poem imagines a spoken question that its final lines do not answer, as if to refuse easy resolution to the issues it raises.

The following companion poem, "Drummer Hodge," extends the scene of decomposition as a dead Wessex-born soldier in is thrown, unceremoniously and uncoffined, into a makeshift grave in the Karoo during the Boer War. Here, in a tragic paradox, the boy's corpse will merge intimately into surroundings he had never understood while he was alive:

> Young Hodge the drummer never knew—
>   Fresh from his Wessex home—
> The meaning of the broad Karoo,
>   The Bush, the dusty loam,
> And why uprose to nightly view
>   Strange stars amid the gloom.
>
> Yet portion of that unknown plain
>   Will Hodge for ever be;
> His homely Northern breast and brain
>   Grow to some Southern tree,
> And strange-eyed constellations reign
>   His stars eternally.

(7–18)

The boy's body becomes absorbed into a natural order that transcends geographical and national markers. The poem's ordering of locations suggests this progression from the familiar and local to the unfamiliar and beyond, to the cosmos, as it proceeds from Wessex to the Karoo and the Bush and on to the "strange stars" and "strange-eyed constellations" that hover over his body and parallel the allusion to Canopus in "A Christmas Ghost-Story." The *NED* gives for "loam" the obsolete definition of "clayey earth, mud; *occas.* 'earth' or 'clay' as the material for the human body." This suggestive definition underscores how Hodge's body mingles with the earth, but it also evokes the religious myth of the first man created from clay. Much as this first man is the type of men to come, so too is Hodge a type of other fallen soldiers who will follow him to the grave.

With the repetition of "strange" Hardy stresses the soldier's uprooting, displacement, and decomposition abroad as a criticism of an imperial conflict that regularly takes the lives of provincial soldiers who barely comprehend its cause. The focus on the imagined inner lives of individual Wessex soldiers does circumscribe the terms of this criticism, so that the emphasis remains on the soldier rather than the people who die at his hands, or on the larger issue of Britain's violent defense of its empire. Hardy's emphasis on the soldier's organic mingling with the "strange" natural features of the Karoo instead calls attention to Hodge's sundering from his Wessex home as a symbol for the broader dissolution of England's rural provinces into the national-imperial cause. For the shading-off of geographic boundaries in Murray's "Preface," Hardy substitutes the fading away of soldiers' bodies, showing how the trope of borderlessness works in service of deadly military conflict and the perpetuation of Britain's overseas empire. He does this by showing the consequences of the vanishing form of the province, making physical, aural, and embodied the rural soldiers and laborers whose lives were written out or effaced in the larger national imperative to war. Through tramping footsteps, lingering, imagined voices, and drifting, dissolving bodies severed from their Wessex homes, Hardy shows how Britain's violent quest for overseas expansion preyed on the lives of many of its vulnerable, newly enfranchised citizens.

Throughout both *Wessex Poems* and *Poems of the Past and Present*, Hardy anticipates concerns about what Erich Auerbach, in "The Philology of World Literature," would later call "the homogenization of human life the world over," a process borne of "the eclipsing of local traditions."[41] Composed and published at a historical juncture in which the philological quest for linguistic inclusion intersected with the last nineteenth-century expansion of the franchise, Hardy's poetry questions both the timing and the flattening effects of this new form of national becoming. The difficulties of lovers' speech rendered in short lyrics and the device of the sympathetic listener in dialogue poems both challenge ready distinctions between town and country in the growing Philological Society literature about the national lexicon. Tropes of snapped threads, forgotten folklore, and drifting phantoms illustrate the consequences of neglecting place and locality in the broader national quest for imperial dominance in the late-Victorian period. Challenging the boundary-collapsing ethos of the *NED*, Hardy instead stresses the tenuous construction of the reformed nation, and resists the political and linguistic appropriation of rural districts for violent ends.

Notes

1 Taylor, *Hardy's Literary Language*, esp. 1–172. Norman Page also discusses the influence of dialect on Hardy's writing in "Hardy and the English Language," 151–172. See also Taylor's analysis of Hardy's blending of both abstract and concrete vocabulary in *Hardy's Poetry*, 3–4. Hardy's unusual word choice has often been noted; see, for example, Hynes, *The Pattern of Hardy's Poetry*, 89–108 and Isobel Grundy, "Hardy's Harshness," 1–17.

2 Taylor, *Hardy's Literary Language*, 253.

3 Ibid., 269.

4 In Dipesh Chakrabarty's influential formulation, to "provincialize" Europe is to resist Marxist historiography's assumption that political modernity takes a similar form in non-Western societies as it did in the West. Instead,

Chakrabarty seeks to show how European thought is both "indispensible and inadequate" for understanding non-Western political modernity, and how that thought may be "renewed from and for the margins" (*Provincializing Europe*, 16). More recently, Richard Bonfiglio has read this project of provincialization back upon mid-century Victorian literature, showing how images of domesticity in Victorian writing helped to generate cosmopolitan sympathies for the Continent and to reveal how Europe worked as "an emerging comity of nations still very much under construction rather than a unified hegemonic power" ("Proximate Cosmopolitanism").

5 On the OED as an imperial production see Willinsky, *Empire of Words*; for an account of the OED that challenges this view see Ogilvie, *Words of the World*.

6 See Hoppen, *Mid-Victorian Generation*, 265 and Michael S. Smith, "Parliamentary Reform," 178. See also Glen, *The Representation of the People Act, 1884*. For a comparison of the effects of the Third Reform Act in England, Scotland, and Ireland see Hoppen, "The Franchise and Electoral Politics in England and Ireland 1832–1885," 217. Hoppen argues that the Act in England helped consolidate middle-class power and to foster Conservative rule; in Ireland, the newly enfranchised voters continued to support Parnell as had their predecessors (217). See also Hoppen's *Elections, Politics, and Society in Ireland 1832–1885*, 87–88. On the Third Reform Act as the "death knell for an old order dominated by the aristocracy" see Smith, "Parliamentary Reform," 168; on the Third Reform Act as the beginning of the era of mass politics see 170.

7 Hayes, *The Background and Passage of the Third Reform Act*, 4. On nineteenth-century debates over citizenship and the franchise see Heater, *Citizenship in Britain*, 99–133.

8 Pugh, *Making of Modern British Politics*, 9.

9 Taylor, *Hardy's Literary Language*, 123.

10 Thomas Hardy to Percy Bunting, 12 October 1883, in Millgate and Purdy, *Collected Letters*, 1: 121.

11 Ibid., 1: 123. Millgate describes Hardy's politics in the 1880s and in the wake of the introduction of the first Irish Home Rule bill as increasingly "disenchanted" and opposed, to some extent, both to aristocracy and democracy. See *Thomas Hardy: A Biography Revisited*, 251.

12 "Dorset in London," 219.

13 Ibid.

14 Ibid.

15 On sixpenny pronunciation and usage manuals see Mugglestone, *Talking Proper*, 39. For an overview of the study of dialect in England see Wakelin, *English Dialects*, 34–63; for the study of dialect in the mid- and late-Victorian period see Petyt, *The Study of Dialect*, 68–81, and Crowley, *Standard English*, 138–151. See also Phillipps, *Language and Class*.

16 Trench, Theodore Goldstücker, Thomas Hewitt Key, et. al., "Canones Lexicographici," 3.

17 Ibid., 4.

18 Peyt, *The Study of Dialect*, 68. See also Crowley, *Standard English*, 140.

19 Ibid., 164.

20 Elworthy, "Dialect of West Somerset," 197.

21 Ibid., 197–198.

22 Ibid., 199.

23 Murray, Preface to Vol. 1 of *A New English Dictionary*, viii.

24 All citations to *Wessex Poems* and *Poems of the Past and Present* are from *The Complete Poetical Works of Thomas Hardy*, edited by Samuel Hynes,

5 vols. (Oxford: Clarendon Press, 1982–1995), and will be given by line number in parentheses within the text.

25 All definitions and references from Wright's *English Dialect Dictionary* in this chapter are taken from the thirty-part edition (New York: G.P. Putnam's Sons, 1896–1905).

26 All definitions and references from the *NED* in this chapter are taken from the ten-volume first edition (Oxford: Clarendon Press, 1888–1928).

27 For a comprehensive study of Hardy's understanding of Victorian metrical theory see Taylor, *Hardy's Metres and Victorian Prosody*.

28 Barrett Browning, *A Drama of Exile*, 1827, also discussed in Chapter 2.

29 Wordsworth, "Strange fits of passion," in Stafford, *Lyrical Ballads*, 223–224. On Wordsworth's influence on the Victorians more broadly see Stephen Gill, *Wordsworth and the Victorians*.

30 "Establishments and Disestablishment," 834.

31 Ibid., 833.

32 Hill, "Canvassing the Rustics," 581.

33 Ibid., 581.

34 Ibid., 584.

35 Anon., "Mr. Hardy as a Poet," 334.

36 Windle, *The Wessex of Thomas Hardy*, 51–52; Lea, *Thomas Hardy's Wessex*, 56.

37 Hardy, "The Dorsetshire Labourer," 170.

38 On the feminization of Italy in Victorian women's poetry see Alison Chapman, *Networking the Nation*, 216–217.

39 Thomas Hardy to Florence Henniker, 17 September 1899 and Christmas Eve, 1900, in Millgate and Purdy, *Collected Letters* 2: 228 and 2: 277.

40 Hardy, "To the Editor of the *Daily Chronicle*," 201.

41 Auerbach, "The Philology of World Literature," 253.

Conclusion
Revisiting Philology

In his *Lectures*, Müller observes that the science of language "was more intimately connected than any other physical science with what is called the political history of man."[1] In this book, I have argued that Victorian poets drew on the study of language to navigate the rise of popular sovereignty. Nineteenth-century theories of language provided authors with an imaginative resource for thinking about the reformed electorate, including the role of women, the working classes, and colonial subjects. Moreover, fantastic accounts of incarnated speech, mystical roots, and divine origins fueled these conversations just as much as evolutionary, physiological, and empirical research did, providing us with a more wide-ranging portrait of the interactions between literature, science, and speculative thought in the period. While previous scholars of nineteenth-century literature and language-science have focused on fiction or on single poets in isolation, I have argued that the mutually constitutive relationship among poets, philologists, and political writers in the period worked to index the changing Victorian social body. Moreover, these poets recognized that the social body was a partial, contested, and incomplete form, and wrote with an eye toward acknowledging its oversights and affirming a more inclusive vision of the reformed state.

In the twentieth century, philology split into the discrete disciplines of linguistics and literary studies and lost some of its emphasis on the historical method and the search for mythical origins that characterized the science in Victorian times. However, the field's importance to poetry and also to cultural debates about democracy has long outlasted its nineteenth-century heyday. In this conclusion, I give a brief account of the major changes in the field around the turn of the twentieth century, with an eye to philology's lasting influence on twentieth- and twenty-first-century poetry. I then turn to recent calls for a new or revived philology, showing how the topics discussed in this book might inform our contemporary debates about the humanities and about the relationship between politics, poetry, and literary form.

As Ferguson notes, the early years of the twentieth century saw a decisive shift away from the work of Victorian philologists like

Müller and toward the monumental work of Ferdinand de Saussure.[2] Saussure himself articulates the shortcomings of the previous age of language-study in the lectures that would become the *Course in General Linguistics* (1916). For Saussure, his predecessors' approach lacked a clear methodology, focused on Indo-European language families to the exclusion of others, and stopped short of explaining the relations among languages that their comparisons revealed. Instead, philologists treated "the development of two languages as a naturalist might look upon the growth of two plants.... Language was considered a specific sphere, a fourth natural kingdom; this led to methods of reasoning which would have caused astonishment in other sciences."[3] Saussure intended his more systematic approach to avoid these kind of groundless, pseudoscientific speculations. Additional developments in linguistics in the twentieth and twenty-first centuries further discredited many of the assumptions about race, civilization, and divine origins that appear in many works of Victorian philology. As Ferguson also notes, contemporary linguistics scholarship rightly dismisses the Victorian categorization of languages into primitive and civilized forms, and the influence of Noam Chomsky's system of Universal Grammar, which posits an underlying, rule-bound, and systematic basis for all languages based in the human brain, has eclipsed the Victorian mission "to determine the specific historical moment in which humans uttered the first words and, by so doing, gained their human status."[4] The field of linguistics in the earlier part of the twentieth century deliberately turned away from some of the more far-fetched explanations of nineteenth-century philology.

The institutionalization of the discipline of English literature in the late nineteenth and early twentieth centuries also shifted the way linguistics and literary scholars thought about their objects of study. As Haruko Momma explains:

> In the twentieth century, the study of language and literature blossomed in the fields of linguistics and literary analysis. These two may be seen as sibling disciplines in that they were born of the same parent, philology, and that they each took after different features of their matrix. Their paths parted almost immediately after birth: literary analysis found its home in the emergent field of modern languages and especially of English, whereas linguistics often claimed its own territory in university programmes bearing its name.... This meant, however, that the study of language and literature was split into two separate subjects, thus dissolving a good portion of the space occupied by philology for more than a century.[5]

Despite this separation between the fields, the new field of literary studies did retain many of philology's guiding concerns, among them the attempt to establish literary analysis as a rigorous field of inquiry, much as the *OED* compilers had in the previous century. In the first volume of the *Transactions of the Modern Language Association of America* (1884–1885, later the *PMLA*), for example, H.C.G. Brandt insists that "All teaching should follow a strictly scientific basis" and that all of the new profession's materials, including textbooks and reference guides, should likewise be authored or compiled according to a scientific model.[6] The reason for this, Brandt claims, is, on the one hand, the presence of classical philologists who "deny that there is a scientific basis for Modern Philology. They assert, that the study of Modern Languages is hardly worthy of the serious pursuit of students and investigators."[7] Then there are the amateur students of modern languages who want to learn a "little French or German or Italian" without recognizing the academic principles that underlay the study of modern languages and literatures: "They are the utilitarians taking the 'bread and butter view' of our study."[8] Brandt looks back to the nineteenth-century philologists William Walter Skeat and Henry Sweet as practitioners of the kind of rigor he expected of teachers of modern languages and literatures. In so doing, he demonstrates how the nineteenth-century instantiation of philology as a discipline continued to shape and influence the field of literary studies that followed in its wake.

Early professional statements about literary studies, too, take part in the border-crossing project of studying multiple linguistic and literary traditions. "The intercourse of people with people, political, social, and literary is becoming constantly more intimate and we may anticipate in the future a more cosmopolitan spirit in the relation of nations," declares W.T. Hewett in the same volume.[9] He urges his readers to recognize that the "very nearness and sympathy of nations politically causes each to present problems which every student of contemporary thought must investigate."[10] Like Müller, whose lectures so frequently imagined the dissolution of national boundaries or looked back to a nostalgically rendered pre-national period, Hewett presents the study of modern languages and literatures as a necessary strategy for navigating a complex geopolitical landscape.

Philology continued to shape the way poets practiced their craft. Cary H. Plotkin and, more recently, Meredith Martin have both shown how mid-century philology at Oxford had lasting influences on the daring experimentation of Gerard Manley Hopkins, who first came to Balliol in 1863 and who composed the bulk of his poetry in the 1870s and 1880s.[11] As Taylor observes, the diachronic method of the *OED* still survived Saussure and extended into the twentieth century and beyond, with the final fascicle of the first edition appearing, to great acclaim, in 1928.[12] Production on the *OED* continued steadily if sometimes slowly and unevenly into the early twentieth century, with lexicographers, volunteers, and assistants working through changes of editorship and through the devastating loss of manpower and material supplies brought on by World War I.[13] Twentieth-century poets responded to the evocative word histories and shades of meaning that the massive dictionary offered. As Charlotte Brewer has shown, T.S. Eliot and W.H. Auden both celebrated dictionaries as tools of poetic vocabulary, with Eliot equating national and linguistic greatness during a 1940 BBC broadcast and Auden proudly displaying the *OED* in his study at his home in Kirchstetten.[14] In the context of the Representation of the People Acts of 1918 and 1928, the democratic impulse of Victorian philology was surely relevant to the *OED*'s long-awaited completion.

The advent of new forms of media in the twentieth century also led to new developments in the study and regulation of language. On the one hand, broadcasting led to the codification of a so-called Received Pronunciation, free from regional and dialectical variation, during the official news programming of the British Broadcasting Corporation.[15] On the other hand, this greater variety of media forms made possible the variety of demotic and elite registers that famously vie for attention in works like Eliot's *The Waste Land*, where snippets of Shakespeare, popular songs, and overheard conversations follow each other in rapid succession.[16] For Vince Sherry, such modernist experimentation responds to a liberal and "rationalistic language" that was used to justify and legitimize the atrocities of the World War I.[17] Projects like the *OED* were tacitly part of this legitimizing language. The war showed "with greater urgency a motive implicit in this initiative [the *OED*] from the beginning: to recover the interior coherence of a specifically English speech."[18] The way modernist poets challenged this coherence recalls Browning's poetic rebuttals to the nationalist vision of Trench in the nineteenth century. In both cases, dissonance and lexical disruption foil the imagined philological project of consensus building among speakers.

The *OED* remains a cultural bulwark of language-use in both traditional and digital formats. Even after the final fascicle was released in 1928, editors continued to work on supplements, adapting to digital formats in 1992 with the release of a CD-ROM version, and work is still being carried out for a fully revised third edition.[19] Digital access to the *OED* has transformed the way users encounter the text, although, as Lynda Mugglestone observes, the cost of a subscription necessarily limits the dictionary's potential audience and qualifies its democratic ethos: "Privilege coexists uneasily with the real and undeniable diversity of English as represented in the dictionary itself."[20] For those with personal subscriptions or institutional access through libraries and universities, the *OED* continues to be a wellspring for poetic experimentation. The late poet Geoffrey Hill was openly indebted to the *OED* and composed critical essays about the dictionary, while the poet Laura Bylenock has credited the *OED*'s entry for "warp" as an inspiration for her 2015 collection of the same title.[21] The poetry guide *Wingbeats II: Exercises and Practices in Poetry* (2015) advises students to consult the dictionary as part of a writing exercise to cultivate awareness of word choice and different shades of meaning.[22] Similar exercises have, no doubt, inspired contemporary poets to think seriously about language and political community. For example, in "Three OED Poems" (2013), David Antoine-Williams rearranges headword entries from the *OED* into poems that create startling effects. The third poem, a poetic reworking of the entry for "*Fantasma*," conjures the specter of the body politic that so fascinated the Victorians:

> Image which appears
> in a dream, which is formed
> or cherished in the mind;
> also, anything that haunts
> the imagination:
> some incorporeal
> body politic, a model
> infant devised by way of pretence.[23]

Antoine-Williams's poem recalls the mingling of metaphysical and material theories of language that informed Victorian poets' engagement with the shifting body politic as he reworks the text into a twenty-first-century digital platform.

Recently, many scholars and writers have looked back to philology as a model for cross-disciplinary work in the contemporary university. As Gerald Graff notes, the philological tradition stands for a "larger cultural vision" than its subsequent pedantic reputation implies, and nineteenth-century philologists like Müller and Bopp understood the term to encompass cultural history more broadly.[24] James Turner explores philology's foundational relationships with anthropology, comparative religion, literary studies, and other fields, ultimately concluding that philology offers the present-day humanities scholar a refreshing model of portability across otherwise quite specialized fields of research:

> Sooner or later, the humanities disciplines must shift their shapes, even drastically shrink in number. The past does not prophesy the future. But perhaps some day humanistic scholarship will, once again, inhabit more wide-ranging academic divisions than it does today. If so, erudition will command a higher premium: more extensive knowledge, multiple languages will be required, to broaden the monoglot, narrowly focused scholarship increasingly common in the humanities during the past half century.... At any rate, when the time for change comes—whatever form change takes—it will help to remember that the humanities amount to more than a set of isolated disciplines, each marooned on its own island. Modern

disciplinarity masks a primal oneness. Today's multiple humanities collectively form the latest version of a millennia-long Western tradition of inquiry into language and its products—inquiry, that is, into worlds that human beings have created for themselves and expressed in words.[25]

It remains an open question whether current funding cuts and dwindling university support for humanistic research are best answered by cutting down on the proliferation of disciplines. Indeed, such cuts are already well underway at many colleges and universities, where those remaining must handle the work of teaching and publishing in several fields or subfields at once without additional training or material resources, and one might object that diminished scholarly rigor could be the inevitable by-product of institutional and administrative disregard for specialization. Turner also has little to say about the nationalistic and ethnocentric underpinnings of philology and how these might be accounted for and transformed in a revived philological practice.[26] Nevertheless, his emphasis of philology's innate multi-disciplinarity is a timely reminder of the collaborative work the field has always performed. As the Victorians discussed in this book knew very well, the study of languages and texts was never an isolated inquiry, but rather one that addressed contemporary and timely issues in politics, religion, poetry, science, and myriad other domains of knowledge. Such calls for a revived philological practice have gained more urgency and momentum as scholars navigate the challenges of the digital archive.[27]

Recent calls for new and revived formalisms also invite a revived philological practice. As Best and Marcus argue, a renewed dedication to New Formalism may encourage critics to move beyond suspicious, debunking readings of literary texts inspired by Marxism and psychoanalysis in order to focus on the "surface" of literary texts themselves.[28] Taking a different approach, Levine maintains that "forms are the stuff of politics" and urges readers to practice a close attention to texts as sites of colliding forms.[29] A renewed philological approach, with its attention to verbal detail as well as broader cultural contexts, might be productively allied with recent New Formalist imperatives to examine literary patterns and forms in conjunction with their wider sociopolitical meanings.[30] As we have seen, both Victorian philologists and their readers were keenly aware of the political circumstances of language's production; because of this, the field can restore an attention to language without bracketing context as the New Critics did. Moreover, such an approach would encourage conversations among disciplines. As this book has shown, the authors examined here—Carlyle, the Brownings, Tennyson, and Hardy—all turned to the science of language as an imaginative forum in which to understand their changing political landscape. Their work serves as a vital and timely reminder of the combined power of poetry, philology, and political reflection that persists even into our moment of intense disciplinary specialization, and that continues to teach us about sovereignty, self-expression, and the ever-shifting dynamics of language and form.

Notes

1 Müller, *Lectures*, 71.
2 Ferguson, *Language, Science, and Popular Fiction*, 3.
3 Saussure, *Course in General Linguistics*, 4.
4 Ferguson, *Language, Science, and Popular Fiction*, 4.
5 Momma, *From Philology to English Studies*, 185.
6 Brandt, "How Far Should Our Teaching and Text-Books Have a Scientific Basis?" 58. DOI: 10.2307/455998.
7 Ibid.
8 Ibid.
9 W.T. Hewett, "The Aims and Methods of Collegiate Instruction in Modern Languages," 25. Hewett references world literature and seems to advocate a borderless approach to literary studies, but the article itself is primarily concerned with instruction in French and German.
10 Ibid.
11 Plotkin, *The Tenth Muse*, 42.
12 Taylor, *Hardy's Literary Language*, 4–5.
13 For the survival of the *OED* through the war years and through the shortage of men and supplies see Mugglestone, *Lost for Words*, 193–195.
14 Brewer, *Treasure-House of the Language*, 191–193.
15 Mugglestone, *Talking Proper*, 267–278.
16 T.S. Eliot, *The Waste Land*, 124–134.
17 Sherry, *The Great War and the Language of Modernism*, 18.
18 Ibid., 187.
19 "History of the *OED*," *OED* blog, Oxford University Press, n.d., http://public.oed.com/history-of-the-oed/. Brewer discusses the ongoing work on this edition in *Treasure-House of the Language*, 237–257.
20 Mugglestone, *Lost for Words*, 220. See also Brewer, *Treasure-House of the Language*, 239.
21 See Sperling, *Visionary Philology*, 1–39 and Allison Bearly and Hannah Brockhaus, "The Force of Words: An Interview with Laura Bylenock, Winner of the T.S. Eliot Prize," Truman State University Press blog, March 31, 2015, http://tsup.truman.edu/tag/oxford-english-dictionary/.
22 See Natasha Sajé, "Poems Aware of History: Using the *Oxford English Dictionary*," 233–239.
23 David Antoine-Williams, "Three OED Poems," *Poetry and Contingency*, 1 February 2013. http://poetry-contingency.uwaterloo.ca/three-oed-poems/
24 Gerald Graff, *Professing Literature*, 68.
25 James Turner, *Philology*, 386.
26 Ibid., xx.
27 Jerome McGann's *A New Republic of Letters* makes the case for a return to textual philology as a way of negotiating our complex twenty-first-century world of digital media. As McGann argues, the digitization of paper-based archives is handled by librarians and, more problematically, by commercial organizations like Google and Gale that elevate profit over public learning (20–21). Scholars are thus obligated to take on the management of these

archives by creating digitized equivalents of the textual scholarly edition, integrating library materials into online environments, and determining how to extend the lifetime of such editions beyond a twenty-year window, all endeavors that philology and textual criticism can help us theorize and undertake (26–27). Here, of course, McGann mainly means by "philology" the text-based scholarship of the Higher and Lower Criticism rather than the science-of-language branch of philology I have analyzed in this book. However, his emphasis on the notion of the revived, global "republic" of philology is very much in line with the democratic impulse of language-study I have traced throughout the Victorian period. Responding to Pascale Casanova's claims *The World Republic of Letters* (2004), which describes a universal republic of literature based in avant-garde writing and removed from political and economic mandates, McGann looks to philology as "the republic of grammarians, rhetoricians, and the poets they study" and to scholarship as a leveling arena where "dialects and dead or disappearing languages are as pertinent as imperial tongues" (205–206). Philology thus acts as a timely critical resource for historically marginalized authors and traditions.

28 Best and Marcus, "Surface Reading," 10.
29 Levine, *Forms*, 3.
30 For a recent study of philology and Romanticism that analyzes philology's productive attention to small parts rather than thematic wholes and its distancing from assumptions of authorial agency see Elfenbein's *Romanticism and the Rise of English*, 1–17 and 185–219.

Bibliography

Aarsleff, Hans. *The Study of Language in England, 1780–1860*. Princeton: Princeton University Press, 1967.

———. *From Locke to Saussure: Essays on the Study of Language and Intellectual History*. Minneapolis: University of Minnesota Press, 1982.

Abberley, Will. "Race and Species Essentialism in Nineteenth-Century Philology." *Critical Quarterly* 53, no. 4 (2011): 45–60.

———. *English Fiction and the Evolution of Language*. Cambridge: Cambridge University Press, 2015.

Alexander, Sarah C. *Victorian Literature and the Physics of the Imponderable*. Abingdon: Pickering & Chatto, 2015.

Alter, Stephen G. *Darwinism and the Linguistic Image: Language, Race, and Natural Theology in the Nineteenth Century*. Baltimore: Johns Hopkins University Press, 2002.

———. *William Dwight Whitney and the Science of Language*. Baltimore: Johns Hopkins University Press, 2005.

Altick, Richard D. and James F. Loucks, II. *Browning's Roman Murder Story: A Reading of "The Ring and the Book."* Chicago: The University of Chicago Press, 1968.

Anderson, Amanda. *Tainted Souls and Painted Faces: The Rhetoric of Fallenness in Victorian Culture*. Ithaca: Cornell University Press.

Anonymous. "The Ring and the Book." *Saturday Review of Politics, Literature, Science and Art* 26, no. 687 (1868): 833. *British Periodicals Collection*. 8 April 2016.

———. "Mr. Hardy as a Poet." *The Academy* no. 1383 (1899): 43–44. Reprinted in *Thomas Hardy: The Critical Heritage*, edited by R.G. Cox (London: Routledge, 2005), 333–336.

Armstrong, Isobel. "*The Ring and the Book*: The Uses of Prolixity." In *The Major Victorian Poets: Reconsiderations*, edited by Isobel Armstrong, 177–198. Lincoln: University of Nebraska Press, 1969.

———. *Victorian Poetry: Poetry, Poets, and Politics*. London: Routledge, 1993.

———. "Browning's 'Caliban' and Primitive Language." In *Robert Browning in Contexts*, edited by John Woolford, 76–85. Winfield: Wedgestone Press, 1998.

———. *The Radical Aesthetic*. Oxford: Blackwell, 2000.

Arnold, Matthew. *Culture and Anarchy*. Ed. by Jane Garnett. Oxford: Oxford World's Classics, 2006.

Ashcroft, Bill, Gareth Griffiths, and Helen Tiffin, eds. *The Post-Colonial Studies Reader*. 2nd ed. London: Routledge, 1995.

Auerbach, Erich. "The Philology of World Literature." In *Time, History, and Literature: Selected Essays of Erich Auerbach*, edited by James I. Porter. Translated by Jane O. Newman. 253–265. Princeton: Princeton University Press, 2014.

Austin, Kay. "Pompila: 'Saint and Martyr Both.'" *Victorian Poetry* 17, no. 4 (1979): 287–301.

Avery, Simon and Rebecca Stott. *Elizabeth Barrett Browning*. Harlow: Pearson Education, 2003.

———. "Telling It Slant: Promethean, Whig, and Dissenting Politics in Elizabeth Barrett's Poetry of the 1830s." *Victorian Poetry* 44, no.4 (2006): 405–424.

Ayers, Michael. *Locke: Epistemology and Ontology*. 2 vols. London: Routledge, 1993. Reprinted as one volume, London: Routledge, 1996.

Bagehot, "Wordsworth, Tennyson, and Browning; or, Pure, Ornate, and Grotesque Art in English Poetry." *The National Review* 19 (1864): 27–67. *British Periodicals Collection*. 21 November 2017.

Bailey, Richard W. "British English Since 1830." In *A Companion to the History of the English Language*, edited by H. Momma and M. Matto, 234–242. Chichester, UK: Blackwell Publishing Ltd, 2008.

Barton, Anna. *Nineteenth-Century Poetry and Liberal Thought: Forms of Freedom*. Basingstoke: Palgrave Macmillan, 2017.

Beer, Gillian. "Darwin's Reading and the Fictions of Development." In *The Darwinian Heritage*, edited by David Kohn, 543–588. Princeton: Princeton University Press, 1985.

———. *Open Fields: Science in Cultural Encounter*. Oxford: Clarendon Press, 1996.

———. *Darwin's Plots*. 2nd ed. Cambridge: Cambridge University Press, 2000.

Beer, John. *Romanticism, Revolution, and Language*. Cambridge: Cambridge University Press, 2013.

Bell, Duncan. *The Idea of Greater Britain: Empire and the Future of World Order, 1860–1900*. Princeton: Princeton University Press, 2009.

———. "Empire and Imperialism." In *The Cambridge History of Nineteenth-Century Political Thought*, edited by Gareth Stedman Jones and Gregory Claeys, 864–892. Cambridge: Cambridge University Press, 2011.

Beltrami, Pietro G. and Simone Fornara. "Italian Historical Dictionaries: From the Accademia Della Crusca to the Web." *International Journal of Lexicography* 17, no. 4 (2004): 357–384.

Best, Stephen and Sharon Marcus. "Surface Reading: An Introduction." *Representations* 108, no. 1 (2009): 1–21.

Bevis, Matthew. "Tennyson, Ireland, and 'The Powers of Speech.'" *Victorian Poetry* 39, no. 3 (2001): 345–364.

Blackburn, Helen. *Women's Suffrage: A Record of the Women's Suffrage Movement in the British Isles*. London: Williams & Norgate, 1902. https://books.google.com/books?id=JjkZAAAAYAAJ.

Blair, Hugh. *Lectures on Rhetoric and Belles Lettres*. Edited by Linda Ferreira-Buckley and S. Michael Halloran. Carbondale: Southern Illinois University Press, 2005.

Blair, Kirstie. *Victorian Poetry and the Culture of the Heart*. Oxford: Oxford University Press, 2006.

———. *Form and Faith in Victorian Poetry and Religion*. Oxford: Oxford University Press, 2012.

Blake, N.F. *Non-Standard Language in English Literature*. London: Andre Deutsch, 1981.

Bonfiglio, Richard. "Proximate Cosmopolitanism: The transnational work of Victorian domesticity, 1848–1875." Ph.D. diss., University of Chicago, 2010.

Bowler, Peter. *Evolution: The History of an Idea*. 25th ed. Berkeley: University of California Press, 2009.

Brady, Ann P. *Pompilia: A Feminist Reading of Robert Browning's The Ring and the Book*. Athens: Ohio University Press, 1988.

Brandt, H. C. G. "How Far Should Our Teaching and Text-Books Have a Scientific Basis?" *Transactions of the Modern Language Association of America* 1 (1884): 57–63. doi:10.2307/455998.

Brantlinger, Patrick. *Rule of Darkness: British Literature and Imperialism, 1830–1914*. Ithaca: Cornell University Press, 1988.

———. *Victorian Literature and Postcolonial Studies*. Edinburgh: Edinburgh University Press, 2009.

Brewer, Charlotte. *Treasure-House of the Language: The Living OED*. New Haven: Yale University Press, 2007.

———. "Johnson, Webster, and the *New English Dictionary*." In *A Companion to the History of the English Language*, edited by H. Momma and M. Matto, 113–122. Chichester, UK: Blackwell Publishing Ltd, 2008.

Brock, Michael. *The Great Reform Act*. London: Hutchinson University Library, 1973.

Brown, Stewart J. "Irving, Edward (1792–1834)." In *Oxford Dictionary of National Biography*. Oxford University Press, 2004. Accessed 28 October 2016. doi:10.1093/ref:odnb/14473.

Brown, Susan. "'Pompilia': The Woman (in) Question." *Victorian Poetry* 34, no. 1 (1996): 15–37.

Browning, Elizabeth Barrett. "A Thought on Thoughts." [1836]. Edited by Sandra Donaldson. Vol. 4 of Donaldson, *The Works*, 275–285.

———. *An Essay on Mind*. [1826]. Edited by Simon Avery. Vol. 4 of Donaldson, *The Works*, 75–131.

———. "Kings." [1831]. Edited by Sandra Donaldson. Vol. 4 of Donaldson, *The Works*, 171–173.

———. "Some Account of the Greek Christian Poets." [1842]. Edited by Sandra Donaldson. Vol. 4 of Donaldson, *The Works*, 347–442.

———. "Thomas Carlyle." In *A New Spirit of the Age*, edited by R. H. Horne. 2 vols. Vol. 2. 253–280. London: Smith, Elder, and Co., 1844.

———. *A Drama of Exile*. [1844]. Edited by Marjorie Stone and Beverly Taylor. Vol. 1 of Donaldson, *The Works*, 3–73.

———. *Sonnets from the Portuguese*. [1850]. Boston: Small, Maynard, 1902. https://archive.org/details/fromportusonnets00browrich.

———. *Aurora Leigh*. [1856]. Edited by Marjorie Stone and Sandra Donaldson. Vol. 3 of Donaldson, *The Works*, 3–74.

———. Frederic G. Kenyon (ed.), *The Letters of Elizabeth Barrett Browning*. Edited by Frederic G. Kenyon. 2 vols. New York: The Macmillan Co., 1899. https://books.google.com/books?id=ADRGAAAAYAAJ.

———, and Robert Browning. *The Browning Letters*. Armstrong Browning Library. Baylor University. http://digitalcollections.baylor.edu/cdm/landingpage/collection/ab-letters.

———. "Two Autobiographical Essays by Elizabeth Barrett." In *Browning Institute Studies*, edited by William S. Peterson, no. 2, 119–134. New York, 1974.

Browning, Robert. *Sordello*. [1840]. Vol. 2 of *The Complete Works of Robert Browning*, edited by John Berkey, 125–335. Athens: Ohio University Press, 1970.

———. "Respectability." [1855]. Vol. 5 of *The Complete Works of Robert Browning*, edited by John Berkey, Ashby Bland Crowder, Jr., Susan Crowl, et. al., 257. Athens: Ohio University Press, 1981.

———. "Caliban upon Setebos." [1864]. Vol. 6 of *The Complete Works of Robert Browning*, edited by John C. Berkey, Allan C. Dooley, and Susan E. Dooley, 259–270. Athens: Ohio University Press, 1996.

———. *The Ring and the Book*. [1868–1869]. Edited by Richard D. Altick and Thomas J. Collins. Peterborough: Broadview Press, 2001.

———. *Dearest Isa: Robert Browning's Letters to Isabella Blagden*. Edited by Edward C. McAleer. Austin: University of Texas Press, 1951.

Bucher, Lothair. "On Political Terms." In *Transactions of the Philological Society 1858*, 42–62. Berlin: A. Asher, 1858. https://archive.org/details/transact185800philuoft/page/n3.

Buckland, Adelene. *Novel Science: Fiction and the Invention of Nineteenth-Century Geology*. Chicago: The University of Chicago Press, 2011.

Buckler, William E. *Poetry and Truth in Robert Browning's* The Ring and the Book. New York: New York University Press, 1985.

Burgess, Michael. "Imperial Federation: Continuity and Change in British Imperial Ideas, 1869–1871." *New Zealand Journal of History* 17, no. 1 (1983): 60–80.

Canovan, Margaret. "The Un-Benthamite Utilitarianism of Joseph Priestley." *Journal of the History of Ideas* 45, no. 3 (1984): 435–450.

Carlyle, Thomas. "Essay on Burns." [1828]. Edited by Cornelius Beach Bradley. Boston: Benj. H. Sanborn & Co., 1901. https://babel.hathitrust.org/cgi/pt?id=hvd.32044097037840;view=1up;seq=15.

———. "Boswell's *Life of Johnson*." [1832]. In *Critical and Miscellaneous Essays*, edited by Henry Duff Traill, 63–135. 5 vols. Vol. 3. London: Chapman and Hall, 1899. https://books.google.com/books?id=1qFDAQAAIAAJ.

———. *Sartor Resartus*. [1833–1840]. Edited by Kerry McSweeney and Peter Sabor. Oxford: Oxford University Press, 1987.

———. *The French Revolution*. [1837]. Edited by K.J. Fielding and David Sorensen. Oxford: Oxford World's Classics, 1989.

———. *Chartism*. [1839]. 2nd ed. London: James Fraser, 1840. https://books.google.com/books? id=kaelVuyDq20C.

———. *On Heroes, Hero-Worship, and the Heroic in History*. [1841]. Edited by David R. Sorensen and Brent E. Kinser. New Haven: Yale University Press, 2013.

———. Prologue to *Oliver Cromwell's Letters and Speeches*. [1845]. 3 vols. Vol. 1. 3–74. London: Chapman and Hall, 1885.

———. *Reminiscences*. Edited by James Anthony Froude. New York: Harper & Brothers, 1881. https://archive.org/details/reminiscencesbyt01carl.

————, and Jane Welsh Carlyle. *The Carlyle Letters Online [CLO]*. Edited by Brent E. Kinser. Durham: Duke University Press, 2007–2016. www.carlyleletters.org.

Carpenter, Mary Wilson. "The Trouble with Romola." In *Victorian Sages and Cultural Discourse: Renegotiating Gender and Power*, edited by Thaïs E. Morgan, 105–128. New Brunswick: Rutgers University Press, 1990.

Carr, Geraldine. "Translator's Preface." In *Condillac's Treatise on the Sensations*, translated by Geraldine Carr, xix–xxvii. Los Angeles: University of Southern California Press, 1930.

Chakrabarty, Dipesh. *Provincializing Europe: Postcolonial Thought and Historical Difference*. Princeton: Princeton University Press, 2007.

Chambers, Robert. *Vestiges of the Natural History of Creation*. Ed. by James Secord. Chicago: The University of Chicago Press, 1994.

Chapman, Alison. "Poetry, Network, Nation: Elizabeth Barrett Browning and Expatriate Women's Poetry." *Victorian Studies* 55, no. 2 (2013): 275–285.

————. *Networking the Nation: British and American Women's Poetry and Italy, 1840–1870*. Oxford: Oxford University Press, 2015.

Chase, Malcolm. *Chartism: A New History*. Manchester: Manchester University Press, 2007.

Chawaf, Chantal. "La chair linguistique" [Linguistic flesh]. *Nouvelles littéraires* 2534 (1976): 18. Translated by Yvonne Rochette-Ozzello. Reprinted in Marks and de Courtivron, *New French Feminisms*, 177–178.

Christie, Ian. *Stress and Stability in Late Eighteenth-Century Britain: Reflections on the British Avoidance of Revolution*. Oxford: Oxford University Press, 1985.

Cixous, Hélène. "Le rire de la méduse." *L'arc* 61 (1975): 39–54. "The Laugh of the Medusa." Translated by Keith Cohen and Paula Cohen. *Signs* 1, no. 4 (1976): 875–893. Reprinted in in Marks and de Courtivron, *New French Feminisms*, 245–264.

Claeys, Gregory. *The French Revolution Debate in Britain: The Origin of Modern Politics*. Basingstoke: Palgrave, 2007.

Clark, Anna. "Gender, class, and the constitution: franchise reform in England, 1832–1928." In *Re-Reading the Constitution: New Narratives in the Political History of England's Long Nineteenth Century*, edited by James Vernon, 230–253. Cambridge: Cambridge University Press, 1996.

Cobbett, William. *A Grammar of the English Language, in a Series of Letters*. 4th ed. London: William Benbow, 1820. https://books.google.com/books?id=IrfUf5nE4VUC&printsec=frontcover&source=gbs_ge_summary_r&cad=0#v=onepage&q&f=false.

Coburn, Kathleen and Bart Winer, eds. *The Complete Works of Samuel Taylor Coleridge*. 16 vols. Princeton: Princeton University Press, 1971–2001.

Coleridge, Derwent. "Observations on the Plan of the Society's Proposed New English Dictionary." In *Transactions of the Philological Society 1860–1*, 152–167. Berlin: A. Asher, n.d. https://archive.org/details/transact186100philuoft.

Coleridge, Samuel Taylor. *Aids to Reflection*. [1825]. Edited by John Beer. Vol. 9 of Coburn and Winer, *The Complete Works*.

————. *On the Constitution of Church and State*. [1830]. Edited by John Colmer. Vol. 10 of Coburn and Winer, *The Complete Works*.

Condillac, Étienne Bonnot. *Condillac's Treatise on the Sensations*. Translated by Geraldine Carr. London: The Favil Press, 1930.

Cowling, Maurice. *1867: Disraeli, Gladstone, and Revolution: The Passing of the Second Reform Bill*. Cambridge: Cambridge University Press, 1967.

Cox, R.G., ed. *Thomas Hardy: The Critical Heritage*. London: Routledge, 2005.

Crawford, Robert. *Devolving English Literature*. 2nd. ed. Edinburgh: Edinburgh University Press, 2000.

Crombie, Alexander. *The Etymology and Syntax of the English Language*. 2nd ed. London: J. Johnson, 1809. https://archive.org/details/atreatiseonetym00 cromgoog.

Crowley, Tony. *The Politics of Discourse: The Standard Language Question in British Cultural Debates*. London: Macmillan, 1989.

———. *The Politics of Language in Ireland 1366–1922*. London: Routledge, 2000.

———. "Class, Ethnicity, and the Formation of 'Standard English.'" In *A Companion to the History of the English Language*, edited by H. Momma and M. Matto, 303–312. Chichester, UK: Blackwell Publishing Ltd, 2008.

Cundiff, Paul A. "The Clarity of Browning's Ring Metaphor." *PMLA* 63, no. 4 (1948): 1276–1282.

Dale, Peter Allan. "'Paracelsus and Sordello': Trying the Stuff of Language." *Victorian Poetry* 18, no. 4 (1980): 359–369.

Darwin, Charles. *On the Origin of Species*. [1859]. Edited by William Bynum. New York: Penguin Classics, 2009.

———. *The Descent of Man, and Selection in Relation to Sex*. [1871]. Edited by James Moore and Adrian Desmond. New York: Penguin, 2004.

Davies, Corinne. "Aurora, the Morning Star: The Female Poet, Christology, and Revelation in *Aurora Leigh*." *Studies in Browning and his Circle* 26 (2005): 54–61.

Dean, Dennis R. *Tennyson and Geology*. Lincoln: Tennyson Research Centre, 1985.

Dever, Carolyn. "Strategic Aestheticism: A Response to Caroline Levine." *Victorian Studies* 49, no. 1 (2006): 94–99.

Dewitt, Anne. *Moral Authority, Men of Science, and the Victorian Novel*. Cambridge: Cambridge University Press, 2013.

Dieleman, Karen. *Religious Imaginaries: The Liturgical and Poetic Practices of Elizabeth Barrett Browning, Christina Rossetti, and Adelaide Proctor*. Athens: Ohio University Press, 2012.

Donaldson, John William. *The New Cratylus, or, Contributions Towards a More Accurate Knowledge of the Greek Language*. London: John Parker, 1839. https://books.google.com/books?id=syhGAAAAcAAJ.

Donaldson, Sandra, et.al, ed. *The Works of Elizabeth Barrett Browning*. 5 vols. London: Pickering & Chatto, 2010.

Dowling, Linda. "Victorian Oxford and the Science of Language." *PMLA* 97, no. 2 (1982): 160–78.

———. *Language and Decadence in the Victorian Fin de Siècle*. Princeton: Princeton University Press, 1986.

Drury, Annmarie. *Translation as Transformation in Victorian Poetry*. Cambridge: Cambridge University Press, 2015.

Elfenbein, Andrew. *Romanticism and the Rise of English*. Stanford: Stanford University Press, 2009.

Eliot, T.S. *The Waste Land*. Edited by Michael North. New York: W.W. Norton, 2001.

Elworthy, Frederick Thomas. "Dialect of West Somerset." In *Transactions of the Philological Society 1875–76*, 197–272. London: Trübner & Co., 1877. https://archive.org/details/transactionsphi13britgoog.

Emsley, Clove. *Britain and the French Revolution*. London: Routledge, 2000.

Engelberg, Edward. "The Beast Image in *Idylls of the King*." *ELH* 22, no. 4 (1955): 287–92.

"Establishments and Disestablishment." *Blackwood's Edinburgh Magazine* 138, no. 842 (1885): 832–846. *British Periodicals Collection*. 15 December 2016.

Evans, Eric J. *The Forging of the Modern State: Early Industrial Britain 1783–1870*. 3rd ed. London: Pearson Education, 2001.

Fabian, Johannes. *Time and the Other: How Anthropology Makes Its Object*. New York: Columbia University Press, 2002.

Falkenstein, Lorne. "Étienne Bonnot de Condillac." In *Stanford Encyclopedia of Philosophy*. Stanford University, 2010. Article published 17 October 2002, revised 6 August 2010. http://plato.stanford.edu/archives/fall2010/entries/condillac.

Faulk, Laura J. "Destructive Maternity in *Aurora Leigh*." *Victorian Literature and Culture* 41, no. 1 (2013): 41–54.

Ferguson, Christine. *Language, Science and Popular Fiction in the Victorian Fin-de-siècle: The Brutal Tongue*. Aldershot: Ashgate, 2006.

Ficke, Sarah H. "Crafting Social Criticism: Infanticide in 'The Runaway Slave at Pilgrim's Point' and *Aurora Leigh*." *Victorian Poetry* 51, no. 2 (2013): 249–267.

Field, George. *Chromatography; or, A Treatise on Colours and Pigments, and of Their Powers in Painting, &c*. London: Charles Tilt, 1835. https://books.google.com/books? id=NBMFAAAAYAAJ

Findlay, L. M. "Taking the Measure of *Différance*: Deconstruction and *The Ring and the Book*." *Victorian Poetry* 29, no. 4 (1991): 401–414.

Fourier, Charles. *The Theory of the Four Movements*. Edited by Gareth Stedman Jones and Ian Patterson. Cambridge: Cambridge University Press, 1996.

Frye, Lowell T. "'Vocables, Still Vocables': Linguistic and Religious Despair in Carlyle's Latter-Day Pamphlets." *Literature and Belief* 25, no. 1 (2007): 196–216. http://literatureandbelief.byu.edu/publications/vocables.pdf.

Fynes, R. C. C. "Müller, Friedrich Max (1823–1900)." In *Oxford Dictionary of National Biography*, Oxford University Press, 2004. Accessed 28 October 2016. http://www.oxforddnb.com/view/article/18394.

Gallagher, Catherine. *The Industrial Reformation of English Fiction: Social Discourse and Narrative Form, 1832–1867*. Chicago: University of Chicago Press, 1985.

Geric, Michelle. "Tennyson's *Maud* and the 'unmeaning of names': Geology, Language Theory, and Dialogics." *Victorian Poetry* 51, no.1 (2013): 37–62.

———. *Tennyson and Geology: Poetry and Poetics*. Abingdon: Palgrave Macmillan, 2017.

Gikandi, Simon. *Maps of Englishness: Writing Identity in the Culture of Colonialism.* New York: Columbia University Press, 1996.

Gilbert, Pamela. *Mapping the Victorian Social Body.* Albany: State University of New York Press, 2004.

Gill, Stephen. *Wordsworth and the Victorians.* Oxford: Clarendon Press, 1998.

Gleadle, Kathryn. *The Early Feminists: Radical Unitarians and the Emergence of the Women's Rights Movement, 1831–1851.* New York: St. Martin's Press, 1995.

Glen, W. Cunningham. *The Representation of the People Act, 1884.* 2nd ed. London: Shaw & Sons, 1885. https://archive.org/details/representationp00glengoog.

Graff, Gerald. *Professing Literature: An Institutional History.* 20th ed. Chicago: The University of Chicago Press, 2007.

Grundy, Isobel. "Hardy's Harshness." In *The Poetry of Thomas Hardy,* edited by Patricia Clements and Juliet Grindle, 1–17. Totowa: Barnes and Noble Books, 1980.

Hadley, Elaine. *Living Liberalism: Practical Citizenship in Mid-Victorian Britain.* Chicago: University of Chicago Press, 2010.

Hair, Donald S. *Browning's Experiments with Genre.* Toronto: University of Toronto Press, 1972.

———. *Tennyson's Language.* Toronto: University of Toronto Press, 1991.

———. *Robert Browning's Language.* Toronto: University of Toronto Press, 1999.

———. *Fresh Strange Music: Elizabeth Barrett Browning's Language.* Montreal: McGill-Queen's University Press, 2015.

Hall, Catherine. "The nation within and without." In *Defining the Victorian Nation: Class, Race, Gender and the British Reform Act of 1867,* edited by Catherine Hall, Keith McClelland and Jane Rendall, 179–233. Cambridge: Cambridge University Press, 2000.

———. "The Rule of Difference: Gender, Class, and Empire in the Making of the 1832 Reform Act." In *Gendered Nations: Nationalisms and Gender Order in the Long Nineteenth Century,* edited by Ida Blom, Karen Hagemann, and Catherine Hall, 107–135. Oxford: Berg, 2000.

———. *Civilizing Subjects: Colony and Metropole in the English Imagination, 1830–1867.* Chicago: University of Chicago Press, 2002.

Hardy, Thomas. "Dorset in London." *Longman's Magazine* 2, no. 9 (1883): 252–269. Reprinted in Orel, *Thomas Hardy's Personal Writings,* 218–225.

———. *Wessex Poems.* [1898]. Vol. 1 of Hynes, *Complete Poetical Works,* 7–106.

———. "To the Editor of the *Daily Chronicle.*" 25 December 1899. Reprinted in Orel, *Thomas Hardy's Personal Writings,* 201–202.

———. *Poems of the Past and Present.* [1901]. Vol. 1 of Hynes, *Complete Poetical Works,* 109–228.

Hare, A. W. and J. C. Hare. *Guesses at Truth, by Two Brothers.* Vol. 1. London: John Taylor, 1827. https://archive.org/details/guessesattruthb03haregoog/page/n9.

Harrold, Charles Frederick. "Carlyle's Sources for *The French Revolution.*" In *A Bibliography of Thomas Carlyle's Writings and Ana,* edited by Isaac Watson Dyer, 582–584. Portland: Southwerk Press, 1928.

Hayes, William A. *The Background and Passage of the Third Reform Act.* New York: Garland Publishing, 1982.

Heater, Derek Benjamin. *Citizenship in Britain: A History*. Edinburgh: Edinburgh University Press, 2006.

Henchman, Anna. "'The Globe we groan in': Astronomical Distance and Stellar Decay in *In Memoriam*." *Victorian Poetry* 41, no.1 (2003): 29–45.

———. *The Starry Sky Within*. Oxford: Oxford University Press, 2014.

Herder, Johann Gottfried. *Essay on the Origin of Language*. Translated by Alexander Gode. In *On the Origin of Language: Two Essays*. Translated by John H. Moran and Alexander Gode. 87–166. Chicago: University of Chicago Press, 1966.

Hewett, W. T. "The Aims and Methods of Collegiate Instruction in Modern Languages." *Transactions of the Modern Language Association of America* 1 (1884): 25–36. doi:10.2307/455996.

Hill, Lucy Birkbeck. "Canvassing the Rustics." *Time* no. 12 (Dec 1889): 581–588. *British Periodicals Collection*. 5 November 2016.

Hilton, Boyd. *The Age of Atonement: The Influence of Evangelicalism on Social and Economic Thought, 1785–1865*. Oxford: Clarendon Press, 1986.

———. *A Mad, Bad, and Dangerous People? England 1783–1846*. Oxford: Clarendon Press, 2006.

Holmes, John. *Darwin's Bards: British and American Poetry in the Age of Evolution*. Edinburgh: Edinburgh University Press, 2009.

———. ""The Poet of Science": How Scientists Read Their Tennyson." *Victorian Studies* 54, no. 4 (2012): 655–78.

Hoppen, Theodore K. *Elections, Politics, and Society in Ireland 1832–1885*. Oxford: Clarendon Press, 1984.

———. "The Franchise and Electoral Politics in England and Ireland 1832–1885." *History* 70, no. 229 (1985): 207–217.

———. *The Mid-Victorian Generation 1846–1886*. Oxford: Clarendon Press, 1998.

Horne Tooke, John. *Epea pteroenta, or, The Diversions of Purley*. Edited by Richard Taylor. 2 vols. London: Thomas Tegg, 1840. https://archive.org/details/epeapteroentaord00took.

Hughes, Linda. *The Manyfacèd Glass: Tennyson's Dramatic Monologues*. Athens: Ohio University Press, 1987.

———. "Come Again, and Thrice as Fair: Reading Tennyson's Beginning." In *King Arthur's Modern Return*, edited by Debra N. Mancoff, 51–64. New York: Garland, 1998.

Hynes, Samuel. *The Pattern of Hardy's Poetry*. Chapel Hill: University of North Carolina Press, 1961.

———, ed. *The Complete Poetic Works of Thomas Hardy*. 5 vols. Oxford: Clarendon Press, 1982–1995.

Irigaray, Luce. "Ce sexe qui n'en est pas un" [The sex which is not one] in *Ce sexe qui n'en est pas un*. Minuit, 1977. Translated by Claudia Reeder. Reprinted in Marks and de Courtivron, *New French Feminisms*, 99–106.

Irving, Edward. "That the Beginning or Origin of the Mystery, that the Eternal Word should take Unto Himself a Body, is the Holy Will and the Good Pleasure of God." In *Sermons, Lectures, and Occasional Discourses*. 3 vols. Vol. 1, 1–66. London: Seeley and Burnside, 1828. https://books.google.com/books?id=VwUeH-wTxZ8C.

Johnson, Samuel, ed. *A Dictionary of the English Language*. 2 vols. Vol. 1. London: W. Strahan, 1755. https://books.google.com/books?id=cNrI9Y4bY_QC.

Jones, Andrew. *The Politics of Reform 1884*. Cambridge: Cambridge University Press, 1972.

Jones, Gareth Stedman. *Languages of Class: Studies in English Working Class History 1832–1982*. Cambridge: Cambridge University Press, 1984.

Jowett, Benjamin. "On the Interpretation of Scripture." In *Essays and Reviews: The 1860 Text and Its Reading*, edited by Victor Shea and William Whitla, 477–614. Charlottesville: University of Virginia Press, 2000.

Kachru, Braj B. "World Englishes in World Contexts." In *A Companion to the History of the English Language*, edited by H. Momma and M. Matto, 567–580. Chichester, UK: Blackwell Publishing Ltd, 2008.

Kantorowicz, Ernst. *The King's Two Bodies*. Princeton: Princeton University Press, 1957.

Kaplan, Cora. Introduction to Elizabeth Barrett Browning's *Aurora Leigh and Other Poems*. Edited by Cora Kaplan, 5–36. London: The Women's Press, 1978.

Keirstead, Christopher M. *Victorian Poetry, Europe, and the Challenge of Cosmopolitanism*. Columbus: The Ohio State University Press, 2011.

Kelley, Philip and Ronald Hudson, eds. *The Brownings' Correspondence*. 23 vols. Winfield: Wedgestone Press, 1984–2016.

Kiernan, Victor. "Tennyson, King Arthur, and Imperialism." In *Culture: Ideology and Politics: Essays for Eric Hobsbawm*, edited by Raphael Samuel and Gareth Stedman Jones, 126–148. London: Routledge and Kegan Paul, 1982.

Killham, John. "Browning's 'Modernity': *The Ring and the Book*, and Relativism." In *The Major Victorian Poets: Reconsiderations*, edited by Isobel Armstrong, 153–176. Lincoln: University of Nebraska Press, 1969.

King, Joshua. *Imagined Spiritual Communities in Britain's Age of Print*. Columbus: The Ohio State University Press, 2015.

Lamarre, Paul. "John Horne Tooke and the Grammar of Political Experience." *Philological Quarterly* 77, no. 2 (1998): 188–207.

Langbaum, Robert. *The Poetry of Experience: The Dramatic Monologue in Literary Tradition*. New York: Random House, 1957.

LaPorte, Charles and Jason Rudy, eds. "Spasmodic Poetry and Poetics." Special issue, *Victorian Poetry* 42, no.4 (2004).

———. *Victorian Poets and the Changing Bible*. Charlottesville: University of Virginia Press, 2011.

Lea, Hermann. *Thomas Hardy's Wessex*. London: Macmillan and Co., 1913. https://archive.org/details/hardyswessthomas00leahrich.

Leask, Nigel. *Robert Burns and Pastoral: Poetry and Improvement in Late Eighteenth-Century Scotland*. Oxford: Oxford University Press, 2010.

Lefort, Claude. *Democracy and Political Theory*. Translated by David Macey. Minneapolis: University of Minnesota Press, 1988.

Leighton, Angela. "'Because men made the laws': The Fallen Woman and the Woman Poet." *Victorian Poetry* 27, no. 2 (1989): 109–127.

———. *Victorian Women Poets: Writing Against the Heart*. Charlottesville: University of Virginia Press, 1992.

Levine, Caroline. "Strategic Formalism: Towards a New Method in Cultural Studies." *Victorian Studies* 48.4 (2006): 625–657.

———. "Scaled Up, Writ Small: A Response to Carolyn Dever and Herbert F. Tucker." *Victorian Studies* 49, no. 1 (2006): 100–105.

———. "Formal Pasts and Formal Possibilities in Victorian Studies." *Literature Compass* 4, no. 4 (2007): 1241–1256.

———. *Forms: Whole, Rhythm, Hierarchy, Network*. Princeton: Princeton University Press, 2015.

Levine, George. *The Realistic Imagination: English Fiction from Frankenstein to Lady Chatterley*. Chicago: The University of Chicago Press, 1981.

———. *Darwin and the Novelists: Patterns of Science in Victorian Fiction*. Chicago: The University of Chicago Press, 1988.

Levinson, Marjorie. "What Is New Formalism?" *PMLA* 122, no. 2 (2007): 558–569.

Lewis, Linda. M. *Elizabeth Barrett Browning's Spiritual Progress*. Columbia: University of Missouri Press, 1998.

———. *Germaine de Staël, George Sand, and the Victorian Woman Artist*. Columbia: University of Missouri Press, 2003.

Lifschitz, Avi. *Language and Enlightenment: The Berlin Debates of the Eighteenth Century*. Oxford: Oxford University Press, 2012.

Lightman, Bernard. "The Popularization of Evolution and Victorian Culture." In *Evolution and Victorian Culture*, edited by Bernard Lightman and Bennett Zon, 286–311. Cambridge: Cambridge University Press, 2014.

Littledale, Harold. *Essays on Lord Tennyson's Idylls of the King*. London: Macmillan and Co., 1893. https://books.google.com/books?id=_sHPAAAAMAAJ.

Locke, John. *An Essay Concerning Human Understanding*. Edited by Roger Woolhouse. New York: Penguin, 2004.

Lootens, Tricia. *Lost Saints: Silence, Gender, and Victorian Literary Canonization*. Charlottesville: University of Virginia Press, 1996.

Lyell, Charles. *Principles of Geology*. 2nd ed., 3 vols. Vol. 2. London: John Murray, 1833. https://books.google.com/books?id=mFkOAAAAQAAJ.

———. *The Geological Evidences of the Antiquity of Man*. London, John Murray, 1863. https://archive.org/details/geologicalevide07lyelgoog.

Margini, Matthew. "The Beast with the Broken Lance: Humanism and Posthumanism in Tennyson's *Idylls of the King*." *Victorian Poetry* 53, no. 2 (Summer 2015): 171–192.

Markovits, Stefanie. *The Crimean War in the British Imagination*. Cambridge: Cambridge University Press, 2009.

Marks, Elaine and Isabelle de Courtivron, eds. *New French Feminisms: An Anthology*. Amherst: The University of Massachusetts Press, 1980.

Martin, Amy E. "Blood Transfusions: Constructions of Irish Racial Difference, the English Working Class, and Revolutionary Possibility in the work of Carlyle and Engels." *Victorian Literature and Culture* 32, no. 1 (2004): 83–102.

Martin, Meredith. "Gerard Manley Hopkins and the Stigma of Meter." *Victorian Studies* 50, no. 2 (2008): 243–253.

———. *The Rise and Fall of Meter: Poetry and English National Culture, 1860–1930*. Princeton: Princeton University Press, 2012.

Marx, Karl. "The Eighteenth Brumaire of Louis Bonaparte." In *The Marx-Engels Reader*, 2nd ed., edited by Robert C. Tucker, 594–617. New York: W.W. Norton, 1978.

Maurice, Frederick Denison. *The Kingdom of Christ*. 2 vols. Vol. 2. London: Darton and Clark, 1837.

Mayhall, Laura E. Nym. *The Militant Suffrage Movement: Citizenship and Resistance in Britain, 1860–1930.* Oxford: Oxford University Press, 2003.

McClure, J. Derrick. "English in Scotland." In *A Companion to the History of the English Language,* edited by H. Momma and M. Matto, 358–365. Chichester, UK: Blackwell Publishing Ltd, 2008.

McCracken-Flesher, Caroline. "Carlyle, Irving, and the Problematics of Prophecy." *Literature and Belief* 25, no. 1 (2005): 25–52. http://literatureandbelief. byu.edu/publications/carlyleirving.pdf.

McClintock, Anne. *Imperial Leather: Race, Gender and Sexuality in the Colonial Contest.* New York: Routledge, 1995.

McGann, Jerome. *A New Republic of Letters.* Cambridge: Harvard University Press, 2014.

McKelvy, William. "Much Better Burnt: Reading Arthur's Return by the Light of Troy." In *King Arthur's Modern Return,* edited by Debra N. Mancoff, 31–50. New York: Garland, 1998.

McKusick, James C. *Coleridge's Philosophy of Language.* New Haven: Yale University Press, 1986.

Mee, Jon. *Conversable worlds: Literature, Contention, and Community, 1762 to 1830.* Oxford: Oxford University Press, 2011.

Mercier, Louis-Sébastien. *Panorama of Paris.* [1781–1788]. Translated by Helen Simpson and edited by Jeremy D. Popkin. University Park: The Pennsylvania State University Press, 1999.

———. *New Picture of Paris.* [1789]. Translator unknown. 2 vols. London: C. Whittingham, 1800. *Eighteenth Century Collections Online,* Gale Group, http://find.galegroup.com.ezp.lib.rochester.edu/ecco/infomark.do?&source= gale&prodId=ECCO&userGroupName=roch18072_rbw&tabID=T001&do cId=CW102340426&type=multipage&contentSet=ECCOArticles&version= 1.0&docLevel=FASCIMILE.

Merivale, Herman. "Review of *The French Revolution.*" *Edinburgh Review* lxxi (July 1840): 411–445. Reprinted in Seigel, *Thomas Carlyle: The Critical Heritage,* 76–87.

Meynell, Alice. "Some Thoughts of a Reader of Tennyson." In *Hearts of Controversy* 1–22. London: Burns & Oates, 1917. *Victorian Women Writers Project.* Indiana University. Accessed 28 December 2018. http://purl.dlib. indiana.edu/iudl/vwwp/VAB7075.

Michie, Helena. *The Flesh Made Word: Female Figures and Women's Bodies.* New York: Oxford University Press, 1987.

Micklethwaite, David. *Noah Webster and the American Dictionary.* Jefferson: McFarland, 2000.

Mill, John Stuart. "*The French Revolution*: A History." *London and Westminster Review* 5, no. 2 (July 1837): 17–53.

———. *On Liberty.* [1859]. In *On Liberty and The Subjection of Women,* edited by Alan Ryan 7–129. New York: Penguin Classics, 2006.

Millgate, Michael. *Thomas Hardy: A Biography Revisited.* Oxford: Oxford University Press, 2004.

Moers, Ellen. *Literary Women.* London: W.H. Allen Co., 1977.

Momma, Haruko and Michael Matto, eds. *A Companion to the History of the English Language.* Chichester, UK: Blackwell Publishing Ltd, 2008.

Momma, Haruko. *From Philology to English Studies: Language and Culture in the Nineteenth Century.* Cambridge: Cambridge University Press, 2012.

"More on Great Britain Confederated." *Fraser's Magazine* 4, no. 20 (1871): 249–250.

Morgan, Lady Sydney. "Review of *The French Revolution.*" *Athenaeum* (20 May 1837): 353–5. Reprinted in Seigel, *Thomas Carlyle: The Critical Heritage,* 46–51.

Mugglestone, Lynda. *Talking Proper: The Rise of Accent as a Social Symbol.* Oxford: Oxford University Press, 2003.

———. *Lost for Words: The Hidden History of the Oxford English Dictionary.* New Haven: Yale University Press, 2005.

———. "The Rise of Received Pronunciation." In *A Companion to the History of the English Language,* edited by H. Momma and M. Matto, 243–250. Chichester, UK: Blackwell Publishing Ltd, 2008.

Müller, Friedrich Max. *Lectures on the Science of Language.* 5th ed. London: Longman's, 1861. https://books.google.com/books?id=BI9DAAAAcAAJ.

———. "Lectures on Mr. Darwin's Philosophy of Language." *Fraser's Magazine* 7, no. 41(1873): 525–541. *British Periodicals Collection.* 13 December 2013.

———. "Lectures on Mr. Darwin's Philosophy of Language." *Fraser's Magazine* 7, no. 42 (1873): 659–678. *British Periodicals Collection.* 13 December 2013.

Murray, James. Preface to Vol. 1 of *A New English Dictionary on Historical Principles,* v–xiv. Oxford: Clarendon Press, 1888.

———, et al. *A New English Dictionary on Historical Principles.* 10 vols. Oxford: Clarendon Press, 1888–1928.

Murray, K.M. Elisabeth. *Caught in the Web of Words: James A.H. Murray and the Oxford English Dictionary.* New Haven: Yale University Press, 1977.

Murray, Timothy. "The Académie Française." In *A New History of French Literature,* edited by Denis Hollier, 267–273. Cambridge: Harvard University Press, 1989.

Newbould, Ian. *Whiggery and Reform, 1830–41.* Basingstoke: Macmillan Academic, 1990.

Olender, Maurice. *The Languages of Paradise.* Translated by Arthur Goldhammer. Cambridge: Harvard University Press, 1992.

Oliphant, Margaret, ed. *The Life of Edward Irving, Illustrated from his Journals and Correspondence.* 2nd ed. 2 vols. Vol. 2. London: Hurst and Blackett, 1862. https://books.google.com/books?id=ckRAAAAAMAAJ.

Orel, Harold, ed. *Thomas Hardy's Personal Writings: Prefaces, Literary Opinions, Reminiscences.* Basingstoke: Macmillan, 1966.

O'Neal, John C. *The Authority of Experience: Sensationist Theory in the French Enlightenment.* University Park: Pennsylvania State University Press, 1996.

Ott, Walter R. *Locke's Philosophy of Language.* Cambridge: Cambridge University Press, 2004.

Page, Norman. "Hardy and the English Language." In *Thomas Hardy: The Writer and His Background,* edited by Norman Page, 151–172. New York: St. Martin's, 1980.

Parry, Jonathan. *The Rise and Fall of Liberal Government in Victorian Britain.* New Haven: Yale University Press, 1993.

Patmore, Coventry. *Coventry Patmore's "Essay on English Metrical Law": A Critical Edition with a Commentary.* Edited by Sister Mary Augustine Roth. Washington, DC: The Catholic University of America Press, 1961.

Pearsall, Cornelia. *Tennyson's Rapture: Transformation in the Victorian Dramatic Monologue.* New York: Oxford University Press, 2008.

Peel, Ellen and Nanora Sweet. "*Corinne* and the Woman as Poet in England: Hemans, Jewsbury, and Barrett Browning." In *The Novel's Seductions: Staël's* Corinne *in Critical Inquiry*, edited by Karyna Szmurlo, 204–220. Lewisburg: Bucknell University Press, 1999.

Peterfreund, Stuart. "Robert Browning's Decoding of Natural Theology in 'Caliban upon Setebos.'" *Victorian Poetry* 43, no. 3 (2005): 317–331.

Peterson, William S., ed. *Browning's Trumpeter: The Correspondence of Robert Browning and Frederick J. Furnivall, 1872–1889.* Washington, DC: Decatur House Press, 1979.

Petyt, K. M. *The Study of Dialect: An Introduction to Dialectology.* Boulder: Westview Press, 1980.

Phillips, John A. *The Great Reform Bill in the Boroughs: English Electoral Behaviour, 1818–1841.* Oxford: Clarendon Press, 1992.

Phillipps, K. C. *Language and Class in Victorian England.* Oxford: Basil Blackwell, 1984.

Philp, Mark, ed. *The French Revolution and British Popular Politics.* Cambridge: Cambridge University Press, 1991.

Plotkin, Cary H. *The Tenth Muse: Victorian Philology and the Genesis of the Poetic Language of Gerard Manley Hopkins.* Carbondale: Southern Illinois University Press, 1989.

Ponting, Clive. *The Crimean War.* London: Chatto & Windus, 2004.

Poovey, Mary. *Uneven Developments: The Ideological Work of Gender in Mid-Victorian England.* Chicago: University of Chicago Press, 1988.

———. *Making a Social Body: British Cultural Formation, 1830–1864.* Chicago: University of Chicago Press, 1995.

Prichard, James Cowles. *The English Origin of Celtic Nations.* Oxford: S. Collingwood, 1831. https://babel.hathitrust.org/cgi/pt?id=hvd.32044024 305419;view=1up;seq=5.

Priestley, Joseph. *English Grammar: Lectures on the Theory of Language and Universal Grammar; and on Oratory and Criticism.* Edited by John Towill Rutt. London: Rowland Hunter, 1833. https://books.google.com/books?id=4JE_AAAAYAAJ.

Proudhon, Pierre-Joseph. "The Collective Force." In *Selected Writings of Pierre-Joseph Proudhon*, edited by Stuart Edwards and translated by Elizabeth Fraser, 113–124. New York: Anchor, 1969.

Pugh, Martin. *The Making of Modern British Politics.* New York: St. Martin's, 1982.

Purdy, Richard Little and Michael Millgate, eds. *The Collected Letters of Thomas Hardy.* 8 vols. Oxford: Clarendon Press, 1980–2012.

Purton, Valerie and Norman Page, eds. *The Palgrave Literary Dictionary of Tennyson.* Basingstoke: Palgrave, 2010.

Radick, Gregory. *The Simian Tongue: The Long Debate about Animal Language*. Chicago: University of Chicago Press, 2007.

Ramanathan, Vaidehi. *The English-Vernacular Divide: Postcolonial Language, Politics, and Practice*. Bristol: Multilingual Matters, 2005.

Rath, Andrew. *The Crimean War in Imperial Context, 1854–1856*. Basingstoke: Palgrave, 2015.

Regier, Alexander. *Fracture and Fragmentation in British Romanticism*. Cambridge: Cambridge University Press, 2010.

Reynolds, Matthew. *Realms of Verse 1830–1870: English Poetry in a Time of Nation-Building*. Oxford: Oxford University Press, 2001.

Reynolds, Margaret. Critical Introduction to *Aurora Leigh, by Elizabeth Barrett Browning*. Edited by Margaret Reynolds. Athens: Ohio Univ. Press, 1992. 1–77.

Ricks, Christopher. *Tennyson*. New York: The Macmillan Company, 1972.

———. *The Poems of Tennyson*. 3 vols. Berkeley: University of California Press, 1987.

Rigg, Patricia Diane. *Robert Browning's Romantic Irony in* The Ring and the Book. Madison: Fairleigh Dickinson University Press, 1999.

Romaine, Suzanne. Introduction to *The Cambridge History of the English Language*, vol. IV: 1776–1997, 1–56. Edited by Suzanne Romaine, gen. ed. Richard Hogg. Cambridge: Cambridge University Press, 1998.

Rosenberg, Daniel. "Louis-Sébastien Mercier's New Words." *Eighteenth-Century Studies* 36, no. 3 (2003): 367–386.

Rosenberg, Philip. *The Seventh Hero: Carlyle and the Theory of Radical Activism*. Cambridge: Harvard University Press, 1974.

Rousseau, Jean-Jacques. *Essay on the Origin of Languages*. Trans. John H. Moran. In *On the Origin of Language: Two Essays*, translated by John H. Moran and Alexander Gode. 5–74. Chicago: University of Chicago Press, 1966.

Rover, Constance. *Women's Suffrage and Party Politics in Britain, 1866–1914*. London: Routledge and Kegan Paul, 1967.

Rudwick, Martin. *Bursting the Limits of Time: The Reconstruction of Geohistory in the Age of Revolution*. Chicago: University of Chicago Press, 2008.

Rudy, Jason. *Electric Meters: Victorian Physiological Poetics*. Athens: Ohio University Press, 2009.

Ryals, Claude de L. *The Life of Robert Browning*. Oxford: Wiley-Blackwell, 1993.

Said, Edward. *Orientalism*. New York: Vintage, 1979.

Sajé, Natasha. "Poems Aware of History: Using the *Oxford English Dictionary*." In *Wingbeats II: Exercises and Practices in Poetry*, edited by Scott Wiggerman and David Meischen, 233–239. Albuquerque: Dos Gatos Press, 2015.

Santner, Eric. *The Royal Remains: The People's Two Bodies and the Endgames of Sovereignty*. Chicago: University of Chicago Press, 2011.

de Saussure, Ferdinand. *Course in General Linguistics*. Edited by Charles Bally and Albert Sechehaye. Translated by Wade Buskin. London: Peter Owen, 1959.

Savage, W.H. *The Vulgarisms and Improprieties of the English Language*. London: T.S. Porter, 1833. https://archive.org/details/vulgarismsimprop00sava.

Saville, Julia F. *Victorian Soul-Talk: Poetry, Democracy, and the Body Politic.* Basingstoke: Palgrave Macmillan, 2017.

Schleicher, August. *Darwinism Tested by the Science of Language.* Translated by Alex V.W. Bikkers. London: John Camden Hotten, 1869. https://books. google.com/books?id=p0Ki6e8f5SUC.

Schneider, Edgar. *Postcolonial English: Varieties around the World.* Cambridge: Cambridge University Press, 2007.

Scrivener, Michael Henry. *Seditious Allegories: John Thelwall & Jacobin Writing.* University Park: The Pennsylvania State University Press, 2001.

Secord, James. "Introduction to Robert Chambers." In *Vestiges of the Natural History of Creation and Other Evolutionary Writings*, edited by James Secord, vii–xlv. Chicago: The University of Chicago Press, 1994.

———. "Introduction to Charles Lyell." In *Principles of Geology*, edited by James Secord, ix–xliii. New York: Penguin Classics, 1997.

Seigel, Jules Paul, ed. *Thomas Carlyle: The Critical Heritage.* New York: Barnes and Noble, 1971.

Shaffer, E.S. *'Kubla Khan' and the Fall of Jerusalem.* Cambridge: Cambridge University Press, 1975.

Shaw, W. David. "Browning's Murder Mystery: *The Ring and the Book* and Modern Theory." *Victorian Poetry* 27, no. 3/4 (1989), 79–98.

Shannon, Brent. "'A Finished Generation, Dead of Plague': Contagion, the Social Body, and the London Poor in Elizabeth Barrett Browning's *Aurora Leigh*." *Studies in Browning and His Circle* 27 (2006): 41–52.

Sherry, Vince. *The Great War and the Language of Modernism.* Oxford: Oxford University Press, 2003.

Sherwood, Marion. *Tennyson and the Fabrication of Englishness.* Basingstoke: Palgrave, 2013.

Shires, Linda M. "On Color-Theory, 1835: George Field's *Chromatography*." BRANCH: Britain, Representation, and Nineteenth-Century History. http:// www.branchcollective.org/?ps_articles=linda-m-shires-on-color-theory-1835-george-fields-chromatography

Slinn, E. Warwick. "Language and Truth in *The Ring and the Book*." *Victorian Poetry* 27, no. 3/4 (1989): 115–133.

Smajić, Srdjan. *Ghost-Seers, Detectives, and Spiritualists: Theories of Vision in Victorian Literature and Science.* Cambridge: Cambridge University Press, 2010.

Smith, F. B. *The Making of the Second Reform Bill.* Cambridge: Cambridge University Press, 1966.

Smith, Harold L. *The British Women's Suffrage Campaign, 1866–1928.* London: Longman, 1998.

Smith, Michael S. "Parliamentary Reform and the Electorate." In *A Companion to Nineteenth-Century Britain*, edited by Chris Williams, 156–173. Oxford: Blackwell's, 2004.

Smith, Olivia. *The Politics of Language 1791–1819.* Oxford: Clarendon Press, 1984.

Solomonescu, Yasmin. *John Thelwall and the Materialist Imagination.* Basingstoke: Palgrave Macmillan, 2014.

Sorensen, Janet. *The Grammar of Empire in Eighteenth-Century British Writing.* Cambridge: Cambridge University Press, 2000.

Sperling, Matthew. *Visionary Philology: Geoffrey Hill and the Study of Words.* Oxford: Oxford University Press, 2014.

Staines, David. *Tennyson's Camelot: The "Idylls of the King" and Its Medieval Sources.* Waterloo: Wilfrid Laurier University Press, 1982.

Stone, Marjorie. "Genre Subversion and Gender Inversion: 'The Princess' and 'Aurora Leigh.'" *Victorian Poetry* 25, no. 4 (1987): 101–127.

——. *Elizabeth Barrett Browning.* New York: St. Martin's, 1995.

——, and Beverly Taylor. Introduction to Elizabeth Barrett Browning's *Poems.* In *The Works*, vol. 1, edited by Sandra Donaldson, lxi–lxxx. London: Pickering & Chatto, 2010.

——. "Elizabeth Barrett Browning." *Victorian Poetry* 50, no. 3 (2012): 330–349.

——. "Criticism on *Aurora Leigh*: An Overview." *Elizabeth Barrett Browning Archive.* Edited by Marjorie Stone and Beverly Taylor. www.ebbarchive. org. 30 August 2016.

Stott, Rebecca and Simon Avery. *Elizabeth Barrett Browning.* London: Pearson Education Limited, 2003.

Straley, Jessica. *Evolution and Imagination in Victorian Children's Literature.* Cambridge: Cambridge University Press, 2016.

Sullivan, Mary Rose. *Browning's Voices in* The Ring and the Book: *A Study of Method and Meaning.* Toronto: University of Toronto Press, 1969.

Taylor, Barbara. *Eve and the New Jerusalem: Socialism and Feminism in the Nineteenth Century.* New York: Pantheon, 1983.

Taylor, Beverly. "Carlyle, Elizabeth Barrett Browning, and the Hero as Victorian Poet." In Carlyle, *On Heroes, Hero-Worship, and the Heroic in History.* [1841], edited by David R. Sorensen and Brent E. Kinser, 235–246. New Haven: Yale University Press, 2013.

Taylor, Dennis. *Hardy's Poetry, 1860–1928.* New York: Columbia University Press, 1981.

——. *Hardy's Metres and Victorian Prosody.* Oxford: Clarendon Press, 1988.

——. *Hardy's Literary Language and Victorian Philology.* Oxford: Clarendon Press, 1993.

Tennyson, Alfred. "Locksley Hall." [1842]. In Vol. 2 of Ricks, *The Poems*, 118–130.

——. *The Princess.* [1847]. In Vol. 2 of Ricks, *The Poems*, 185–296.

——. *In Memoriam.* [1850]. In Vol. 2 of Ricks, *The Poems*, 304–459.

——. *Maud.* [1855]. In Vol. 2 of Ricks, *The Poems*, 513–584.

——. *Idylls of the King.* [1859–1885]. In Vol. 3 of Ricks, *The Poems*, 255–563.

——. *Idylls of the King.* Edited by Hallam Lord Tennyson. London: Macmillan, 1908. https://books.google.com/books?id=j5Y-AAAAYAAJ.

——. "By an Evolutionist." [1889]. In Vol. 3 of Ricks, *The Poems*, 202.

Tennyson, Hallam. *Alfred Lord Tennyson: A Memoir.* 2 vols. New York: The Macmillan Company, 1896. https://archive.org/details/alfredlordtennys01 tennuoft.

Thackeray, William Makepeace. Review of *The French Revolution. The Times* (3 August 1837). Reprinted in Seigel, *Thomas Carlyle: The Critical Heritage*, 69–75.

The Brownings: A Research Guide. Armstrong Browning Library, Baylor University. http://www.browningguide.org.

"The Ring and the Book." *The Dublin Review* 13, no. 25 (1869): 48. *British Periodicals Collection.* 8 April 2016.

Thomas, David Wayne. *Cultivating Victorians: Liberal Culture and the Aesthetic.* Philadelphia: University of Pennsylvania Press, 2004.

Thompson, E. P. *The Making of the English Working Class.* Harmondsworth: Penguin, 1977.

Tomalin, Claire. *Thomas Hardy.* New York: Penguin, 2007.

Tomalin, Marcus. *Romanticism and Linguistic Theory: William Hazlitt, Language, and Literature.* Basingstoke: Palgrave Macmillan, 2009.

Trench, Richard Chenevix. *On the Study of Words.* 6th ed. London: John W. Parker, 1855.

———. *On some Deficiencies in our English Dictionaries. Being the Substance of Two Papers Read before the Philological Society.* London: John W. Parker, 1857. https://archive.org/stream/onsomedeficienci00trenrich#page/n8/mode/1up.

———. Theodore Goldstücker, Thomas Hewitt Key, Thomas Watts, et.al. "Canones Lexicographici." In *Transactions of the Philological Society 1857*, Part 2: 3–11. London: The Society for George Bell, n.d. https://archive.org/details/transactions00philuoft.

———. *Proposal for the Publication of a New English Dictionary, by the Philological Society.* London: Trübner and Co., 1859. https://archive.org/stream/proposalforpubl01britgoog#page/n7/mode/1up.

Tucker, Herbert. "Dramatic Monologue and the Overhearing of Lyric." In *Lyric Poetry: Beyond New Criticism*, edited by Chaviva Hošek and Patricia Parker, 226–243. Ithaca: Cornell University Press, 1985.

———. *Tennyson and the Doom of Romanticism.* Cambridge: Harvard University Press, 1988.

———. "Representation and Repristination: Virginity in *The Ring and the Book*." In *Virginal Sexuality and Textuality in Victorian Literature*, edited by Lloyd Davis, 67–86. Albany: State University of New York Press, 1993.

———. "The Fix of Form: An Open Letter." *Victorian Literature and Culture* 27.2 (1999): 531–535.

———. "Tactical Formalism: A Response to Caroline Levine." *Victorian Studies* 49.1 (2006): 85–93.

———. *Epic: Britain's Heroic Muse 1790–1910.* Oxford: Oxford University Press, 2008.

Turner, James. *Philology: The Forgotten Origins of the Modern Humanities.* Princeton: Princeton University Press, 2014.

Turner, Frank M. "Victorian scientific naturalism and Thomas Carlyle." *Victorian Studies* 18 (1975): 325–343. Reprinted in *Contesting Cultural Authority: Essays on Victorian Intellectual Life*, 131–150. Cambridge: Cambridge University Press, 1993.

Tylor, Edward. *Primitive Culture: Researches into the Development of Mythology, Philosophy, Religion, Art, and Custom.* 2 vols. Vol. 1. London: John Murray, 1871. https://books.google.com/books?id=AucLAAAAIAAJ.

Ulrich, John M. *Signs of Their Times: History, Labor, and the Body in Cobbett, Carlyle, and Disraeli.* Athens: Ohio University Press, 2003.

———. "Thomas Carlyle, Richard Owen, and the Paleontological Articulation of the Past." *Journal of Victorian Culture* 11, no. 1 (2006): 30–58.

[Unsigned]. Review of *The Ring and the Book. Spectator* 41 (1868): 1464–66. Reprinted in Browning, *The Ring and the Book*, edited by Collins and Altick, 774–777.

Vanden Bossche, Chris R. *Carlyle and the Search for Authority.* Columbus: Ohio State University Press, 1991.

———. *Reform Acts: Chartism, Social Agency, and the Victorian Novel, 1832–1867.* Baltimore: Johns Hopkins University Press, 2014.

Van Riper, A. Bowdoin. *Men Among the Mammoths: Victorian Science and the Discovery of Human Prehistory.* Chicago: The University of Chicago Press, 1993.

Vernon, James. *Politics and the People: A Study in English Political Culture, c. 1815–1867.* Cambridge: Cambridge University Press, 1993.

Wakelin, Martyn F. *English Dialects: An Introduction.* London: The Athlone Press, 1972.

Walker, William. "*Pompilia* and Pompilia." *Victorian Poetry* 22, no.1 (1984): 47–63.

Ward, Candace. "'Damning Herself Praisworthily': Nullifying Women in *The Ring and the Book.*" *Victorian Poetry* 34, no. 1 (1996): 1–14.

Wasserman, George. "The Meaning of Browning's Ring-Figure." *Modern Language Notes* 76, no. 5 (1961): 420–426.

Webster, Noah. *Dissertations on the English Language.* Boston: Isaiah Thomas and Co., 1789. https://archive.org/stream/dissertationsone00webs#page/n6/mode/1up.

———. Preface to *An American Dictionary of the English Language.* [1828]. Edited by Noah Webster. 2 vols. Vol. 1. n.p. New York: S. Converse, 1828. https://archive.org/details/americandictiona01websrich.

Wedgwood, Hensleigh. *On the Origin of Language.* London: N. Trübner & Co., 1866. https://books.google.com/books?id=241DAAAAcAAJ.

Wheeler, Michael. *St. John and the Victorians.* Cambridge: Cambridge University Press, 2012.

Whewell, William. *Indications of the Creator.* London: John Parker, 1845. https://books.google.com/books?id=YV0XAAAAYAAJ&num=11.

———. *History of the Inductive Sciences, From the Earliest to the Present Time*, 3rd. ed. Vol. 3. London: John Parker, 1857. https://books.google.com/books?id=b3EIAAAAIAAJ.

Whitney, William Dwight. *The Life and Growth of Language.* London: Henry S. King, 1875. https://archive.org/stream/lifeandgrowthla03whitgoog#page/n7/mode/1up.

———. *Language and the Study of Language.* London: N. Trübner & Co., 1867. https://books.google.com/books?id=ufOeAnt3gV8C.

Williams, G. A. *Artisans and Sans-Culottes: Popular Movements in France and Britain during the French Revolution.* London: Routledge, 1989.

Williams, Raymond. *Culture and Society: 1780–1950.* 2nd ed. New York: Columbia University Press, 1983.

Willinsky, John. *Empire of Words: The Reign of the OED*. Princeton: Princeton University Press, 1995.

Willis, Martin. *Vision, Science, and Literature 1870–1920: Ocular Horizons*. Abingdon: Pickering & Chatto, 2011.

Winchester, Simon. *The Meaning of Everything: The Story of the Oxford English Dictionary*. Oxford: Oxford University Press, 2003.

Windle, Bertram. *The Wessex of Thomas Hardy*. London: John Lane, 1902. https://archive.org/details/wessexofthomasha00windrich.

Wolfson, Susan. *Formal Charges: The Shaping of Poetry in British Romanticism*. Stanford: Stanford University Press, 1997.

Wordsworth, William. "Strange fits of passion I have known." [1800]. In William Wordsworth and Samuel Taylor Coleridge, *Lyrical Ballads: 1798 and 1802*, edited by Fiona Stafford, 223–224. Oxford: Oxford University Press, 2013.

———. Preface to *Lyrical Ballads*. [1802]. In William Wordswoth and Samuel Taylor Coleridge, *Lyrical Ballads*, edited by Fiona Stafford, 95–115.

Woodworth, Elizabeth. "Elizabeth Barrett Browning, Coventry Patmore, and Alfred Tennyson on Napoleon III: The Hero-Poet and Carlylean Heroics." *Victorian Poetry* 44, no. 4 (2006): 543–560.

Wright, Joseph. Preface to Vol. 1 of *The English Dialect Dictionary*. Edited by Joseph Wright, v–viii. London: Henry Frowde, 1898. https://archive.org/details/englishdialectdi01wriguoft.

———. *The English Dialect Dictionary*. 30 parts. New York: G.P. Putnam's Sons, 1896–1905.

Zonana, Joyce. "The Embodied Muse: Elizabeth Barrett Browning's *Aurora Leigh* and Feminist Poetics." *Tulsa Studies in Women's Literature* 8, no. 2 (1989): 240–262.

Index

Note: Page numbers followed by "n" denote endnotes.

For Product Safety Concerns and Information please contact our EU
representative GPSR@taylorandfrancis.com
Taylor & Francis Verlag GmbH, Kaufingerstraße 24, 80331 München, Germany